THE HOUSE & HOME KITCHEN PLANNING GUIDE

THE HOUSE & HOME KITCHEN PLANNING GUIDE

McGraw-Hill Book Company

New York
St. Louis
San Francisco
Auckland
Bogota
Dusseldorf
Johannesburg
London
Madrid
Mexico
Montreal
New Delhi
Panama
Paris
Sao Paulo
Singapore
Sydney
Tokyo
Toronto

the housing press

New York

The editors for this book were Hugh S. Donlan and Jeremy Robinson. The production editor was Patricia Mintz. The designer was Mary Puschak. It was set in Newton by The Call; printed and bound by Halliday Lithograph Corp.

1234567890   HDHD   7654321098

Library of Congress Cataloging in Publication Data
Main entry under title:

The House & Home Kitchen Planning Guide
Includes index.
        1. Kitchens.   2. Interior decoration.   I. the housing press.   II. Title: Kitchen Planning Guide.
NK2117.K5H68   728   77-7553
ISBN 0-07-030472-6

CONTENTS

Introduction

This book was written primarily for the homeowner who is planning either to have a custom-made house built or to have an old kitchen remodeled. Although the homeowner will probably not carry out the major structural work, the information in this book will stimulate interest in kitchen design and crystallize needs and wishes so that they can be discussed with a kitchen remodeler, architect or professional builder.

We would like to thank the following for their special assistance: Raymond W. Afflerbach of the American Institute of Kitchen Dealers; William J. Ketcham of the General Electric Company; Lewis P. Thompson of St. Charles Manufacturing Company; and Henry R. Spies of the Small Homes Council/Building Research Council — University of Illinois. (Some of the material that appears in Chapters 8 and 9 was originally prepared for the American Institute of Kitchen Dealers by the Council and reprinted in part with the permission of the Council.) We would also like to thank all the companies and photographers listed in the illustrations acknowledgments on page 191. Most of the drawings in this book were prepared by Joseph G. Andrachick of Robert Scharff and Associates.

CHAPTER I

THE ROOM THAT MAKES THE HOUSE

The kitchen is the room that can sell you on a house. Any builder knows that if there is any one room that can turn you on — or off — it is the kitchen. Once you have made the primary decisions as to price, financing, location, and size of the home you are seeking, it is you the designer who really has the greatest influence on which specific home is eventually bought. And the kitchen ranks *very* high in your priorities. Here is why.

The kitchen is the most lived-in room in the house. Besides being a food-preparation area, today's kitchen is an eating area, a planning area, sometimes a laundry area and, in most cases, the control center of the whole house. As a result, it is the room you consider most carefully. If you are shopping for a second or third house, you have usually lived with less-than-good kitchens, and know instinctively whether a model kitchen will be easy or hard to work in. And, because today's informal living patterns mean guests in the kitchen, you want it to be attractive as well.

The kitchen is the most expensive room in the house. Starting with bare walls, today's builder will put thousands of dollars worth of cabinets, appliances, flooring, and lighting into models. Custom kitchens, either new or remodeled, will cost a great deal more. So it just does not make economic sense to give the kitchen less than the best in plan and design.

In addition to looks, the homemaker wants the most efficient kitchen possible. More and more women are working outside of the home today and kitchen chores are often shared by all members of a household. Working people need efficient kitchens to complete tasks quickly.

The kitchen is important not only with a new house, but in an old one as well. The kitchen is the most remodeled room in the home. It is often the room that causes other remodeling projects to begin and frequently it is the only area to be remodeled.

Why is this true? Actually, any number of things can make a person start thinking about redesigning a kitchen. A change in the family is often one reason.

When the children are small, parents often like to have them in the kitchen where they watch over them and enjoy their presence. When the children grow older, parents might never find them in the kitchen except for snacktime. And the kitchen should accommodate these changes in living style.

Once the children are gone, the functions and design of the kitchen may change. Do the householders want a family kitchen with room for the grandchildren? Will they want to entertain more? Can they now afford the kitchen they have always dreamed of? Thus, when the family situation undergoes a major change, so often does the kitchen.

Of course, one of the major reasons for remodeling a kitchen is a change in life-style. While this affects planning throughout the entire house, it is most apparent in the redesigning of the kitchen. In the first years of homeowning, for example, young people might well like a small but intimate kitchen (and it might be all they can afford). There, two can work together in close harmony. However, if children arrive, the couple then needs a family kitchen — a bigger room with space for a playpen and room for the toys. Perhaps even a rocking chair to help provide solace for the bumps and falls of childhood.

As children grow older, families may find themselves entertaining more. So a kitchen that is pretty enough to entertain in is needed. Then when the children are gone, that intimate kitchen of earlier days may again be planned. Anyhow there will be changes — perhaps more special equipment for gourmet cooking, a wine cellar, or extra space for storing gourmet foods. Even later, families might want a very compact, efficient kitchen that will not tie them down with extra work in the retirement years. Thus, as you can see, kitchen requirements generally change with life-style and as life-styles change, the kitchen should change with them.

When Shakespeare wrote the famous line "To thine own self be true," he never dreamed that it would become the first rule of successful kitchen planning. That is, the kitchen must reflect the individual needs, work habits, and lifestyle of the homemaker and the family, not those of anyone else.

The project builder will design kitchen plans around a mythical "average" homemaker and a "typical" life pattern. Builders, designers and architects keep up to date on all trends in kitchen styles and equipment. Surveys conducted by building and architectural publications often reveal interesting trends among homebuyers. For instance, a survey published in June 1976 was conducted by Walker & Lee, a Los Angeles-based realty firm which annually sells more than 5,000 new houses and also recommends floor-plan and marketing ideas to its builder clients. In this survey, published in *House & Home,* one of the questions asked was "Which is the preferable plan for kitchen space — breakfast bar, small nook area, or just table space?"

As shown in the accompanying graphs, small nooks won hands down in every age category. Its strongest fans were the 56-and-overs — 66.6 percent; second strongest support came from 25-or-unders — 54.4 percent. The nook's weakest showing — only 42.8 percent — came from 36-to-45 year-olds who gave breakfast bars second place, as did the two youngest age groups. Second choice for the two oldest groups was kitchen-table space, which got its biggest share of votes — 33.7 percent — from 46-to-55-year-olds. And the breakfast-bar plan came in first with 36.3 percent of the 26-to-35-year bracket.

While trend-setting surveys are good indicators as to what goes into homebuying decisions, the best advice to follow is to use a good kitchen plan. Also a bad kitchen costs just as much money as a good one.

People who buy a house may not understand everything about electronics or thermodynamics, but unless they are very new at homemaking, they will know at a glance whether they will like the kitchen offered. They will know whether it will be a pleasant and easy place in which to work and whether it is conveniently located to answer the door bell, watch the children, and enjoy guests. As mentioned earlier, second- and third-time homebuyers are generally sophisticated and judges of kitchen design. They notice faults like too-small dining areas or a doorway half blocked by counter corners. An

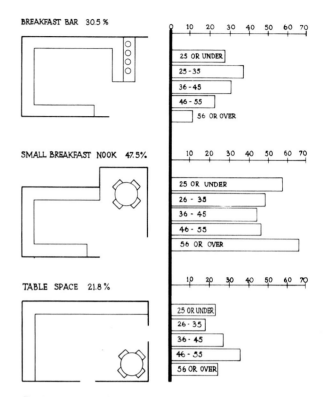

Results of owner's kitchen eating area preference survey.

experienced homeowner usually rates design ahead of quality.

The original version of the kitchen shown on the opposite page had problems. But an experienced kitchen designer got the blueprint before the job was started and made the big improvement shown in the revised version. In the original, split work area hindered traffic flow by flanking the corner archways. The dining area was much too small — only 3 by 5 feet. By moving all three archways, the window and plumbing connections, the designer enlarged the work area, concentrated the cabinets and appliances, and doubled the dining space.

Do not start planning the kitchen by deciding how much to spend. It is the design that is going to make the kitchen and help coordinate the house so set the budget to accommodate the design rather than the other way around. This approach need not be overly expensive especially if the plans are based on stock dimensions for cabinets and appliances.

Since kitchens are often sold by the foot, a good design is bound to stand out. Details like the planning desk, breakfast bar, kitchen greenhouse or storage wall in the remodeling plan make the difference between a unique design and a so-so one that simply fills the walls with cabinets.

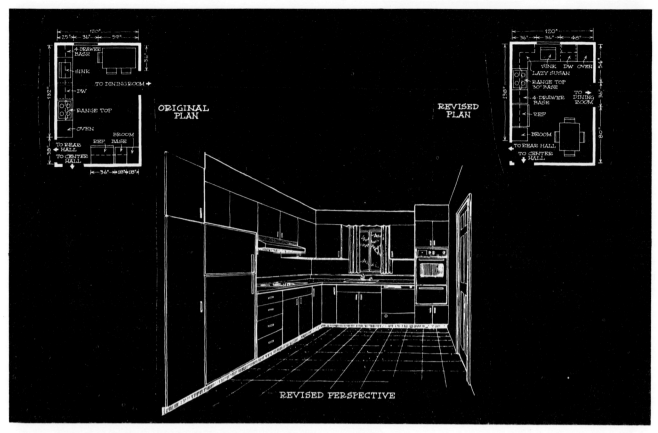

ORIGINAL PLAN

REVISED PLAN

REVISED PERSPECTIVE

Builder's kitchen plan needed only slight structural changes to make layout more useful.

It is design, not price, that will win you over, especially if you have grown impatient with the inefficiency and drabness of the old kitchen. The first thing you will want in the new one is practical and attractive features. Do not ignore price, but place it second to design.

Detailed planning also brings hidden costs out into the open and helps you buy competitively. The word-picture remodeler, selling kitchens by the foot on time payments, cannot offer the kind of improvements shown here because of unwillingness to draw plans that would show, for example, what could be done by moving a door (the key to the plan above). Such remodelers have only a vague idea of costs, so they must protect themselves with a steep markup. If they do not get the job on the first call, they will not go back because they know that you can, after a little shopping around, easily find a better price.

The remodeling of an existing kitchen does present problems. For instance, the physical limitations of the space available for a kitchen is perhaps one of the first considerations which must always be met. A completely free plan usually occurs only in the planning stages of a house and very seldom in remodeling work. The kitchen remodeler is limited by the space already allotted for the kitchen. Even then,

cost and limitations of size and proportions of space with relation to the rest of the house frequently restrain the designer from complete freedom of design. Therefore, the size, the number of square feet within the space for the kitchen, is important.

Often, simple square footage does not permit the designer an ample layout of the necessary appliances, storage, and equipment. Is the room narrow, square, broken up with many small projections? Just what is the basic plan? These considerations are a vital part in determing the appearance of the kitchen. For example, how does the designer achieve the look of a spacious kitchen in a relatively confined space? Can a ceiling which appears quite low be raised visually without actual architectural changes?

The location of the kitchen with reference to other rooms is often a determining factor in the design. Kitchens are frequently found adjacent to the living areas of the home, next to the sleeping areas, and even at considerable distance from eating areas. The fact that some houses have closed plans and others have open plans can also affect the design considerations of the kitchen. Houses with closed plans are those which have the space designated for various uses separated by walls. Movement from one space to another is usually

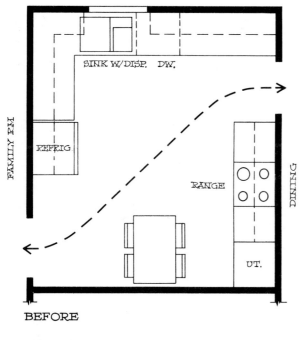

BEFORE

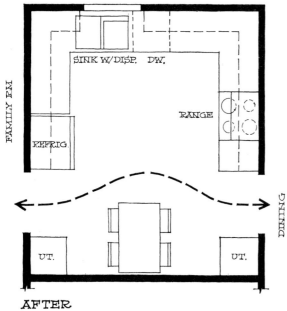

AFTER

The eating and working areas of the original kitchen were not clearly defined. But by moving both doors, traffic was pulled out of the work zone creating a separate eating area. The new plan also has room for an extra utility closet.

through openings such as doors, to dining rooms, bedrooms, living rooms, etc. An open-plan house does not have walls separating the functional spaces. One space flows, visually and actually, into another, and terms like living area, dining space, study alcove, are often used. Quite frequently, a combination of open plan and closed plan is found in a house. The kitchen designer must be aware of this. Perhaps the kitchen is placed so that there are no visual barriers separating the area of food preparation from that of the living and entertaining spaces. This can be quite desirable, or it can be an unwanted and frustrating arrangement. The personality of the cook must be heeded and the designer must plan accordingly.

Doors and windows are often troublesome components of a kitchen's design. Frequently, there seem to be more openings than wall space and the functional arrangement must be carefully planned around them. Unnecessary doors can often be eliminated with little difficulty and cost, thus making for a better working arrangement. Instances have been found where the most used door is located in what could be the most functional area of the kitchen, and the relocation of the troublesome door is most desirable. Traffic patterns and furniture arrangements of the adjacent spaces must, of course, be altered. Necessary but less frequently used doors can also be "visually" eliminated, or at least minimized, with the final design appearing less fragmented.

It Is Important whether a door leads to the outside and is frequently used by the family, or whether it leads to an unused porch or whether it is an interior door leading either to another room or to a storage area. The placement of the various parts of the kitchen often is governed by the major exterior and interior entrances to the kitchen.

Windows play another important part in the total design. What exposure is the kitchen; what direction are the windows facing — east, west, north, south? Is there a problem of glaring sunlight in the late afternoon? Is there a view, or does the window look out on a dingy building, an air shaft, or a service area with garbage cans, as so often happens in urban living? Again, the placement of the windows, as with doors, is a determining factor. Frequently, to obtain more wall cabinet space, a window is moved or eliminated completely.

But, despite such physical limitations, you have a much greater chance of coming up with the "perfect plan" if you ask yourself a series of pertinent

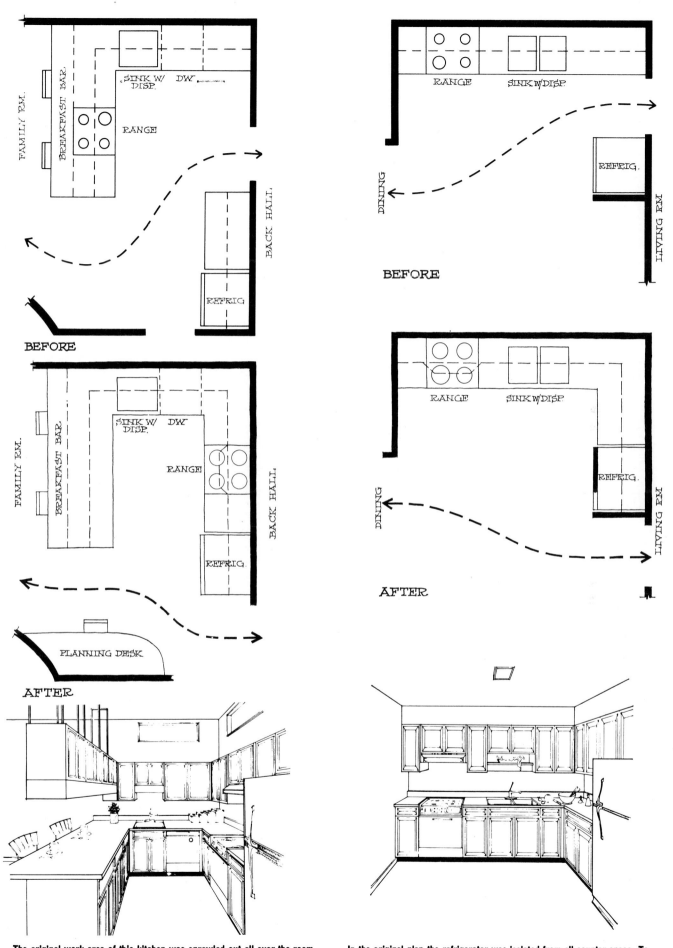

The original work area of this kitchen was sprawled out all over the room. With the shifting of one counter the kitchen was turned into a compact U which eliminated cross-traffic. And by moving the range top the snack bar was made much more useable.

In the original plan the refrigerator was isolated from all counter space. To correct this, one door was moved. The kitchen was thus turned into an L, which also eliminated a traffic lane through the work area and added a corner cabinet space.

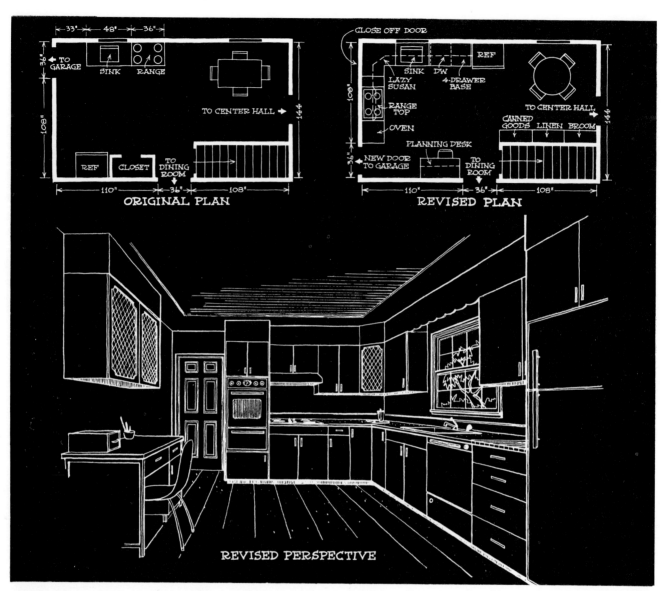

ORIGINAL PLAN

REVISED PLAN

REVISED PERSPECTIVE

Remodeler's plan improves an over-sized kitchen by eliminating an old structural problem.

questions. It is then easy to design the kitchen around your lifestyle.

1. *Are you the only cook in your household?* If other members of the household aid in making cooking a joint project, certainly there will be a need to duplicate certain utensils and increase counter space.

2. *How do you work best?* If the homemaker enjoys talking while cooking, plan a kitchen that allows room for extra people to congregate far enough away from the work, while still close enough to talk. Or if he or she is the "I-want-to-be-alone" kind of cook, then consider a compact working unit isolated from traffic areas and gathering places, such as family rooms and eating areas.

3. *What kind of cook are you?* A love-to-cook person who enjoys trying out the latest recipes and collecting recipes and cookbooks needs space and a well-organized kitchen. Such a cook needs a place to have several projects going simultaneously, and, literally, to be messy. A cook who leans to frozen food dinners and instant everything has far less use for the super kitchen. If the cook is gourmet minded, the need for a large assortment of special-use tools, utensils, spices, and herbs will govern the kitchen storage requirement. Such a design may even call for a small herb garden planter.

4. *Will you want to incorporate other activities in the kitchen?* Perhaps the only place to install a laundry in the home is in the kitchen. Plan to

separate it from the cooking area. Does the homemaker have a hobby, such as painting, sewing, weaving, writing? If the answer is yes, devote some working space close enough to the cooking area so the cook can combine pop art with popovers, basting seams with basting a roast. Also a planning desk makes a lot of sense if the homemaker works outside the home. If room does not permit that, a file drawer nearby for organizing papers, menus, recipes, and so on is a good touch.

5. *How large is your family?* Obviously, a big family eats more than a small family. This translates into a need for more storage space for food, cooking utensils, and the paraphernalia of eating. It does not necessarily require more floor space in the kitchen, unless the kitchen is a family gathering place, which leads to the next question.

6. *Is yours a white-tie-and-tails family with formal dinner in the dining room every night?* A small pull-out counter table for quick breakfasts may be adequate for the kitchen. But the everyone-winds-up-in-the-kitchen family will welcome a sizable dining area in the kitchen or immediately adjacent, with no solid partitions to keep the "lookers" and "cookers" from carrying on their conversation while the pot boils.

7. *Do you entertain a lot?* Does the family prefer large parties or smaller, more intimate dinners? Depending upon the way the members of the family entertain, storage needs will vary. If they like large holiday parties or "big bash" barbecues, they will need storage space for large platters, bowls, and extra dishes. Again, if they entertain informally and everyone ends up in the kitchen, the chances are they will welcome a sizable dining area in the kitchen or family room. They might even want to consider duplicating appliances. Two dishwashers can be a welcome addition after a large party. Or an under-counter refrigerator might provide additional storage space for prepared party foods.

8. *Do you have small children?* Do your preschoolers like to follow their parents into the kitchen to "help" or just ask them to "look at the effalunt I colored?" Some family-centered kitchens provide a child-height desk top for a play/study center. Or, it may be better to plan a play/work area for them in a family room/kitchen.

9. *Are you a trend-setter?* If the homemaker is, he or she will want a kitchen that incorporates all the latest, most advanced designs in appliances, fixtures, and gadgets. Or does he or she treasure the

(Top) A cook-top and eating island combination solves many a problem in a small kitchen. (Bottom) a built-in sewing machine arrangement is ideal for the sewing hobbyist.

(Top) A family room right off the kitchen is frequently good design, especially when there are small children in the family. (Right) A laundry area need not be big to be successful.

mellow charm of some of the loved possessions that have come to be a part of living? The kitchen will need to make room for the familiar — to harmonize the new with the old.

The answers to these and similar questions will go a long way towards providing a solid basis as to what your exact needs and desires are. Satisfactory design cannot be formulated without a thorough investigation of your needs, wants, and living habits. To assure individuality, satisfy the functional requirements, and obtain the preferred appearance of a kitchen, you must be aware of the variables and work within the limitations. Each kitchen should be different, as each home-owner is different. It is up to the designer to ascertain what these differences are and to incorporate their satisfactory solutions in the design. A designer must also bring to the problem elements and principles which will help provide the needed answers. But, every designer knows that it is possible to wind up with a kitchen that is technically

"correct" and efficient according to all the rules, standards, and statistics, but in which he or she will be disappointed in one or more important respects.

A big help to any kitchen designer are three lists of wants and needs. The first is an "I wish . . ." list. On this list, the home-owner should be encouraged to let herself or himself go by ignoring the practical considerations of what he or she believes is possible or impossible. Make this a rapid-fire enumeration of what you would most like. You may be pleasantly surprised to find that some of the things you thought completely impossible for your kitchen can be taken care of in ways that had not occurred to you.

For instance, some families like to take living outdoors when the weather permits. They would like a kitchen that opens up to include the patio in its area of service. Conversely, the barbecue enthusiasts who miss the campfire flavor of a charcoal fire when winter comes will be happy to learn that their kitchen can include "indoor campfires."

The point being to ask yourself what you want. And try to be confident in your ability to see what you want, but keep an open mind toward suggestions from the contractor, architect, or kitchen designer.

Next, make a list of "must haves." After this, have them make a list of "taboos," such as a particularly strong aversion to some color, material, texture, or feature. Maybe you have a collection of trivets (or Toby mugs, Cranberry glass, or earthenware pitchers) that have to be featured in any kitchen you can call your own. Perhaps lingering

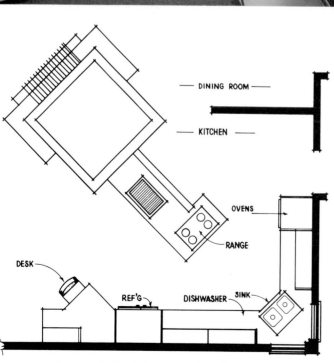

A modern kitchen design as seen from three different points.

cooking odors particularly bother you, so that a carefully engineered exhaust system will have special priority in your kitchen. Of course, you can adopt or adapt ideas that come from other sources, such as magazines, picture books, and manufacturer's brochures.

Now that the certain personal standards that must be conformed to in the kitchen are established, let us take a look at some of the standards in the next chapter that have been set up by the kitchen planning experts. Keep in mind, however, that the suitability of individual needs or preferences can cancel out any statistical norm. Remember that a kitchen is for you, its owner. A familiarity with these formulae can help in the evaluation of efficiency of the various kitchen plans that may be up for consideration. Of course, if all the basic rules of kitchen designing are known, it is much easier to judge when and how to bypass them wisely. In all cases, however, you are the one who is going to live with the design, so you are the only one who can really evaluate it as good or bad. The most certifiably great product of the most famous designer in the world cannot be considered really good if it makes you uncomfortable. It might be interesting, it might be trend-setting, it might even be revolutionary by ordinary design standards, but if it does not make you feel good or happy or pleased, then it is not really good design.

SQUARE MEASURE

U.S. Unit	Metric Unit
1 square inch =	645.16 square millimeters
	6.4516 square centimeters
1 square foot =	929.03 square centimeters
	9.2903 square decimeters
1 square yard =	0.092903 square meter
	0.83613 square meter
0.0015500 square inch	= 1 square millimeter
0.15500 square inch	= 1 square centimeter
15.500 square inches	
0.10764 square foot	= 1 square decimeter
1.1960 square yards	= 1 square meter

CUBIC MEASURE

U.S. Unit	Metric Unit
1 cubic inch =	16.387 cubic centimeters
	0.016387 liter
1 cubic foot =	0.028317 cubic meter
1 cubic yard =	0.76455 cubic meter
0.061023 cubic inch	= 1 cubic centimeter
61.023 cubic inches	= 1 cubic decimeter
35.315 cubic feet	= 1 cubic meter
1.3079 cubic yards	

LINEAR MEASURE

U.S. Unit	Metric Unit
1 inch =	25.4 millimeters
	2.54 centimeters
1 foot =	30.48 centimeters
	3.048 decimeters
1 yard =	0.3048 meter
	0.9144 meter
	1609.3 meters
0.03937 inch	= 1 millimeter
0.3937 inch	= 1 centimeter
3.937 inches	= 1 decimeter
39.37 inches	
3.2808 feet	= 1 meter
1.0936 yards	
3280.8 feet	= 1 kilometer
1093.6 yards	

CHAPTER 2

BASIC PRINCIPLES OF KITCHEN DESIGN

"Form follows function," our great designers tell us. And certainly nothing could be more true than when planning a new or remodeled kitchen. While everyone wishes for a kitchen to be beautiful, he or she also wants it to be efficient. No matter how beautiful it is, if it is not functional, it is not good.

To be functional, the kitchen plan for either a new or remodeled house must take into consideration its location within the home, its size and shape, and the arrangement of its equipment and work centers.

KITCHEN LOCATION

While this book is primarily concerned with the planning of the kitchen itself, some mention should be made of the location of the kitchen within the home.

With regard to traffic in the home, there are several important connections between the kitchen and the other areas of the house. First, there should be a direct connection from the kitchen to both indoor and outdoor eating and entertainment areas. Second, there should be a reasonably direct outside entry route to the garage or driveway. Delivery of groceries into the kitchen should be easy, quick, and not across carpeted dining or living areas. Third, the refuse disposal area should be directly accessible, without the need to pass through living areas or the main entrance. Fourth, the kitchen should not be too distant from the front door in order that the homemaker may answer the bell quickly.

While the kitchen should be situated to enable it to function as the home's center of activity and should be easily accessible from all parts of the house, the kitchen should not be a main thoroughfare for the rest of the house. Since passageways and access routes into the kitchen interrupt the continuous wall space for cabinets and appliances, a kitchen can be arranged to utilize floor space more efficiently if there are only two or at the most three access ways, and if these access ways are located primarily in one part of the space.

An outside view can be another important factor in selecting the kitchen location, as well as the size and placement of the windows in the kitchen. Observation of community life and enjoyment of nature will enhance the outside view. If there are young children in the house, the kitchen, if possible, should be located with a good view of, and access to, their play area.

SIZE AND SHAPE

When remodeling an old kitchen, of course, there is usually a limit to work within the area, although it is sometimes possible to expand the room by moving a wall or rearranging the existing space to obtain a more workable plan. With a new home — regardless of the size or price — the area

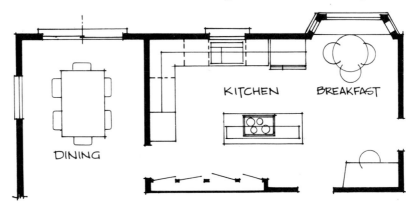

For serving convenience, a good plan locates the kitchen between the dining room and the breakfast nook.

DINING

KITCHEN   BREAKFAST

allocated for the kitchen work centers should not be less than 80 to 100 square feet, and not more than 150 to 160 square feet. Areas in excess of this result in too great a distance between the work centers. Areas smaller than recommended create cramped, tight arrangements, difficult to work in.

Frequently, many people make the mistake of assuming that more space is the solution to any problem of kitchen design. Sometimes it is. Other times, it may simply mean that the homemaker has farther to walk before he or she gets to other problems. Usually, inefficiency is the fault of poor planning (often in older homes) rather than of size. Thus, if more than 160 square feet is available, it is best to make it part of a separate dining or sitting area, a laundry room, or a playroom.

Functional kitchens must have adequate, organized storage located at each work center. In addition, kitchens should have those "extras" — planning centers, pantries, and eating areas — so necessary for the easy, efficient functioning of the kitchen. However, while the location of the kitchen within the home is important, the efficiency of a well planned kitchen depends on its size, shape, and the arrangement of its work centers.

WORK CENTERS

The basic kitchen is a place for storage of all the implements and ingredients necessary to the preparation of a meal. The activities of homemaking that are concentrated in the kitchen are complex, so they must be carefully planned in sequence of movement or work from storage, through preparation, to cooking and serving. To accomplish this, there should be three main or basic activity areas — commonly referred to as work centers — in every kitchen: (1) the refrigeration or storage area; (2) the sink or preparation/clean-up area; and (3) the range or cook area. The organization of these three main activity centers should be the first step in the formulation of any new kitchen plans since they are the basis of any good design.

An ideal kitchen installation includes proper distribution of appliances, work counter surfaces, and cabinets within these three activity areas. Each work center should include the major appliances, the food, the cooking equipment, and any other supplies used in that activity. In other words, each activity center should provide efficient working conditions for the particular activities that are performed at each appliance — the refrigerator, sink or range.

The Refrigeration or Storage Area

The refrigeration or storage area should be arranged to expedite storing and removing of foods. Perishables must be moved to and from the refrigerator and the freezer. Canned goods, cereals, and staples are contained in the base, wall, and pantry cabinets that surround and are fitted to this center. In recent years, the refrigerator/storage center has become increasingly more important as food processing and prepackaging has changed. More and more ready-to-use foods are appearing on

The refrigerator is the center of the storage area.

the scene, and many of them require freezer storage. And, with families using more prepackaged foods, the pantry of yesteryear has returned and is now considered an essential storage space in any well planned kitchen.

To expedite the storage and handling of foods, the refrigerator/storage center should be located immediately adjacent to the kitchen's service entrance. A refrigerator/freezer combination or a separate freezer unit allows longer storage of many foods. (As a separate freezer is not used as many times a day as the refrigerator, it may be located out of the main kitchen work area: in a line of tall cabinets or another wall if it is an upright model, or in a garage or utility room.) Allow at least 15 to 18 inches of countertop next to the refrigerator, with the refrigerator door opening on the side toward the counter. With a side-by-side refrigerator/freezer, remember it is easier to reach across the closed freezer door to load and unload the fresh food section than to reach around an open door to a counter on the wrong side. Of course, with a side-by-side refrigerator/freezer, it is a good idea, when possible, to have an equal amount of space beside the freezer.

Some refrigeration models have doors that can be hinged to swing in either direction. Consider this carefully before ordering a new unit. Also check the specifications of the intended model for the height of the box and recommended clearance for air circulation as well as for width. Avoid putting a refrigerator in a corner, beside a wall or next to a line of cabinets. It is usually necessary to open the door more than 90 degrees to remove crispers and shelves.

When designing a kitchen, if you like pantries, the refrigerator/storage center is where the pantry belongs. If you prefer cabinet food storage, this is where the appropriate cabinets belong. Tailor everything to your habits and preferences, but be sure to group it all efficiently so you do not have to keep walking from one side of the kitchen to the other. When planning the storage space for the refrigerator/storage center, be sure to include several adjustable shelves to allow for odd-sized packages and bottles. The refrigerator/storage center should be placed next to the cleanup center, and there should be at least 42 inches of uninterrupted countertop between the two.

The Cook Center

The main piece of equipment of the cook center is the range. Whether a free-standing, a built-in, a drop-in or slide-in unit, the cooking equipment should be the latest design, offering all of the labor- and time-saving devices. Ideally, the range should be handy to the dinner area used most often by the family. However, do not place it next to a door that may open onto a constant parade of children. A cabinet or counter surface at least 15 inches wide between the door and the range will cut down the number of accidents. Do not forget that space should be provided on each side of the range for elbow room and pan handles, with at least 24 inches of counter on one side for serving and 12 inches on the other. Also the range or built-in surface unit should not be installed under a window. Any curtains could catch fire, and the operation of such a window could be hazardous. Frequently local building codes have something to say about range placement. Check their requirements first.

While a built-in range top and separate oven(s) are generally considered the most convenient of all

A typical cook center containing a range with oven, grill, and vent hood unit.

range styles, they use up the most wall space. They also cost more to install, and replacement of the oven is difficult if the new model does not fit the cabinet for the old one. A separate oven should not be located directly next to the range; counter space is needed next to each. If necessary, locate the oven, as discussed later in the chapter, out of the busiest kitchen area. A wall oven should be installed so the inside top surface of the fully opened door is 1 to 7 inches below elbow height. If a double-oven unit is used, the bottom of the upper oven at counter height (36 inches) is about right for most people. Never install a built-in oven too high. High mounting makes it difficult to remove pans and can result in burns. Allow 24 inches of counter on at least one side of the oven. A heat-resistant surface of stainless steel or ceramic glass here is a joy to busy bakers. A plastic laminate countertop should never be subjected to heat over 270 degrees F (132.2 degrees C). Avoid having the wall oven at the end of a line of cabinets where the door will open into a traffic lane. Also avoid installation in a corner. Easier loading, unloading, and cleaning are possible with space all around the open oven door.

As to the range itself, there are several kinds available. There are the familiar freestanding units of counter height as well as freestanding units of the "over and under" design (with an oven on the top, an oven on the bottom, and the cooktop in between). There are also drop-in or slide-in units with a separate built-in cooktop and wall oven or an eye-level oven and cooktop stacked on a base cabinet.

The most common cooking facility for the least space is a 30-inch-wide range with an eye-level oven above the range top and another oven below it. However, a very short person often finds it difficult to handle a hot roasting pan in the high oven while a very tall person may find the view of the back burners on the range blocked by the upper oven. Stand in front of the model being considered and go through the motions of cooking to see if you can work with it safely and comfortably. Ideally a portion of the counter surface around the range should be heat resistant, allowing hot cooking utensils to be placed directly on it.

All styles of ranges and ovens are available with either gas or electricity as the fuel, and if both types of fuel are available in the area, consideration should be given to their individual advantages carefully before any choice is made. Both gas and electric models offer a wide variety of special features such as automatic timers, rotisseries, special broiling devices, and special colors.

Whenever possible the fumes from the cook center should be vented to the outdoors. The most efficient arrangement is to have a hood and exhaust fan with a grease filter over the range, with the shortest possible duct to the outdoors. The duct may go through a wall, but avoid directing cooking odors toward an outdoor sitting area. The duct may also go through the roof; it should never end in an attic. Check the local codes for installation standards. A ceiling or wall fan located away from the range will draw the cooking fumes over the intervening surfaces. A nonducted hood and fan will trap most of the grease and some of the odors, but none of the heat and moisture from cooking. These hoods are recommended only for interior locations from which outdoor venting is impossible.

Storage space is needed in the cook center for small appliances, skillets, pans, pots, cooking utensils, seasoning, spoons, spatulas, and so on.

Sink and Clean-up Center

The sink and cleanup center involves the beginning and the end of the kitchen activities, and consequently should be located where it is most convenient — usually between the other two centers. There should be a minimum of 30 inches of counter surface on either side of the sink, and part of that should contain a chopping block or cutting board. The sink itself should be a double or triple bowl sink with one of the bowls deep enough and wide enough to allow the washing of pots and pans. In addition to

the sink, the center should contain a disposer, dishwasher usually adjacent to the sink, and a trash compactor. (If the dishwasher or trash compactor is not in the budget now, it is wise to plan ahead by installing proper-sized base cabinets which can later be replaced with an automatic dishwasher and/or trash compactor.) The sink and cleanup center must have good lighting, both natural and artificial. A light fixture should be located directly over the sink, and when possible, the sink placed close to a window since many people like this. But this is, however, a matter of personal preference. If there is only one window allotted to the area, some people like it better in the eating area. Also installation of a sink along an interior plumbing partition will usually cost less, if permitted by the local plumbing code.

A typical cleanup center containing dishwasher, sink, food waste disposer and trash compactor.

As a general rule, store items in this center that use water. Sufficient storage should be provided for fruits, vegetables and other foods that do not require refrigeration and must be washed or soaked, as well as space for small pots, coffee pot, everyday dishes and glassware, dish towels and cloths (or sponges), brushes, and dishwashing and cleaning supplies.

Supplementary Work Centers

Two supplementary work centers are also included in most well-designed kitchens. Although a considerable amount of preparatory work is done at the sink work center, studies of kitchen activities indicate that there is usually a need for a special preparation or *mix center*. Not as clearly defined, nevertheless needed, is a *serve center*, which is often incorporated with the range center.

Mix Center. For the sake of convenience, there is little difference whether the mix center is between the refrigerator and sink or between the sink and range. However, the latter arrangement involves more travel because the distance between mix center and refrigerator is usually longer. In recent years, the mix center has become unique in that the countertop height is lower than the normal countertop (32 inches instead of 36 inches), making it more comfortable for rolling dough and mixing. Plan on a counter 36 to 48 inches long with storage space to house such things as the mixer, blender, flour bin, baking pans, casseroles, larger canisters, mixing bowls of assorted sizes, and utensils for measuring and mixing. (Most packaged, canned, and bottled foods used in baking should also be stored near the mix center.) The mix center also requires a high intensity of illumination (at least the equivalent of two 100-watt incandescent lamps) mounted either under the cabinets or in hanging fixtures. The specialized storage can be supplied by most standard base cabinets and can be designed to roll out at the touch of a finger and spring up to counter height for easy use.

While separate wall ovens are most frequently a part of the cooking center, sometimes they are included in the mix area and the complete unit is known as a *mix/bake center*. As such it will interrupt normal counter usage unless the oven is installed near the cooking surface. A single counter between the two may serve both, but if the oven and cooking surface are separated a considerable distance, each should have an adjacent counter with cabinets. If both the built-in oven and refrigerator must be placed at one end of an assembly, a counter should be installed between them. The refrigerator should be closest to the sink/cleanup center.

Serve Center. The serve center is not used in conjunction with any specific appliance, but it is generally located between the range or cook center and the dining area. A counter area of at least 30 inches should be provided to facilitate food serving. In this center, keep in mind that moist and crisp warming drawers are a joy for party givers and those who dine in shifts. If space prohibits a separate small appliance center (see page 101), it is a good idea to use small appliances near the range rather than close to the sink. A multi-outlet strip will accommodate a good number of them. Warming lights in this center are nice extras, too.

The mixing center can often be more convenient to use if it is lower than the standard 36-inch base cabinet. A height of 32 inches is suggested, although anything from 30 to 34 inches is acceptable.

A low serving counter near the cook center is handy.

Storage for such items as a toaster, trays, serving platters and dishes, table linens, napkins, and cookies, cakes, and other foods that are purchased ready to eat should be included in the serve center. Of course, accessibility to the eating area is most important.

Combination Centers. Frequently in small kitchens of studio apartments and similar areas, as well as in some second kitchens, the space is so limited that it is necessary to combine basic work centers. That is, the cabinets and appliances of one center may be combined with those of the neighboring center to form a continuous assembly. It is usually best to combine at least two centers into one continuous assembly, with corresponding storage above and below.

One of the best ways to determine the proper counter space is to select the widest desirable counter of the two centers and then add 12 inches to it. For instance, if combining the refrigerator and storage center with sink and cleanup center, the counter required for the former is 18 inches, while the minimum for the latter is 30 inches. Thus the widest counter — 30 inches — plus the 12 inches

would mean that the combined counter should be a minimum of 42 continuous inches. The resulting counter permits both centers to operate simultaneously.

It is important to keep in mind when designing a kitchen with combination centers that it must contain at least 10 feet (linear) of full-use base cabinets plus 10 of full-use wall cabinets. Never cut down on counter space at the expense of base cabinets. Every kitchen needs at least 10 lineal feet of base cabinets and 10 lineal feet of wall cabinets. These are absolute minimums.

Specialty Centers

While most kitchens would probably function adequately with only the three main work centers, there are some "extras," or specialty centers, that — like the supplementary work centers — make the kitchen more workable and more pleasant to work in. Depending on the householder's specific needs and the available space, such items as eating areas, planning centers, pantries, barbecues, and laundry centers are no longer considered "extras." They have become essentials.

Eating Area. Kitchen eating facilities can range from a counter-height eating bar to an almost-formal dining space. When planning for a kitchen eating space, a convenient location is of primary importance. The eating area should be easy to serve, yet away from the kitchen's main work areas. It should be large enough to contain a table and chairs and still allow easy circulation.

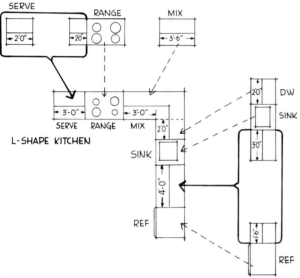

When two or more separate counters are combined, total counter length for the combination is the sum of the widest one plus 1 foot.

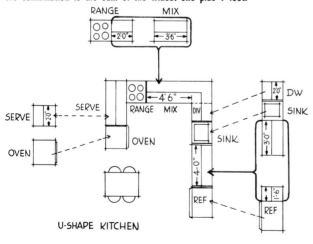

An eating counter is ideal for snacks.

If there is a peninsula dividing the kitchen work area from the dining area, a snack bar built onto it solves the quick meal problem. Children love eating at the counter and innumerable steps can be saved by the homemaker. A dining bar should be about 29 inches high if chairs are used, about 40 inches with high stools. Allow 2 feet of counter or table space for each place setting. A counter should be at least 15 inches deep for meal service.

Planning Center. Since the kitchen is where most household activities are likely to be organized, a planning desk, drop-leaf counter, or complete office space is a desired kitchen item. The work area of the planning or office center should be large enough to be functional (30 inches long at least). It should have a telephone, a recipe file, cookbook shelves, and space for miscellaneous storage, with the work surface at desk height — 29 to 30 inches. The knee space should allow room for storing the chair, and the desk top must be well lighted by natural light and/or by artificial light. Since the planning desk is, in fact, the homemaker's "office," every effort should be made to make it as pleasant as possible.

Pantry. Before kitchens were "modern" in the sense of equipment and materials, the bulk of the kitchen's storage was in the pantry. Usually a closet-like space with a few shelves, it served as storage space for both food and cleaning equipment. Today there is a revival of the pantry, but its similarity to the pantry of yesteryear is minute.

Today's pantry (and, every kitchen should have one) is a compact cabinet, within easy reach of the work area. It should be handsomely designed. Thus, when wall space is limited, plot the pantry with pull-out shelves or drawers that use the full height and depth of the line of cabinets and bring all the stored items within easy reach. Pantry units can also be cleverly designed with hinged shelf sections on both sides, opening like leaves of a book to make everything accessible. Some manufacturers offer ready-made ones. Slanting shelves, supermarket style, can also be used for canned goods storage with cans lying on sides so that a replacement rolls into position as one is removed. Although most cabinet manufacturers offer pantry cabinets as part of their standard line, many builders prefer building

A well-designed planning center.

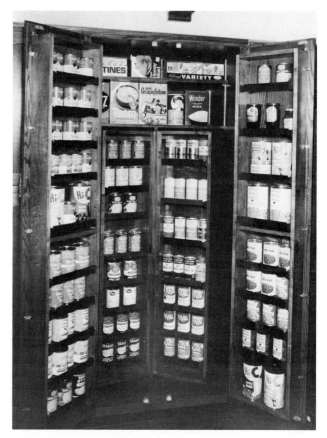

Pantry units are now available that offer plenty of storage for canned goods.

A pantry unit combined with pull-out storage shelves.

their own. And, as previously discussed, this pantry is correctly located as part of the refrigerator/ storage center.

Barbecue. Outdoor cookery has become so popular that the barbecue grill has inevitably moved indoors, allowing the devotee of charcoal-broiled steak to enjoy this succulent treat the year round. Drop-in models are available. They use charcoal, gas, or electricity for fuel. Whichever type is used, indoor barbecues require a powerful exhaust system. Ideally, they should be located against a wall and enclosed on one or both sides.

Laundry Center. If space can be found for a clothes washer and dryer in another convenient location it is better not to put them in the kitchen. Clothes and food just do not mix well together. It is convenient, though, to have the laundry center near the kitchen to help in dovetailing tasks.

If the laundry appliances must be in the kitchen, try to place them out of the refrigerator/sink/range area. Allow at least four-and-a-half feet of wall space for a standard size washer and dryer. Be sure to check the measurements of the models that are to be used. When space is very limited or a standard washer cannot be installed, a compact spinner washer 24 inches wide by 30 inches high by 15 inches deep can be stored out of the way and rolled to the sink for use. A matching compact dryer of the same size may be operated on 120-volt electricity. It can be hung on a wall, parked on a base cabinet, or

A drop-in type barbecue unit.

The laundry center in a kitchen need not be large.

placed standing on the floor. If there is room for a washer, but not enough space or the required utility connections for a standard size dryer, a compact dryer can be mounted on top of some washers with the use of a special kit.

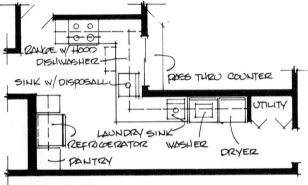

This laundry and kitchen are together but separate so each can function in its own best way.

More details on eating areas, planning centers, family rooms, and laundry centers as well as other kitchen extras are given in Chapter 7.

THE WORK TRIANGLE

The three work centers should be placed in the kitchen so that movement between them is as efficient and direct as possible. The normal work sequence is from right to left. The ideal arrangement for a right-handed person, therefore, is to have the refrigeration/food-storage area on the right with a preparation area adjacent to it. The clean-up center, or sink center with storage for dishes, sink, and dishwasher should be next. Then on the left, the cooking and serving center with storage for pots, pans and serving dishes should be placed.

Such a triangular arrangement fits well a typical work pattern that occurs in the kitchen. Food is taken from the refrigerator and storage center, and is

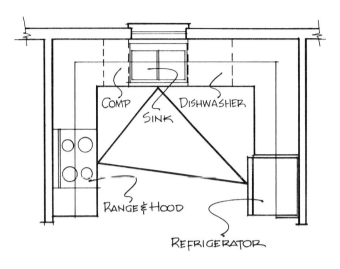

The basic work triangle.

made ready for cooking (or eating) at the preparation center. Since water is likely to be needed in the process, the sink center will be used. Once prepared, the food may be moved directly to the serve center and then to the dining area, or it may go through a cooking process at the cook top or oven.

Under certain conditions a compromise may be needed and the centers may be placed out of sequence, reversed or even separated. A work center can be isolated as on an island or in a separate wall unit. When used in this fashion, it should be a complete center or unit. In any case, whether the sequence is left-to-right or right-to-left is not nearly so important as arranging the kitchen so as to minimize the length of trips between the pairs of work centers. At the same time, ample room for counter and storage at each center should be allowed.

In arranging the three main work centers in a kitchen, a "triangle of convenience" (also known as the work triangle, the magic triangle, the step-saving triangle, etc.) is the prime consideration. This triangle represents the flow of work from one center to another. The sum of the three sides of the triangle should not exceed 22 feet. This is to conserve the homemaker's energy. Nor should the triangle be less than 13 feet. This is to avoid an overcrowded work

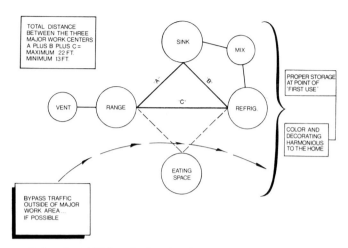

Basics of good kitchen planning at a glance.

pattern. No single arm of the triangle should measure less than 4½ feet.

The most trafficked leg of the triangle is that between the sink and the range. Therefore, this would ideally be the shortest leg of the triangle. The next most heavily traveled route is between refrigerator and sink. This leg of the triangle might be from 5 to 8 feet. When measuring the distance between two appliances, measure from the center front of one to the center front of the other. By the way, since the separate-type oven is used relatively infrequently, it is often convenient to separate the oven center from the other centers of the kitchen and it need not be located on the triangle at all.

Before leaving the subject of kitchen traffic flow, it is worth remembering that common sense is most important. Obviously, no doorways should funnel traffic directly into the middle of the work triangle. The layout should not lead the children to traipse through the entire kitchen just to hang up their coats after school. The number of doorways, their location, and the direction of door swing affect the efficiency of the kitchen arrangement. Generally, doorways in corners should be avoided. It is also desirable to avoid door swings that conflict with the use of appliances or cabinets, or with other doors. When remodeling a kitchen, rehang the door on the other side of the jamb or hinge it to swing out rather than in. In the latter case, make certain that the door does not swing into the traffic path in halls or other activity areas. A sliding or folding door avoids such a problem. But aside from such general thoughts on good traffic movement throughout the triangle, there are no hard and fast rules of traffic flow.

It is also important that adequate aisles between work centers be provided, so that there is room to move about easily. Two people should be able to bend down back to back, without touching. Between opposite work counters, allow at least 48 inches. If two or more people are likely to be sharing the kitchen allow 54 to 64 inches. The same clearance is needed from a counter front to a table, a wall, or to the face of a storage wall if the space is a work area.

KITCHEN TYPES

Although it is possible to have almost infinite numbers of arrangements and combinations of work centers, the most commonly used and generally the most efficient kitchens are U-shaped, L-shaped, corridor, one-wall, or island arrangements. The arrangement used depends on the size and shape of the area allocated for the kitchen; the location of windows, doors, and services (plumbing, electricity, etc.); and the proximity of the kitchen to the home's other rooms and outdoor living spaces. It depends also on getting the most efficient arrangement of work centers arranged in a triangular pattern with the sequence of work centers being — refrigerator/ storage center, sink/cleanup center, and cook center. This triangular arrangement and the sequence of the work centers along the triangle as mentioned earlier, should not exceed 22 feet nor be less than 13 feet. The distance between any two centers should not be more than 7 or 8 feet. In the case of a U-shaped or L-shaped kitchen, the maximum distance between the two extreme centers should not be more than 10 feet.

In planning a kitchen around the triangle, keep all other kitchen activities away from the three main work centers. This way, when one of the children feeds the family pet, for example, she or he will not keep bumping into the person preparing the family dinner. Also, try to prevent the normal traffic lanes between other areas of the house from crossing the triangle, thus cutting down on the plan's efficiency. Such through traffic may generally be avoided by U-shaped, L-shaped, and one-wall kitchen layouts. With some arrangements, such as the corridor and island types, cross traffic often can pass through the work triangle. However, this need not interfere with kitchen activities if the plan provides an alternate route of travel.

Architectural design dictates, as has been noted, to a great extent the type of kitchen plan. However, imagination and basic knowledge of traffic

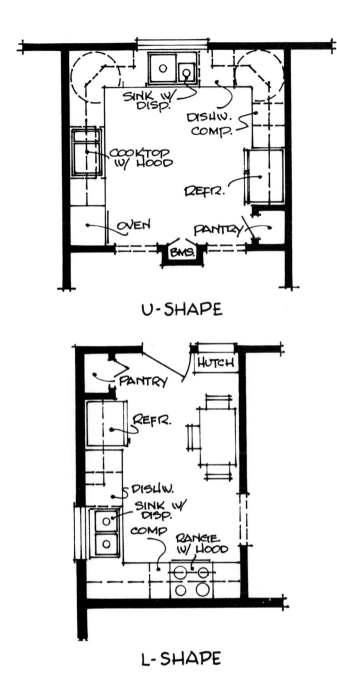

U-SHAPE

L-SHAPE

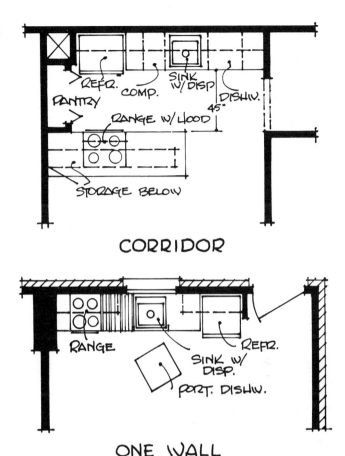

CORRIDOR

ONE WALL

The U-Shaped Kitchen

In spite of the fact that experts seldom agree on anything, most kitchen design experts seem to agree that the U-shaped arrangement is the most desirable kitchen plan from the standpoint of efficiency. This arrangement divides the work centers and their appliances among three walls that are placed in a "U" configuration. The sink/cleanup center is usually placed at the base of the "U," with the refrigerator and cook centers installed on the facing legs. This creates a tight work triangle that eliminates wasted effort. In fact, the U-shaped kitchen's greatest advantage is the short distance between work centers and the privacy it insures for the cook.

Because of its shape, traffic patterns form naturally outside the work area and thus do not affect the U-shaped kitchen's efficiency. Counter space is continuous, and ample storage is generally made available. The U-shaped plan is also adaptable to both large and small kitchens. However, if the "U" is less than 6 feet between base cabinets, the work area gets too cramped. More than 10 feet across the

patterns in the kitchen can help the planner overcome most any obstacle in planning a beautiful new kitchen. And by becoming acquainted with the five basic shapes, one can soon know what to look for in arrangements. Of course, all five basic kitchen types have numerous variations. The U-shaped, for example, can become round, or octagonal. But, it should be remembered that each one is planned for a specific type of use and each has its unique advantages and disadvantages. Select the plan that best suits the needs of the cook and the available space.

The U shape allows great flexibility in arrangement.

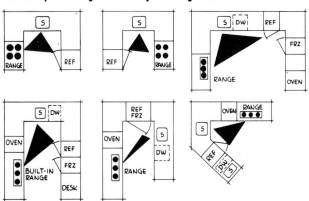

Six arrangements for a U-shaped kitchen.

work area results in too many steps between work centers. Yet, a 5-foot aisle and another wall storage and counter space is better than more aisle and no counters.

Frequently, one leg of the "U" may extend into the kitchen without wall support. Such an arrangement is generally used in connection with an informal dining space, with one leg of the "U" serving as a room-dividing peninsula to separate the kitchen and dining area, or kitchen and family room.

The minor disadvantages of the U-shaped kitchen are the extensive countertops and the need for special cabinets to fit the corners. In the U-shaped plan, it is important to locate the dishwasher so that the door can open without hitting the adjacent corner cabinet. In a tight "U" plan, this can be accomplished with a filler at the corner.

The L-Shaped Kitchen

The L-shaped kitchen divides the work centers and their appliances between two walls that meet at right angles. Another variation of this layout extends

the base of the "L" into the kitchen area. The "L" shape is a good plan for a large kitchen and its openness permits more than one cook to work at a given time. Ideally, the two work spans should not be broken by openings other than windows.

While the L-shaped kitchen permits less space for counters and storage, it has the advantage of creating an eating area without sacrificing space from the work area. This free space on the two unoccupied walls can also be utilized for a laundry, child's play space, or other activity center. The L-shaped kitchen also keeps the work triangle free of through-room traffic and allows an efficient arrangement of the work centers. In any L-shaped kitchen, the sequence of work centers should provide a work flow from refrigerator to sink to range. Any other arrangement would be awkward and difficult to work with. But, keep in mind that if the refrigerator, sink, and range are too far apart, the work triangle would be

An L-shaped kitchen gives a feeling of spaciousness.

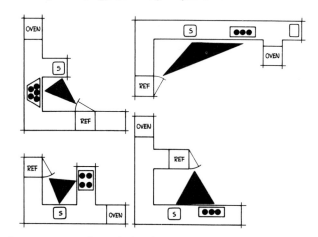

Four arrangements for an L-shaped kitchen.

such that serving a meal could be a very exhausting task.

In most L-shaped kitchens, the sink/cleanup center is placed on the window wall. Sometimes the short leg of the "L" can be widened to create a peninsula between the eating space and the work area, with the cook center placed on the kitchen side of the peninsula and eating bar on the other side.

It may be necessary because of doors, windows, or offsets to adapt one of the five basic kitchen types. For example, the most efficient utilization of space may result in a "broken U" or a "broken L" where doors interrupt the wall pattern. As a rule, however, a broken "U" or "L" layout is a sign of failure in the house's design.

The Corridor Kitchen

The corridor type of kitchen, sometimes called a *galley kitchen*, divides the work centers and their appliances between two parallels walls, two work areas on one wall and one on the other. Because this arrangement is well suited for long narrow spaces, it is one of the most popular kitchen types used in apartment construction. The corridor kitchen is also particularly useful in homes where there is a premium on space. Often its compact dimensions

limit it to one or two cooks, but when well planned, this design can squeeze the maximum number of work surfaces, cabinets, and appliances into the smallest space. The aisle in the corridor should be at least four feet wide, and if possible should reach a dead end to prevent casual traffic from passing through the work triangle. When this happens, the corridor kitchen resembles a small "U," and contains many of its advantages. It is also perhaps the most economical type since there are no corners to turn. However, if the corridor is open at both ends, the corridor is a passageway from one part of the house to another, which could drive the cook crazy.

The One-Wall Kitchen

The one-wall type, frequently called a *pullman*, *line-a-wall*, or *strip kitchen*, positions all work centers and their appliances along one wall. Where space is very limited — mini-kitchens in studio apartments, second kitchens in a family room, or a vacation home kitchen — this plan is frequently employed. It also finds favor in some contemporary open-plan houses where the kitchen is part of the social space. But, because of the cramped space, there is no possible way of forming the step-saving triangle of convenience. Thus the challenge in planning a one-wall kitchen is to provide adequate storage and work surfaces without the distances between the work centers becoming too great for efficiency.

Although the decoration may not be conventional, the layout of the corridor kitchen is.

Single-wall kitchens are suitable for a second home such as this. Notice that the portable dishwasher is also used as a serving cart.

To overcome some of the disadvantages of the one-wall kitchen, consider converting a nearby closet to a pantry for canned foods or for cleaning supplies. Or let a mobile cart or two give some extra counter work space. A portable dishwasher will also add to counter space by serving as a traveling work surface. As far as an eating area is concerned, that will probably have to fit into an adjoining room where space is available — either the family room or a dining room. In this plan, as in all others, route traffic so it bypasses the important kitchen work areas.

The Island Kitchen

All layouts except the one-wall kitchen can benefit from the addition of an island. In recent years, this type is usually a modification of either the U-shaped kitchen or the L-shaped kitchen and should not be confused with what is normally called a "broken U-shaped" plan. The island kitchen retains much of the efficiency of both the U-shaped and the L-shaped kitchens while providing a focal point and design feature. Island kitchens should be used when space is not a problem, or as part of a combined kitchen/family room — the island serves as an excellent room divider. Sometimes, one of the work centers may be moved from the normal sequence and placed on the island. When this is done, care must be taken not to increase or decrease the distance between work centers more than recommended. The island should be a minimum of 25 by 48 inches, and permit an aisle between island and nearby work counters of at least 3 feet. If the range and sink are on opposite walls, never place the island between them unless the homemaker is out to set some sort of a hiking record.

The island counter immediately adds storage space. Base cabinets can fit on all sides, or shelving may be fitted into one or both ends. On the counter

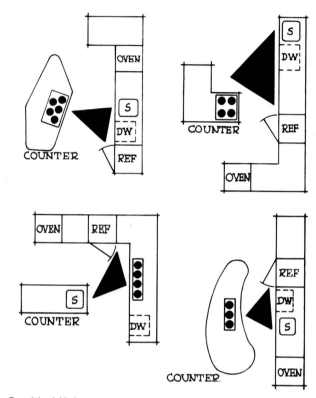

Four island kitchen arrangements.

Islands may be stationary (left), movable (center), and portable (right).

can go many of the items that cannot be fitted onto counters along the kitchen wall — a bar or vegetable-washing sink, a barbecue grill, a hard maple cutting board, or a small appliance center. If space permits, the island might be widened to add a food-serving extension, or even a dropleaf for quick snacks.

Where there is not enough floor space for a permanent island, the so-called "floating" type, which is an island counter on heavy-duty casters, may be an ideal solution. In addition to providing an extra work surface in the kitchen where it is needed, the floating island can be rolled to other rooms in the house, or outside to the terrace.

The peninsula feature in a kitchen is closely akin to the island. A peninsula can bring the three kitchen work centers closer together and reduce the size of the work triangle. Often, the center floor space in a kitchen is not put to good use. A large, old, square kitchen or an open, new kitchen can

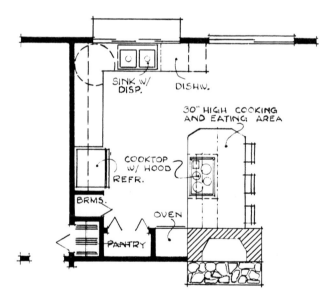

The four-wall for spacious, gracious freedom of design.

benefit from the addition of a peninsula. Even a short line-up of cabinets extending into the center of the room can divide the working and eating areas and give additional storage and work tops. A peninsula is often designed so cabinets open from both sides. This feature is particularly good if the table-setting supplies are housed in the peninsula. Wall cabinets can be hung over the top of the peninsula, or you can leave the view open. The use of a peninsula also per-

mits the so-called "four-wall" type of kitchen for spacious, gracious freedom of design.

The base cabinet at the end of the peninsula should have a toe or kick space on the end side, as well as on the kitchen side, so a person can work in a normal manner. Also, depending on how the peninsula is employed, it may be necessary to have toe space on both sides of all base cabinets. Most island units have a toe space all the way around them.

Peninsula wall cabinets are usually layed out so that their run is shorter than the base cabinet units. Besides reducing head bumping incidents, it contributes greatly to a more open appearance for the entire kitchen. To cut down on bruised arms and hips, it is wise to figure on curved corners rather than square ones at the end of the peninsula.

The Family Kitchen

The so-called "family" kitchen is just an open version of any of the five basic plans. Its function is to provide a gathering place for the entire family in addition to providing space for the everyday kitchen functions. Because of its dual function, a family kitchen is normally divided into two sections. One

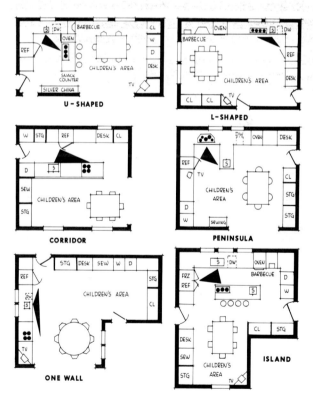

Six family kitchen plans.

section includes the three work centers, while the other contains the dining area and family-room facilities.

COMMON MISTAKES

Frequently, a very little replanning can make a kitchen easier to work in and cut the builders' costs in the bargain. In the two plans shown here, the "befores" were taken from actual builders' plans and the "afters" were taken after a little replanning.

Kitchen No. 1 began as a shallow "U" in which the counter range could not be correctly positioned. A room-divider counter changed it to a straight-line plan which easily accommodated the range and, as a bonus, provided an eating bar.

Kitchen No. 2 suffered from badly allocated work surfaces, a poorly positioned refrigerator, and lack of room for both a washer and a dryer. The first revision provides work space around all centers and room for a separate dryer, but leaves the refrigerator blocking part of the window. The second revision

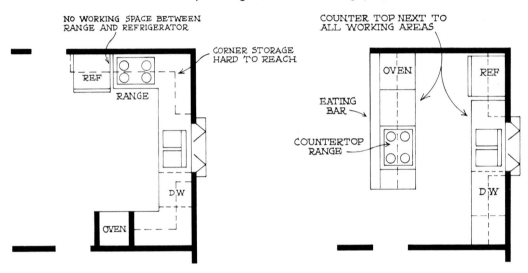

BEFORE

AFTER

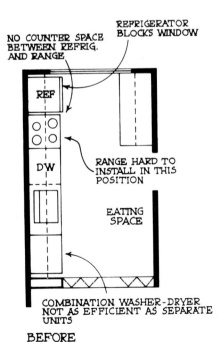

BEFORE

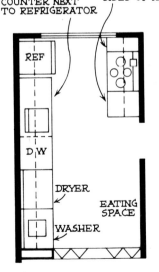

AFTER

AFTER

clears the window and puts the dryer on the outside wall where it is easier to vent.

All the mistakes shown here were taken from actual builders' plans. For example, the dishwasher's location is the problem in Nos. 1 and 2. Since homemakers often leave the machine open

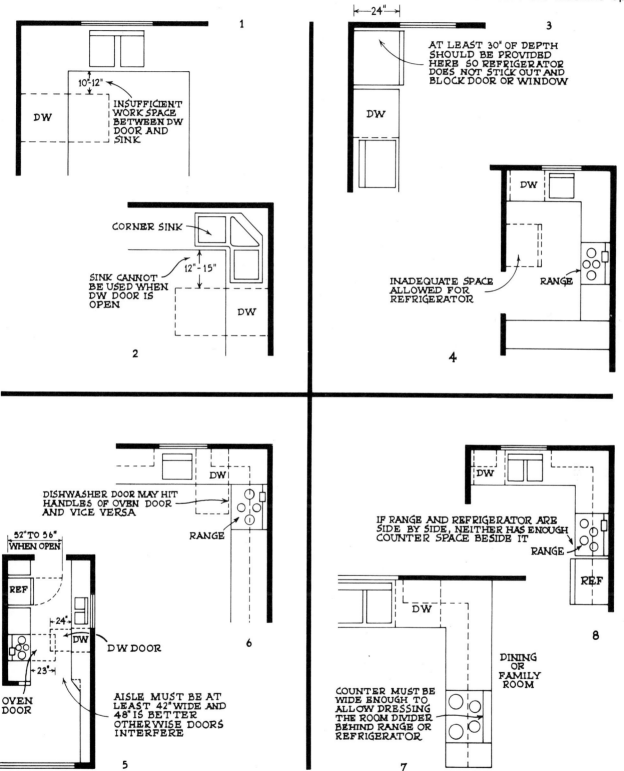

1

10"-12" INSUFFICIENT WORK SPACE BETWEEN DW DOOR AND SINK

DW

CORNER SINK

SINK CANNOT BE USED WHEN DW DOOR IS OPEN

12"-15"

DW

2

24"

3

AT LEAST 30" OF DEPTH SHOULD BE PROVIDED HERE SO REFRIGERATOR DOES NOT STICK OUT AND BLOCK DOOR OR WINDOW

DW

DW

INADEQUATE SPACE ALLOWED FOR REFRIGERATOR

RANGE

4

DISHWASHER DOOR MAY HIT HANDLES OF OVEN DOOR AND VICE VERSA

DW

RANGE

52" TO 56" WHEN OPEN

REF

24"

DW

DW DOOR

23"

OVEN DOOR

AISLE MUST BE AT LEAST 42" WIDE AND 48" IS BETTER OTHERWISE DOORS INTERFERE

5

6

DW

IF RANGE AND REFRIGERATOR ARE SIDE BY SIDE, NEITHER HAS ENOUGH COUNTER SPACE BESIDE IT

RANGE

REF

8

DW

COUNTER MUST BE WIDE ENOUGH TO ALLOW DRESSING THE ROOM DIVIDER BEHIND RANGE OR REFRIGERATOR

DINING OR FAMILY ROOM

7

while it accumulates dirty dishes, it must be positioned so its door will not block a work area.

Mistake No. 3 stems from the fact that a refrigerator is deeper than other appliances. No. 4, surprisingly common, results from just plain forgetting that a refrigerator will have to be moved in when the kitchen is finished. Appliance-door clearances, easy to overlook on paper, create mistakes Nos. 5 and 6. No. 7 is usually the result of trying to jam appliances into inadequate space. And No. 8 occurs when a freestanding appliance is set into a counter that also serves as a room divider.

To summarize the important points of designs let us list the "Ten Basic Rules for Kitchen Planners."

1. Plan the layout around the concept of the work triangle; keep its dimensions within proper limits.
2. Make certain there is sufficient counter space, preferably arranged in a continuous layout.
3. Provide adequate light to counter tops.
4. Plan for adequate storage cabinets; mount them within easy reach.
5. Position the refrigerator so that there is room for counter space adjacent to it; not in a corner or next to the range.
6. The dishwasher should be easily accessible from the sink.
7. Provide a food waste disposer and trash compactor to inhibit growth of insects.
8. Allow enough space between work areas so appliances and cabinets can be opened easily and are accessible.
9. Remember that the kitchen must be highly functional; do not allow decorations to interfere with the logical work sequence.
10. Strive to direct traffic away from the work triangle.

CHAPTER 3

THE WORK CENTER APPLIANCES

Each of the work centers described in the preceding chapter is planned around one or more of the major appliances. The sink/cleanup center includes a disposer, a dishwasher, and a trash compactor; the storage center a refrigerator/freezer; and the cook center the range and possibly a ventilating hood. Since the appliances are usually the most important equipment in the kitchen, they should be selected with great care and consideration. Most new appliances offer a wide choice of sizes and colors and come in either built-in or free-standing designs. In fact, never before have there been so many products from which to choose. New textures, bolder colors, more practical surfaces, and care-free appliances — a dazzling array of beautiful and useful products that really make today's kitchens the wonder room of the American home — are widely available.

Built-in panels give appliances and cabinets the same appearance.

In choosing the many products that go into today's kitchen, consider style and color. It is important to produce a unified and well coordinated effect for maximum impact. Equally important, however, is performance. Choose appliances with a proven record of dependability. Also make certain that the materials meet local building codes and minimum HUD/FHA standards.

While the remodeling of a kitchen does not automatically call for new appliances, it is a good time to take a long look at the ones you have, and at the ones you do not have. For a small outlay, you can save a lot of extra steps, and there is never a better chance to put a whole dream kitchen together than right now. In the case of a new home, of course, the appliances for the kitchen are usually included in the cost of the house. All HUD/FHA and S & LS agencies will let the builder finance them on 20- to 30-year low-interest credit under the package mortgage instead of three-year high-interest consumer credit. But getting the appliances as part of the house means that you will be paying for them over the life of the mortgage, perhaps 20 or 30 years, longer than the usual life of the appliance — but it does keep the monthly cost low. Look at the total cost of credit over the duration of the loan as well as at the payments. You may decide to pay a higher price for the benefit of low payments, particularly if your needs are great now because you are young and expect your income to rise. But you should know what you are doing. Find out what will happen if you cannot meet a payment. Would you be better off with a personal loan than an installment payment? Would it be possible or wise to refinance your house for a major remodeling job?

Installation costs are not usually quoted as part of the price of built-in appliances because the amount of carpentry, electrical work and plumbing needed varies with the job. Replacing an existing built-in is simple. Remodeling will raise the cost. Check into what is needed and what it will cost for materials and labor.

To avoid costly "call backs" or annoying minor repairs, be sure that adequate service is available for the appliances selected. Most manufacturers offer warranties and service policies that make repairs and adjustments much less of a problem than they once were. But, it is still very important to compare warranties and servicing policies. Is it a so-called "full warranty" with a specific period of coverage? Who is responsible for paying for parts? For how long? Are there parts excluded from the warranty? Who pays for the service to replace the parts? For how long? What if you move? Does the warranty apply to the new buyer of the house? Does the warranty apply to the new buyer of the house if it is a built-in appliance?

If retailers are to be responsible for servicing appliances, evaluate them. How long have they been in business? Do they have a good reputation in the community for fair dealing, prompt and courteous service? in many cases, service is handled through a separate factory-owned or factory-approved agency, so the reliability of the manufacturer rather than of the retailer is what counts. The answer to these questions are important consideration to all — the homeowner, the kitchen designer, and the builder or contractor.

Quality standards for gas appliances are set by the American Gas Association (AGA), while the National Electrical Manufacturers Association (NEMA) and Association of Home Appliance Manufacturers (AHAM) sets the quality standards for electrical appliances. The Underwriters Laboratories, Inc. (UL) certifies that electrical appliances have been submitted by the manufacturer for testing and have met standards regarding life, fire, and casualty. HUD/FHA requires all gas appliances to carry the AGA seal of approval and all electrical appliances to carry the NEMA or AHAM seal.

Let us now take a closer look at the three major work centers and the appliances that make them tick.

REFRIGERATOR/STORAGE CENTER

The main appliance of the refrigerator/storage center is the refrigerator or refrigerator/freezer. In recent years, advances in design and insulation have made it possible to put a refrigerator of surprisingly large capacity into the floor space formerly required for a unit with much smaller capacity. This is primarily due to the discovery of new urethan insulation materials, which permit the walls of the unit to be thinner, thus increasing the interior capacity.

In addition to the refrigerator, this work center may also house a separate freezer and ice maker.

Refrigerators

Besides the general cold storage space for fresh foods, the most elementary refrigerator will usually contain a small freezer compartment in which frozen foods may be stored and ice cubes may be made. Since storage space is so important, most modern refrigerator manufacturers pay special attention to shelf and compartment design. Crispers and meat keepers should have tight covers to keep fresh vegetables, fruits, and meats from drying out. Adjustable shelves, pullout shelves, and door storage, portable egg trays, and butter conditioners all are stretch space. It is important for the family to consider what they generally like to put into the refrigerator when they shop — watermelons, turkeys, tall bottles, and other large items can influence their selection.

As to the amount of refrigerator space needed, experts agree that a minimum of 6 to 8 cubic feet should be allowed for a family of two. Then, add one cubic foot for each additional person. If the family entertains regularly, add another 2 cubic feet to the required amount. Incidentally, this footage is for fresh food refrigerator space only; it does not include the freezer compartment.

Basically, all refrigerators fall into three general types as outlined here.

1. *Compact* units can be as small as 2 cubic feet for use in office, family room, nursery, or den. Some have a cart so that they can be rolled out to the pool or patio. There are also undercounter and wall-cabinet compact refrigerators, usually about 7 cubic feet in size, that will fit in with standard kitchen cabinets. These are popular for apartments and vacation homes. Compacts usually have a manual defrost.

Compact refrigerator.   **Conventional upright refrigerator.**

2. In the *conventional* upright model, the freezer compartment is enclosed by an inner door, inside the fresh foods section. Temperature in the freezer stays at 10 to 20 degrees, adequate for short-term storage. Generally this model is available in 9- to 13-cubic-foot sizes and is the lowest in price of standard types.

3. *Two-door* standard upright refrigerator/freezer combinations have separate doors for each compartment. In many two-door units the freezer door is at the top of the appliance. Other designs provide a freezer space alongside the refrigerator space, while still others have the freezer compartment in the lower section. The two-door side-by-side model seems to be gaining in favor. This type offers storage at a convenient height for both refrigerator and freezer. Doors do not require as much space to open because they are narrower than other types. A few models even have three doors, with the third compartment designed for ice cube production, water cooling, etc.

Both the compact and the various standard types can be had in free-standing or built-in models. The latter are frequently preferred because of their ability to fit into the overall design of the kitchen. However, the built-in models are quite a bit more expensive than the free-standing types.

Sizes of refrigerator/freezers vary — 30 to 42 inches being the overall range except for a few side-by-side units that are as wide as 60 inches. The most common cabinet opening required is either 33 or 36 inches wide and 66 inches high. While the exact measurements of the refrigerator/freezer unit should be used for the final layout a 36-inch opening can be used as "good" average for a preliminary design if the model has not yet been selected.

Some refrigerator/freezers are somewhat deeper than the usual 24-inch depth of the base cabinet assembly. This extra depth may create some problems of access to base cabinets, particularly drawer cabinets, where a refrigerator is located close to an inside corner of the base assembly. Of course, flush-mount refrigerators are built with the condenser coils (usually on the refrigerator back) under the refrigerator cold-food compartment. This allows the refrigerator to be pushed back against the wall and saves room space. A fan cools the condenser coils when the refrigerator is running.

As mentioned in Chapter 2, careful attention must be paid to the manner in which the doors are hinged, particularly when the refrigerator door is to be swung open against a wall. Some doors are hinged so that when the door is opened 90 degrees, the space occupied is 4 or 5 inches wider than the refrigerator cabinet width, the added space being due to the thickness of the door. Other designs keep the 90-degree door swing within the width of the refrigerator, but this arrangement may cause some difficulty in removing shelves, vegetable crispers meat keepers, etc.

The so-called "manual" defrost refrigerator must be defrosted, usually about once a month by the homemaker. With automatic defrost and "frost-free" or "no-frost" styles, the refrigerator portion never requires manual defrosting. The latter category has devices which prevent the formation of frost. This convenience increases operating costs to a substantial degree, as power is used for both the heating and cooling operations which may be going on simultaneously. The no-frost feature may be available in both the fresh-food and freezer compartment. With automatic defrost equipment, the freezer compartment must be defrosted manually. Temperatures in frost-free refrigerators, of course,

Two-door upright freezer/refrigerator. Two-door upright refrigerator/freezer.   Two-door side-by-side refrigerator/freezer.   Three-door refrigerator/freezer.

are even throughout the unit, and foods cool to safe storage temperatures faster. But unless foods are carefully wrapped and sealed they will dehydrate. The cost of operating a frost-free refrigerator may be almost double that of automatic defrost refrigerators with manual defrost freezers. A few frost-free models feature "power-saver" switches that let the householder reduce power consumption and operating expense under certain circumstances.

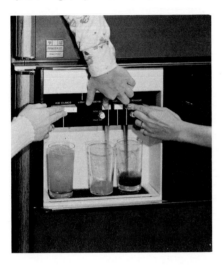

"Four on the door" — ice cubes, two separate beverages and chilled water are available with a touch of the finger.

Some modern refrigerator/freezers have features such as automatic ice cube makers and door water cooling facilities. Both these features necessitate the installation of a water supply for the refrigerator — usually a small diameter copper tube is all that is required. While these devices are usually in a refrigerator compartment, some models are constructed so that cooled drinking water and ice cubes may be obtained without opening the door of either the freezer or fresh-food compartment. By the way, many of the automatic icemakers, which eliminate the tray filling job, are designed so that they can be installed either at the time of purchase or later on. In the latter case, be sure to consider the cold water line in planning the kitchen. Nearly all new refrigerators are electric and operate off standard 120-volt wall outlets.

Freezers

Home freezers are enjoying a spurt in popularity. The types and amounts of frozen foods have more than doubled in the last 10 years. We can expect them to double again in the next 10.

A separate freezer when used properly can help a large family save money by buying food in quantity. Also, it can help supply emergency meals when unexpected guests arrive and it can cut down the number of trips to the supermarket. This latter advantage is especially important if the supermarket is at a distance. The freezer seems to fit nicely with the trend toward busy family lives and more working women. In addition, many families enjoy freezing fresh foods and preparing foods to freeze for later use as well.

There are two types of separate freezer units — upright and chest. The former type, the most popular, has shelf space that is both easy to see and easy to use. Some uprights now also offer a "no-

Refrigerator placement considerations .

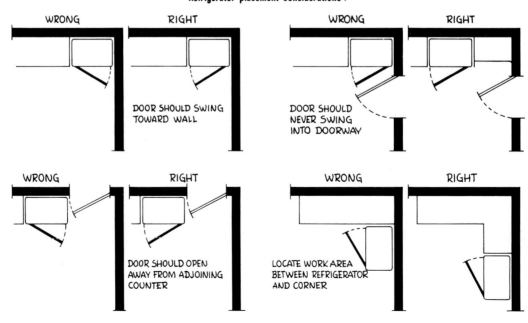

An upright freezer (left) and a chest freezer (right).

frost" feature, as well as door locks, signal lights to warn of current interruptions, adjustable shelves, and rollers or wheels for easy cleaning.

A chest-type freezer costs less to operate than an upright, but takes more floor space and makes reaching foods at the bottom more difficult. It needs defrosting one to three times a year. Some types have push-button flash defrost and a bottom drain to help.

Both types of freezers are available in sizes from 3.2 to 30 cubic feet. The most popular size is 15 cubic feet. Generally speaking, allow 2 cubic feet for each member of the family. Sometimes freezer capacities are quoted in pounds. To convert to cubic feet, remember that 35 pounds of produce can be stored in one cubic foot of space.

As mentioned in Chapter 2, separate freezers are not always installed in the kitchen. Frequently they are found in a basement, attached garage, or in some other secondary space in the house. But there are some facts to remember about the installation of separate freezers. For example, depth of upright u-nits with door open may be nearly 60 inches and height of chest-type units with lid open may be near-ly 63 inches. Condenser units on some models re-quire top ventilation. Some models require 2¼ in-ches side clearance for door lock to allow key inser-tion. Therefore, be sure to check the manufacturer's specifications very carefully before installing a unit.

All home freezers and combination refrigerator/freezers (except for those of the con-ventional refrigerator) will pull down to 0 degrees F (-17.8 degrees C). This can be accomplished by set-ting the control at colder. However, it is not man-datory to have zero degrees F if food is kept for less than a year. Foods can be kept for 3 to 4 months at plus 10 degrees without harm and from 6 to 9 months at plus 3 to plus 8 degrees. Even at zero degrees or less, food kept more than a year will deteriorate in appearance, taste, and nutritive value.

Most refrigerators, refrigerator/freezers, and freezers are finished with an acrylic lacquer-type finish, and a variety of colors are available. Several manufacturers make provisions for the installation of a decorative panel on the door surface. This panel may be replaced from time to time so that the refrigerator appearance may be modified to comply with changing decor requirements.

A built-in refrigerator/freezer unit.

Ice Makers

Ice makers are now available as separate appliances. They are usually available as a base cabinet, ordinarily 15 or 18 inches wide. They are in-tended for use in bar areas or where abnormal sup-ply of ice cubes is necessary. Ice makers must be connected to a 120-volt ac electric power source and to the cold water supply.

CLEAN-UP CENTERS

As every homemaker knows, the clean-up center is used before, during, and after meals, so it is a good idea to get it located as centrally as possible. The center consists of the sink, garbage disposer, trash compactor, and automatic dishwasher, as well as adequate counter space on both sides.

Sinks

Whether or not the sink is actually an appliance is something that will be discussed later. Suffice it to say that it is probably the most important single piece of equipment in the kitchen. It is used more often, for more things, and in more ways than any other item in the kitchen. Thus, locating it in the best possible spot is vital to the whole kitchen plan. For instance, if there is a window at least 40 inches

A triple-bowl stainless steel sink installed in clean-up island.

above the floor (enough to allow for a backsplash), you may want to place the sink under it. If there is a peninsula dividing the work area of the kitchen from the dining area, this makes an excellent site for a sink. Gourmet cooks often favor putting the sink in an island work counter in the middle of a kitchen.

Sinks come in four basic types:

1. *Enameled cast-iron* sinks are manufactured with a heavy wall thickness of iron. A fused-in enamel is applied to all exposed surfaces. The enamel on cast-iron sinks is four times thicker than other types of sinks. This provides much greater resistance to cracking, chipping, and marring. Cast-iron sinks are available in colors or in white. The solid, heavy construction makes them less subject to vibration and, therefore, extremely quiet when installed with a disposer.

2. *Porcelain-on-steel* sinks are formed of sheet steel in one piece and are sprayed and fired to produce a glasslike finish much like the surface found on cast-iron sinks. But, because of the unique physical characteristics of the material used, the finish on porcelain-on-steel sinks is only one-fourth as heavy as that on cast-iron sinks. These porcelain sinks are available in colors and in white.

3. *Stainless-steel* sinks are the lightest of the three and will provide a lifetime of service. The surfaces are easy to keep clean and are stain resistant. Since stainless steel is the finish, this type of sink is not available in colors. But the natural finish blends well with most color schemes. Stainless-steel sinks are graded by gauge (thickness) and nickel and chrome content of the steel. For example, 18-8 stainless steel would mean that there is an 18 per cent chrome content and 8 per cent nickel content. Nickel gives the steel the ability to withstand corrosion, while chrome enhances the sink's ability to

stand up and keep its finish over the years. Eighteen or twenty gauge are the most satisfactory thicknesses for sinks.

4. *Fiberglass* or *plastic-formed* kitchen sinks are relatively new and have not been tested heavily. They appear to be resistant to cracking, chipping, and marring. These sinks are available in several colors, but have been used more in bathroom installations than in kitchens to date.

Sinks are no longer limited to one shape and one size. Now they come in an almost limitless number of sizes, shapes, and bowl combinations. There are single-bowl, double-bowl, and even triple-bowl sinks. The sink bowls can be had in a variety of depths and widths. Let us take a closer look at some of the shapes:

1. *Single-bowl* sinks are usually used where space is limited and for a family that does an average amount of cooking and has a dishwasher. The bowl should be large enough (usually from 21 to 25 inches wide) to handle big pots and pans.

2. *Double bowls* permit one side to be used for soaking pots and pans while the other is employed in the preparation of food. Both bowls might be the

Various shapes of porcelain-on-steel sinks.

42

same size, or one could be shallow and the other deep. While most prefer the double-bowl sink, it is wise to remember that one large sink (24 inches) takes less space than an average double one (33 inches, for example) and is quite satisfactory if there is a dishwasher.

3. *Triple-bowl* sinks are excellent for kitchens where more than one person works at the sink area at the same time, or if the householder does a lot of freezing, canning, and baking. A typical triple-bowl sink may have a small vegetable sink (about 3½ inches deep) between two standard bowls. The standard bowl depth is about 7½ inches, but can vary somewhat among manufacturers. The average triple-bowl sink ranges from 40 to 48 inches long.

4. *Vegetable* sinks have one bowl of standard depth while the other is rather shallow. It may come with or without a cutting board.

5. *Corner* sinks contain two standard bowls in a pie-cut angle configuration. They are used for corner installations.

Most ledge-type sinks are 21 or 22 inches from front to back, and the bowl itself usually is 16 inches from front to back, but these dimensions vary slightly according to manufacturer and style. Most sinks today are drop-in units that rest on the countertop surface. They are held in position by either a clamp-down Huddee-type rim or a self-rimming unit that is held in place with adhesives and sealants. Either type is suitable for most kitchen applications.

The final selection of style, color, and arrangement is up to the householder. Frequently, if space permits, it is a good idea to have two separate sinks in the kitchen for two work centers, or an extra small sink for bartending, plant watering, or fingerpainting. Also consider installing a sit-down sink. This is a sink that puts homemakers close to the work and takes them off their feet at the same time. It makes no difference if they are short or tall. The sink can be installed at the most convenient height. Where space is at a premium and a double-bowl type is desired, there are sinks available in which one of the bowls is shallow enough (5 inches) to fit over a built-in dishwasher. Another good space saver is a single-bowl sink that has a small, raised bowl in one corner to house the the food waste disposer.

There are other sinks made to fit special needs or problems. For instance, for the person who prefers to rack or rinse dishes, single- or double-bowl sinks with drainboard on either right or left side can be had.

Faucets sometimes come with the sink, other times only holes are punched in the sink so that faucets can be purchased separately. There are many different styles of faucets available — standard two-faucet types, single-lever types, color-coordinated faucets, and so on. Other attachments such as sprays and hot-water dispensers may also be installed in the sink unit. The latter is an under-sink heater, which serves at a tap instant near-boiling water for coffee, dehydrated soups, gelatin desserts, and the like.

The installation of a kitchen sink must be made in accordance with local plumbing codes. In remodeling work, the location of existing plumbing is important in deciding where to place the sink in the new kitchen. The maximum allowable distance from the sink drain to the vent stack for various sizes of pipes is given below:

Drain Line Size	Maximum Distance Trap to Vent
1¼"	2'-6"
1½"	3'-6"
2"	5'-0"
3"	6'-0"
4"	10'-0"

Therefore, unless the remodeling plans call for a new vent stack, the sink should be located within the limits of the existing stack. One way of increasing the distance between the sink trap and vent stack is to increase the drain line pipe size.

Automatic Dishwashers

An automatic dishwasher was a luxury appliance 15 years ago. Today, it is considered a kitchen "must" and for good reason. It provides not only for the washing and drying of dishes but also acts as a storage spot for either soiled or clean dishes, out of the way until the homemaker chooses to store them in cabinets. Most new dishwashers also boast a plate-warmer cycle that bypasses the last minute annoyance of oven warming. Many new units also have a device that brings the water temperature up to the heat of sanitization (above 180 degrees F; 82.2 degrees C). This makes the dishwasher a very important family health help that cuts down on colds and other contagious illnesses. In addition, most new dishwashers come with special equipment that disposes of soft, solid food particles, eliminating the need for most scraping and rinsing of dishes before loading. Other features, such as pot and pan wash cycles, automatic dual detergent and rinse agent

While most built-in under-counter automatic dishwashers are installed as shown at left, there has been a growing trend to place them at waist height as illustrated at right.

dispensers, and "electric-saver" controls, can be obtained, too. Incidentally, the electric-saver control featured in some models provides an energy-conserving wash cycle and no-heat drying system.

Automatic dishwashers are usually classified as built-in under-counter, portable, or convertible from portable to built-in. (Some dishwasher-sink combination units are also available as are small countertop models with very limited capacity, but the three main classifications are those given above.) Portable dishwashers are usually top-loaded. The undercounter and convertible dishwashers are generally loaded from the front.

The portable or mobile dishwasher, ideal for apartments and small kitchens in vacation homes, are finished on all sides and come in a choice of colors. Their tops may be matching enamel or plastic laminate, or they may incorporate a chopping board or food warmer. When equipped with a chopping block or other easily maintained top, the portable can serve as a work island if it is not in use for washing, simply being moved to wherever the cook may need it. Soiled dishes can be stored in it wherever it happens to be. When there is a full load, it is wheeled to water connection.

Convertible dishwashers are finished in the same manner as portable ones, but because they are front-loaded they can be built into a line of cabinets. The under-counter models are finished only in the front. Cabinet finishes vary with the manufacturer, but are generally of the acrylic enamel type. Provisions are sometimes made for decorative door panels.

The type of dishwashing action varies to some

A portable automatic dishwasher (left) is easily moved about the room and can be stored in a cabinet such as the one on the right.

degree with each manufacturer. Rotating arms, fan jets, etc., are used. In most machines, the water is filtered and recirculated during the washing process, thereby reducing the amount of water required. The best water temperature for dishwashing is in the 140- to-160-degree F (56.6- to 71.1-degree C) range. Since most home water heater thermostats are ordinarily set at 110 degrees F (43.2 degrees C) a booster heater may be desirable and some dishwashers are so equipped. All dishwashers have one or more wash cycles, one or more rinse cycles, and a drying cycle. Drying is generally done by warm air. More elaborate controls make it possible to obtain various cycles in the machine, including light-wash cycles for slightly soiled dishes, warmer cycles, etc.

A typical space requirement for a built-in dishwasher is 34 inches high, at least 24 inches wide, and 24 inches deep. The dishwasher fits into the space of a standard 24-inch base cabinet. In an existing set-up, if there is a 24-inch base cabinet that can be removed, well and good. If not, it is possible to take out a wider cabinet or two cabinets that total at least 24 inches and use fillers on each side to fill the remaining space. Fillers are usually available from cabinet suppliers and some lumber yards. When existing cabinets were built on the job, some carpentry or cabinetmaking may be needed to open the space and finish the adjacent cabinets. Do not place the dishwasher at an immediate right angle to the sink. If the dishwasher must be around the corner from the sink, allow an intervening space of at least 18, and preferably 24, inches from the corner. Also, because the refrigerator generates cold and a

dishwasher produces heat and steam, these two appliances will last longer and work better if they are separated by a 3-inch insulated filler strip. As a general rule, if the person using the dishwasher the most is left-handed, it should probably go to the right of the sink and to the left of the sink if that person is right-handed.

A dishwasher takes a 120-volt, 60-hertz ac individual circuit, fused for 20 amperes. Three-wire electrical service to the dishwasher is recommended for connection to the terminal block and for grounding. To avoid the hazard of electrical shock, the dishwasher must be installed before it is used.

The water supply needed is, as already mentioned, 140 to 160 degrees F at 15 to 120 pounds per square inch pressure. The water pipe should be ½-inch outside-diameter copper, with a ⅜-inch female pipe thread connection at the valve. A ½-inch by ⅜-inch male compression elbow is provided as an accessory. An 8-foot flexible drain hose with a ½-inch inside diameter is furnished. It is not recommended that the drain line be extended beyond the length of the hose provided, but should this be necessary, attach the hose to a line with a larger inside diameter.

The most desirable drain system for a built-in dishwasher is through a drain air gap mounted at the sink or at countertop level. This accessory protects against a siphoning of the wash or rinse water and also prevents the possibility of food waste entering the dishwasher in the event of a plugged drain line. Many plumbing codes now require such an arrangement and prohibit a direct connection.

Portable dishwashers vary somewhat. One

(Left) A chalkboard front is a handy dishwasher front panel, especially if there are young children in the family. (Right) A dishwasher should be well insulated to cut heat loss and noise.

model, for example, is 33⅛ inches from the top to the bottom including the caster, 23¼ inches wide, and 27¾ inches deep. The handle projects another 2 inches. This portable dishwasher has a hose 34 inches long from the cabinet to the end of the faucet connector, and an electric cord 6 feet long. It requires a 120-volt, 60-hertz, 20-ampere circuit and it has a three-prong plug that must be connected to a properly grounded electrical outlet. The inlet and drain hoses are handled through a single connector to the faucet.

Food Waste Disposers

A food waste (garbage) disposer installed under one sink will eliminate messy food waste and simplify clean-up after meals, since you can peel fruits and vegetables, scrape plates, dump coffee grounds, and empty cereal bowls directly into the sink. The quality disposer can handle bones, fruit pits, egg shells, shrimp shells, in fact, almost any food waste. Some of the more efficient models have cutter blades that can handle fibrous waste such as corn husks, celery stalks, and artichoke leaves. Disposers are so efficient in handling food waste that today approximately 100 cities require their installation in all new housing starts or major improvements. But just as some cities require them in all new kitchen installations, a few areas prohibit or restrict the use of disposers because local sewage systems are not able to handle the extra waste. Therefore, check the local plumbing code before installing a disposer.

Speaking of waste, research by the United States Public Health Service proves that septic tank soil absorption systems that meet the HUD/FHA minimum property standards can handle the additional loads from food waste disposers. The addition of ground food waste may reduce the time between tank cleanings by approximately one-third. Only cold water should be run through the disposer since it is a must to solidify fats so they will not congeal in drain pipes and clog them.

There are two basic types of disposers — the batch-feed and the continuous-feed. The former is controlled by a built-in switch. Waste is placed in the chamber, the cold water is turned on, and the lid is put in place. In some cases, the lid must be turned or positioned a certain way to start the motor. In others, a sealed-in magnet activates a hermetically sealed switch so that the disposer starts as soon as the lid is dropped into place. A continuous-feed model means

you can feed waste into the disposer as it is operating. Because the batch-feed type will operate only with the cover on, it may be safer when the children are around, but may prove to be slower.

To free jams caused by some food or refuse, anti-jamming devices are built into the disposer. Units with rigid impeller hammers usually have an automatic or self-reversing feature. Models with swinging impeller hammers often have a manual reverse switch to prevent jamming. All disposals have a reset overload button incorporated in the body of the disposer which protects the motor from overheating and allows the householder to get the disposer back into operation when stalled.

The vast majority of disposers are designed to fit any single or double sink with a 3½- to 4-inch opening. (When installing in a double sink with two different depths, put the disposer in the shallower section.) As a rule, disposers can be installed without major changes in the drain lines. But check local plumbing codes and requirements to determine the amount of fall necessary and the method of connection. Most disposers are designed to receive the discharge of dishwashers. Detailed instructions for installation are provided with each model and, of course, they should be followed to the letter. The disposer requires a 120-volt ac outlet.

Trash Compactors

Waste compactors are a new favorite in many households. They reduce the volume of trash leaving the home and simplify waste disposal. That is, these units are designed for compacting dry garbage into small disposable packages, usually 20 to 25 pounds in weight. Dry garbage is compacted under pressure of 2,000 to 3,000 pounds. Though some manufacturers claim a compactor can handle a normal amount of wet garbage, it is best to put such waste into the disposer. Also avoid smelly items such as fish and poultry trimmings and combustibles such as chemical containers, oil, and rags.

Compactors are available in free-standing and built-in models. The former are usually top-loaded while the built-in are drawer-loaded. For built-in installation, the compactors come in the form of a base cabinet, usually 15 to 18 inches wide. All models offer an invaluable safety feature that locks the unit when not in use. The compactor will not operate unless the keylock is in the "on" position, the unit is completely closed, and the operating switch on.

Several models use a charcoal filter arrange-

Built-in (top) and portable (bottom) waste or trash compactors.

ment to purify the air in the compactor while others automatically release a measured amount of deodorant spray into the trash container every time the drawer is closed. Some trash compactors feature a reusable vinyl caddy with handles that

facilitates trash removal. In others, the trash bag rests in a heavy reusable plastic container and the whole unit can be taken to the trash can. The waste compactor requires no plumbing or special wiring, and can be used wherever it can be plugged into an ordinary 120-volt outlet.

Hot water heaters and water softeners could also be considered clean-up center appliances. As mentioned earlier, a continuous supply of hot water is a necessity if the dishwasher is operated properly. Soft water can help in the cleaning process of a dishwasher, too. More information on these two appliances can be found in Chapter 8.

COOK CENTER

There are a variety of processes used in cooking. The more common of these processes are boiling, poaching, frying (including sauteing, pan-frying, and deep-frying), braising, broiling, baking, and roasting. Most of these cooking processes can be performed using two basic cooking devices — the oven and the surface cooking unit — but many other cooking devices described in this chapter are available. Some of these additional devices are frequently included in the range. Others are included in only the more expensive cooking appliances.

Ranges, Cooktops, and Ovens

There are a wide variety of designs and types of ranges on the market today. The more popular ones are:

1. *Free-standing ranges* rest on the floor and are completely independent of the adjoining walls, cabinets, etc. Such a range usually has side panels with a finish which is the same as the ones to the front. However, it is usually installed as part of a continuous kitchen assembly of appliances, cabinets, and counters. Many free-standing ranges now are available with squared sides and corners which give a built-in appearance. The free-standing counter-height ranges are available with one or two ovens and/or broiler below the surface cooking unit, the high level type with oven above the surface unit, and the high-low (bi-level models) style with ovens above and below the cooktop. (Eye-level ovens and high broilers are real back-savers, but if the homemakers are less than average height, lifting foods in and out of an eye-level oven may be rather difficult.) The controls may be in the front, along the side, on top, or on a backsplash. As for widths, the free-standing

Free-standing single-oven range.

ranges vary from a minimal 20 inches to as large as 54 inches, with 30 and 36 inches being considered "standards."

Free-standing double-oven range.

2. *Built-in* ranges are designed to be fully integrated into the kitchen and counter area. The various forms of built-in ranges are constructed so

Built-in single-oven range.

Drop-in single-oven range.

that connections to adjoining cabinets and counters are relatively tight thereby eliminating many of the cleaning problems that exist with free-standing ranges.

For example, the *slide-in* or *slip-in range* may be considered a transition design between a free-standing range and a built-in range. In fact, some slide-in ranges can be used in either manner. Slide-in ranges rest on the floor and are usually supplied without side panels. (When side panels are available, the range may be transformed into a free-standing range.) The configurations of these ranges and their sizes are very similar to those of free-standing ranges.

The *drop-in range* differs from the slide-in range in that it does not rest on the floor, but on the adjoining counter or upon a special base cabinet. In some instances the range may extend down to the top space and rest on a framework behind the space. Some units that extend back to the wall have a back panel above the range top. Others are fitted into a cut-out in the cabinet countertop.

A *stack-on range* is essentially a drop-in range in which the oven has been placed at eye level rather than below the surface cooking units. The range is supported by flanges which rest on the countertop.

3. *Built-in Ovens and Cooktops.* In recent years built-in separate ovens and cooktops (surface cooking units) have become increasingly popular. The popularity of the built-in oven stems from two factors: (1) its eye-level placement is easier to use, and (2) built-in installations eliminate a considerable amount of exterior surface cleaning that is necessary with the free-standing range. A disadvantage of the use of separate ovens and cooktop units is that more kitchen space is needed. Some separate oven

appliances actually have more than one oven in the appliance. A microwave cooker may be added to this unit, or, in some instances, two standard ovens are included.

The standard built-in oven is generally designed to fit into 24-, 27-, 30- and 36-inch wall oven cabinets. But remember not to install the built-in oven too high. High mounting makes it difficult to remove pans and can result in burns.

A cook center with a built-in cooktop and double ovens.

Built-in cooktops are available in several forms. Some cooktops are available as drop-in units with backsplash panels, but the majority are designed for installation in cut-outs in counters. In this case, the unit may rest directly on top of the counter or it may be fastened into the counter with a Huddee rim or

Range placement considerations

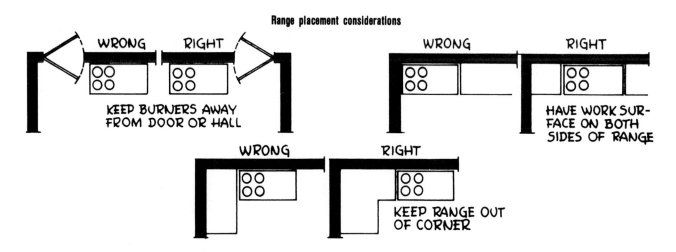

WRONG   RIGHT

KEEP BURNERS AWAY FROM DOOR OR HALL

WRONG   RIGHT

HAVE WORK SURFACE ON BOTH SIDES OF RANGE

WRONG   RIGHT

KEEP RANGE OUT OF CORNER

similar device. Cooktops are available with various numbers of burners, 2 to 6 burners on the average with 4 being the most common. Separate units of 2 burners each range in standard widths of 9 to 15 inches. Placement of the burners and the controls also varies.

All three types of cooking appliances are available in either electric or gas. Utility rates in the area will dictate which is the most readily available and economical to use. In most areas, gas is considered less expensive, but this depends partly on the methods used by the homemaker. Electric cooking is extremely efficient if used properly. If the homemaker has never cooked on a standard electric unit, the smooth top may require a major adjustment. The latter can have five or more heat settings or be entirely thermostatically controlled. Electric ranges require a 240-volt operation, so that cost of wiring may be an additional factor to consider, but most houses built since World War II provide space for this circuit at the service entrance.

Most cook/work-center appliances are finished in either stainless steel, brushed chrome, porcelain enamel, or a combination of these finishes. The porcelain enamel finish offers the possibility of incorporating color into the kitchen appliance; however, porcelain enamel can chip. Stainless is less colorful, but cannot chip although it can dent. Abrasive cleansers should not be used on either finish. Interiors of ovens are generally finished in porcelain enamel. A special finish is required for catalytic-process continuous-cleaning ovens, as described later in the chapter.

When installing a range, remember that handles of pots and pans in use on the range can constitute a hazard in two ways. Handles over adjacent burners in use can become overheated with the result that the hand of the user may be burned. If handles are placed so that they extend beyond the range surface, they may be struck by the kitchen user, and the pans upset, with consequent burns from hot liquids, etc. To avoid these hazards and to provide added convenience, it is best to provide counter surface on both sides of the range burners. The minimum permissible frontage space adjacent to a burner is 12 inches. Also unprotected wood or metal wall cabinets should be kept at least 30 inches above the cooking surface. If the bottom of the wall cabinet is protected with ¼-inch asbestos millboard, covered either with sheet metal or a metal ventilating hood, the vertical clearance may be reduced to 24 inches. Asbestos millboard is a pressed asbestos board not to be confused with cement-asbestos board.

As mentioned in Chapter 2, the range should not be installed under a window or within 12 inches of a window. In the act of reaching over the range to open a window, or to close or open curtains or draperies, the individual is likely to expose himself or herself to a flesh burn or to clothes ignition. Furthermore, if flammable curtains are installed at the window, the potential fire hazard is substantial. In addition to the safety hazard, the location of a range under a window is likely to create a constant cleaning problem as the window tends to accumulate grease and dirt rapidly.

Let us take a closer look at the two major parts of any cook/work center — the surface cooking units and the oven — and how they are heated.

Electric Cooktops. Electric surface units are usually equipped with heating elements of the metallic-sheathed resistance wire and consist of two elements built in a flat spiral. The two elements may be placed side by side in a continuous spiral or one element may be wound in the central portion of the burner, while the second element forms the outer periphery. This latter form is especially useful when it is necessary to place a small pan on a larger burner. The intensity of heat of the burner is usually controlled by an infinite heat-type switch or by push button switches which are arranged to give various levels of heat.

In some instances, one or more units may be equipped with a thermostatic control. At the lower temperatures the resistance heating elements do not glow — they appear much the same as burners which are not in use. For this reason most surface cook units are equipped with indicator lights which show that a burner unit is operating. Indicator lights may be attached to each burner or to push button controls, or one light may be used to indicate that one or more burners are in the "on" position.

In the typical electric surface unit, the heating elements are mounted in an opening in the top surface panel of the appliance. Under the top surface panel is a space which is used for certain necessary wiring connections to the burner and also for the positioning of reflector pans, drip cups, and drip trays. The primary purpose of this arrangement is to facilitate cleaning of the appliance. When spills or overflows occur, they pass down through the opening in which the heating element is located and are collected in the drip cups and drip trays. Access to the space is through the heating element opening or

Electric (left), gas (center) and flat-surface (right) built-in cooktops.

by means of a top surface panel which can be tilted upward.

Surface cooking units should not be located close to an internal corner of a kitchen counter assembly. A person standing at a counter which is adjacent and perpendicular to a range or counter containing a cooktop can inadvertently extend an arm or elbow over a burner and be injured. This hazard potential can be reduced by keeping surface units 12 inches away from the internal corners of counter assemblies.

Gas Cooktops. Gas burners are designed to give a circular flame pattern, the size of which can be controlled to some degree by the amount of gas delivered to the burner. The burners are usually controlled by a throttling valve which resembles a rotary switch in appearance. The intensity of the flame can be controlled on a graduated basis from low to high. Some burners are equipped with special simmer units which are, in effect, a very small burner located in the center of the main burner. Burners are lighted by a centrally located pilot light or by electric ignition. When the gas supply of a burner is turned on, a portion of the gas is guided through a small open-ended pipe toward the pilot light. Once the gas reaches the pilot, the burner is ignited.

Gas burners are mounted in the top surface panel of the appliance in the same manner as are electric elements. Most gas burners are designed so that the burner grill, the burner, and the piping can be removed easily for cleaning.

Flat-Surface Cooking. A smooth ceramic-glass cooking surface unit is basically a flat glasslike plate which is approximately ¼ inch thick. On some units, a separate plate is provided for each unit. Other manufacturers use a one-piece plate to accommodate several units. The heating elements are placed immediately beneath the glass plate. One manufacturer recommends that its unit be used with glass cooking utensils which are specially ground on the bottom so as to fit closely to the surface of the cooking unit. Other manufacturers suggest only flat-bottom pans of any material. In any case, the unit performs most effectively when the pans used have flat bottoms which fit closely to the surface of the unit.

The major advantage of this type of surface cooking unit lies in the ease with which it can be kept clean. There are no drip cups or drip pans. Spills can be wiped clean from the surface. One interesting feature of the ceramic-glass material is that it readily transmits heat upward directly to the cooking utensil, while at the same time little heat is lost laterally through the panel.

Controls on some ceramic cooktops are more sensitive than those of the usual burner. As in the ordinary range, the controls can be set for a typical range of temperatures, but the burner contains a sensor which shuts down the unit when temperatures exceed the selected level. The heat-up and cool-down times on ceramic-glass cooktops are longer than on the conventional electric types.

Another smooth- or flat-surface cooking unit has recently been introduced that uses a magnetic field to stimulate ions in cast-iron cooking utensils, creating friction heat within the cooking vessel itself. The cooking results are similar to those obtained in a microwave unit, which are discussed later in this chapter.

Ovens. Baking and roasting are the basic cooking operations performed in the conventional oven, but many ovens are equipped with broiler units.

Some may incorporate microwave cooking units.

In electric ovens, the heating elements are usually of the metallic-sheathed resistance-coil type. Metallic-sheathed coils are self-cleaning and generally will withstand more severe use than the unsheathed resistance-coil type. The resistance heating units are frequently installed as plug-in units so that they can be removed and replaced relatively easily.

Controls in the typical conventional oven, whether gas-fired or electric, are designed to provide thermostatic control of the temperature in the baking and roasting range, that is, from 140 to 550 degrees F (92.2 to 287.7 degrees C). The broiler units usually operate in the full "on" position. Many oven units are equipped with timers which will operate the oven for a given period of time. Others have programmed timers which will start oven operation at a predetermined time, operate the oven at a selected temperature for a period, and, upon completion of the cooking operation, hold the temperature of the oven at a uniform keep-warm temperature until the operation is terminated by the user. Programmed cooking lets the cook leave the house while dinner is being cooked.

Some ovens are equipped with a probe thermometer which is connected to a thermostatic control unit. This device is particularly useful in cooking meat. Once the temperature of the meat at the point of the probe reaches a predetermined level, the cooking process is stopped and the oven is maintained at a warm level.

Broilers, as already mentioned, usually are incorporated in ovens. The broiling process itself is a rapid, dry, radiant-heat cooking process used primarily for cooking meat, poultry, and fish. The item to be cooked is placed 1½ to 2 inches away from (usually beneath) the broiler heating unit, and the heat controls are set at the highest temperature. Most gas ranges have separate broiling compartments, so one oven is sufficient unless you have a large family or do a lot of entertaining. Two electric ovens are desirable so that you always have one available for broiling. Two small ovens are usually more useful than one large one.

The broiler's heating burners or elements are located at the top of the oven, and the controls are incorporated in the oven controls. Special separate broiler units are also available and are sometimes incorporated in ranges or ovens. In this case, broiling can be done at the same time the oven is being used for baking. Some ovens with broiler units are equipped with ventilating hoods or other ventilating systems designed to overcome any ventilation problem. Rotisseries are also found in many conventional ovens.

Most modern gas or electric conventional ovens employ one of two systems to clean themselves — pyrolitic (self-cleaning) and catalytic (continuous cleaning). The pyrolitic method of oven cleaning is a chemical decomposition of cooking soils by the application of high heat. When the oven needs cleaning, controls are set that lock the door shut for safety, and the oven is heated to a point between 850 and 1050 degrees F (490 and 921 degrees C). At the end of the complete cycle which takes 2 to 3½ hours, after a cool-down period, all that remains of the food soil is a powdery ash that is easily removed with a damp cloth.

Advocates of the pyrolytic, or self-cleaning, system claim the following advantages: all six sides of the oven interior are cleaned completely; no special care is required to prevent scratching or damaging oven surfaces as with the catalytic finish. In addition, the extra insulation provided for the cleaning cycle results in a cooler range during normal cooking operations.

In a catalytic continuous-cleaning oven, there is a catalyst in the porcelain enamel of the interior oven panels that helps to oxidize spatter as it hits the surface. The oven never gets terribly soiled, unless there is a spill-over, but it may look entirely clean. Grease that is deposited on oven surfaces from meat cookery tends to disappear as the oven is used for baking. The catalytic system does not require extraordinary temperatures so no door latch is needed, and the oven is not taken out of use for cleaning. But, manufacturers using the continuous-cleaning method emphasize three points: (1) heavy spill-overs will not be cleaned without first wiping up the excess with a damp cloth; (2) harsh abrasives and scouring pads should not be used on excessive soil or stubborn stains; and (3) certain types of food stains may not disappear in one operation but will fade away during subsequent use of the oven.

Proponents of the catalytic approach point out that the oven is always available for cooking since cleaning is continuous under normal usage. This continuous cleaning prevents any build-up of dirt and very little basic redesign is required since high temperatures are not employed. The consumer gains an economic advantage from this because the initial cost is lower for the catalytic oven than for the pyrolitic.

Convection Ovens. The convection oven is a rather new cooking device in home kitchens. It is really like the conventional ovens just described except that it uses increased air circulation within the oven to speed up the cooking or baking process. The air inside a conventional oven is almost static and cooking depends on the gradual conduction of the heat from the outside of the food to the center. In the convection oven, both upper and lower elements are on during baking and a fan keeps the air circulating evenly around the food, making the whole process more efficient. Cooking temperatures can be reduced 50 degrees F (10 degrees C) and still shorten cooking times up to about a third. So the convection oven is both a time and an energy saver.

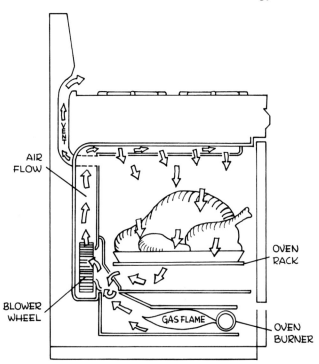

The forced-air principle of convection oven.

Convection ovens have been standard equipment in restaurants and commerical bakeries for many years because more food could be crowded into them, side to side and top to bottom while still achieving even baking and browning results. In the case of meat cookery, less shrinkage of the meat meant thousands of dollars of savings on a commercial or institutional scale.

To take advantage of the time and energy savings of the convection oven, the cook has to adjust familiar cooking habits only slightly. For favorite recipes, simply lower the usual temperature by 50

degrees F and then check for doneness after about two-thirds of the customary cooking time. Food may be cooked in either glass or metal containers. An especially desirable feature of the convection oven is that it lends itself to fast cooking of foods from the frozen state — a real plus for a working person who forgot to take the meat out of the freezer. It is also helpful when there are unexpected guests. A frozen roast put into the convection oven requires very little more cooking time than meats started at room temperature. Frozen convenience foods such as TV dinners cook in half the recommended time with a 25-degree F (-3.9 degrees C) reduction in temperature.

Microwave Units. Microwave units are generally called "ovens" because they look like ovens. Their use is, however, not confined to oven cooking. With a conventional range, roasting, and baking are done in the oven, frying, and boiling on top of the range. Many foods, such as bacon, eggs, cereals, and vegetables, which are usually done on top of the conventional range can be done in a microwave unit.

While microwave or electronic cooking offers many advantages, the most outstanding is its time- and energy-saving features. Food can be cooked much more rapidly by microwaves than by the heat generated in a conventional oven or even in a convection oven. Microwaves are very short waves of radio frequency. When these waves penetrate the material to be cooked, movement is created between molecules, and this action cooks the food. The cooking action takes place almost simultaneously throughout the object being cooked rather than progressively as in cooking by heat penetration. In addition to rapid cooking, the microwave unit is very useful for quick thawing of frozen foods. Still another important advantage of electronic cooking is that it is clean. Because the dishes stay cool, there are no grease vapors caused by sizzling fat, nor are there any grease splatters baked on. When a roast is cooked, splatters do occur as in conventional cooking, but because oven walls are cool, the splatters stay in a semi-liquid state and are very easily cleaned off. Similarly, when a pie filling runs over, it does not bake on. All microwave units are easy to keep clean both inside and out.

The difference in the electronic cooking action and its rapidity usually result in a piece of meat becoming cooked without the surface being browned. Most people are accustomed to seeing a browned crust on roasted meat. To overcome this aspect of microwave cooking, many manufacturers have in-

A microwave is usually placed on a countertop or is part of the conventional oven-range unit.

cluded a browning unit in the microwave oven. By the way, contrary to popular belief food prepared in a microwave oven is not cooked from the inside out, but is cooked all the way through at the same time, with more cooking being performed on the exterior of the food. It is, therefore, possible to prepare a rare, medium, or well-done roast in the electronic oven.

The fact that food is heated throughout, as mentioned earlier, is the reason why it is possible for the microwave oven to cook food fast. Time required to cook an item in the microwave oven is solely dependent upon how much heat is required, and, in turn, the amount of heat required of the food and the weight of the food. In the conventional process only the surface of the food is heated directly by the oven or grill. The heat required to cook the inside portion has to be conducted from the surface. Three factors govern the time required to cook an item in the more conventional way. A minor one of these is how much heat is required. The major ones are how well the food conducts heat and how much the surface of the food can be heated without causing serious defects. Let us take water, for example. Water is a good conductor of heat, and its surface can be overheated without deterioration; therefore, water can boil fairly quickly on a range. On the other hand, let us take milk. Milk is also a good conductor, but the surface cannot take overheating. If you try to boil milk quickly, the milk will burn; therefore, milk has to be cooked slowly. Cake is an example of a food that conducts heat poorly. Although a small amount

of heat is required to bake a cake, it must be cooked rather slowly because the conduction to the center is poor.

The illustration here shows how the microwaves are reflected inside the oven. Generated by the magnetron, the microwaves travel in straight lines much the same way as light. The microwaves follow the waveguide channel into the oven. At the end of the waveguide the microwaves strike the stirrer which is a slowly rotating fan. The fan blades reflect the microwaves, causing them to bounce off the walls, ceiling, back, and bottom of the oven. (Some

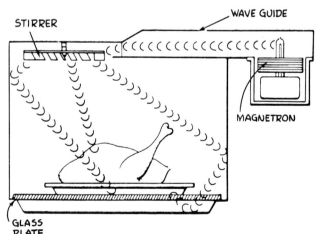

OVEN CAVITY, WAVE GUIDE, AND MAGNETRON

How microwaves are reflected inside a microwave oven. These reflected microwaves enter the food from all sides, thus cooking the food more rapidly.

54

manufacturers use a slowly revolving shelf rather than a stirrer.) The microwaves enter the food from all sides, accomplishing cooking inside and outside from all directions. The food, in an appropriate utensil of glass, ceramic glass, china, pottery, paper, and some plastics on the shelf, is positioned about 1 inch above the bottom of the oven. The microwaves pass through the special glass shelf and are reflected off the bottom of the unit to enter the bottom of the food. Since the cooking utensil is made of materials that transmit the electronic energy it does not heat up. Ordinary metal cooking ware should never be used in the electronic oven as they would reflect waves away from the food to be cooked.

Some concern has been voiced about leaks of microwave energy creating hazards. It is important to point out, however, that microwave rays are longer than visible light and their effect is to create heat. They should not be confused with cosmic rays, gamma rays, X-rays, and ultraviolet rays which are all shorter than visible light and when strong enough can alter living cells. Also microwave ovens are required to comply with rigid federal regulations on leakage. But, some heart pacemakers are affected by microwave energy, so if there is a pacemaker wearer in the family, consult with the physician involved before installing a microwave oven in the kitchen. Presently the Federal Communications Commission has assigned three frequencies for the operation of microwave units and other related types of equipment. They are 915 magahertz (MHz), 2450 MHz, and 5800 MHz. While little difference in overcooking results can be found at the various frequencies, most microwave ovens produced today operate at 2450 MHz.

While microwave units are most frequently sold as portable appliances for use on the countertop or table top, electronic cooking may be combined in a single oven with a conventional electric element, or as the second oven in a freestanding or drop-in range. When combined with a conventional element, a 240-volt hookup is required to microwave and brown simultaneously. Where the two types of cooking are combined in a portable model operating on 120 volts, the two operations, as mentioned previously, can be done simultaneously. The smaller portables have no conventional browning element. In some ovens, browning of meats is done on a plate made of a special material that can attain an unusually high temperature. Portable units are available in sizes that will fit into 24- and 30-inch cabinet spaces. The standard models are usually 30

inches wide. There are several convenient locations for a microwave oven in a kitchen as described below.

A modern cook center: microwave oven (top), convection oven (bottom) and a grill.

1. Stacking a microwave unit and a conventional oven as a built-in double-oven unit makes a useful working arrangement. Where the kitchen plan requires this space-saving setup, the microwave oven should be on top. This is handier because food is taken in and out of the oven repeatedly and in short intervals whereas food is generally placed in a conventional oven for longer periods, requiring few return trips.

2. The microwave oven can be enclosed in a space between the bottom of the existing cabinet and the countertop. Steam accumulates quickly in a microwave cavity. This below-eye level makes opening the door comfortable, especially for a cook of average height or less. Frequently, the location of oven can be away from the regular cook/work center. But, with any built-in installation, be sure there is clearance at top and back for ventilation.

3. A special shelf can be constructed under a high wall cabinet to house the microwave oven. This height works well for anyone 5 feet 7 inches or taller. If the oven is used frequently for entertaining, it should be located near a dining serving counter and adjacent family room.

4. A portable microwave unit can be used on a cart or small movable island and wheeled to within the area of the house or outside. The portable oven should always be plugged into a *grounded* 120-volt ac outlet.

Various locations for the installation of a microwave oven.

Other Cooking Devices

While cooktops and ovens are basic tools of the cook center, some ranges contain such features as a grill and a warming drawer. These items are available as spearate appliances for built-in installation, too.

Grills. Cooking by grilling is similar to broiling as it involves cooking by radiant heat; however, the item to be cooked is above the heat source rather than below it. The grill is located in a horizontal position above the source of heat, and the item to be

A standard grill unit.

cooked is placed on top of the grill. A considerable amount of smoke can be generated in this process as the drippings from the cooking process may fall on the heating unit and be burned. Ventilating hoods or similar smoke-gathering devices are essential.

As already mentioned, grills are sometimes incorporated in ranges or cooktops along with standard surface units, which can be used for cooking meats, pancakes, and the like. In essence, the griddle serves as the pan as well as the heating element for certain types of frying operations. Some manufacturers offer griddles as optional cooking devices for range-top cooking. Frequently, the grill cooktop can be interchanged with ceramic-type or standard electrical elements. Other cooktop options include deep-fat fryers and rotisseries.

Barbecue Grills. Modern barbecue units, which may be installed in standard wood or metal kitchen cabinets, bring barbecue cooking conveniently indoors for year-round enjoyment. Prefabricated barbecue units are available with regular charcoal firing, as well as with gas burners or electric cooking elements. In the gas models, radiant ceramic "coals" above the burner hold and evenly distribute the cooking heat. The electric models usually have a layer of ceramic below the element to distribute the heat. The drop-in type units, which are most commonly used, can be had in the following type models, in units of different widths from 24 to 48 inches:

1. Top controls, countertop cabinet model.

2. Top controls, masonry model.
3. Front controls, countertop cabinet model.
4. Front controls, masonry model.

Barbecues can also be had as part of surface units. Some cooktop grills have a charcoal plate that permanently gives food a charcoal-like flavor. This special charcoal plate keeps its flavor in spite of occasional washing in a dishwasher.

A barbecue unit can bring the outside in.

Most of the standard drop-in units are encased in insulated shells and can be safely installed in wood or metal kitchen cabinetry or built into brick, stone, or concrete block, indoors or out. Some units are designed for masonry only, with open sides, back, and bottom, so make sure to buy the right type for the desired purposes. Most units also offer a motorized rotisserie as an extra. To exhaust cooking aromas and charcoal smoke adequately from indoor areas, a hood and fan is recommended (see page 60).

Food Warmers. While there are several different types of food-warming appliances, the most popular are still in the form of a drawer approximately 12 inches high and 24 inches wide which may be installed in the base cabinet assembly. An opening will have to be provided in the base or oven cabinet for the appliance. A 240-volt power supply is normally required. Frequently, wood trim kits are available for these drawer food warmers so they accept paneling to match the cabinets.

Another popular food warmer, especially in a food serving center, is the wired rectangular glass-ceramic plate that is recessed into the countertop.

This unit has the added advantage of providing a place to put hot pans from a cooking surface. Other food warmers include infrared radiation lamps which can be installed under the wall cabinets or vent hoods.

KITCHEN VENTILATION SYSTEMS

Every kitchen needs a good ventilation system. Odors, smoke, excessive heat, and moisture are by-products of good cooking. A properly installed ventilation system will remove these before they fill up the kitchen and spread throughout the home. But perhaps even more serious, cooking produces over 200 pounds of grease-laden moisture in the average home each year (according to the Home Ventilating Institute). Thus, good kitchen ventilation eliminates the cleaning and maintenance problems this causes in the kitchen and nearby rooms.

While the wall or ceiling exhaust fans are still being made, hood-fan combinations are installed in nearly all new kitchens today. The reason for this is because the hood-fan units are by far a more efficient way to exhaust the odors and smoke than exhaust types.

Types of Hood Fan

There are two basic types of hood ventilating systems available — ducted and non-ducted. They come in various grades, prices, sizes, styles, and colors. In addition, some built-in cooking equipment, as discussed later in this chapter, comes complete with its own ventilating system.

With a ducted system, venting is achieved to the outside by the shortest and most direct route possible to keep the efficiency of the system at its highest. Most hoods offer two-way discharge, horizontal or vertical through standard-sized ducts. It may be installed directly on an outside wall or it may carry its discharge via ducts through attic (to roof or eave), or through a soffit or false beam to the outside wall. But remember when laying out the duct work that extra elbows drastically reduce the flow of air. Also, avoid changes in the duct size along the run, since duct size changes waste fan power and create a place for grease to collect.

Non-ducted ventilating systems can be hung on the wall above a freestanding range or cooktop, or can be suspended beneath the wall cabinets over the cooking surface. They are ideal for any location where ducting to the outside is either difficult or not

A vent hood can be small and decorative (top) or massive and imposing (bottom).

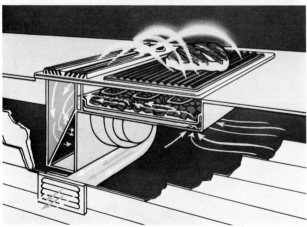

A popular ventilation system that moves odors, smoke, and grease downward and outward.

desirable (such as over an island installation or in apartment kitchens). They are very easy to install. They draw air through a filtering system and then return it to the room, filtering out the smoke, grease, and odors with special charcoal filters. While they do a fairly good job of removing smoke, grease, and odors, the ventless or non-ducted hoods are not effective on heat and moisture.

Certain range models, as mentioned earlier in the chapter, come with a built-in vent system. The vent system uses channels behind the top oven to the cooktop platform. These built-in vent systems either require ducts or are ductless.

As for the hood fan, four types of blades are used:

1. *The propeller type* is a fan with three or more blades, much like an ordinary portable household fan. Its blades are pitched to deliver a maximum volume of air against relatively low resistance. It is often less expensive and uses less power than the other, but it is not recommended where high air resistance is a factor, as with a duct having numerous elbows.

2. *The axial flow type* has blades resembling the contour of an airplane propeller. This is actually a refinement of the propeller principle. It works by driving air at a high velocity through a close-fitting tube. This type is used more often commercially than residentially.

3. *The centrifugal blower* is commonly called a "squirrel cage" fan. Its open revolving drum sucks in air and discharges it at right angles through blades (or vanes) set vertically around the circumference of the drum. This fan has a higher-powered motor than the propeller type.

4. *The mixed flow impeller* combines the principles of squirrel cage and propeller types. On the intake parts, the blades are pitched like a propeller type. On the discharge ends, they are like blower blades. As a rule, these take less power than the squirrel-cage blower.

Today, most good hoods employ the centrifugal blower type fans. It is seemingly the most effective. It overcomes resistance most efficiently, thus giving quieter operation. The propeller-type fan is frequently used where there is little or no resistance in the system (no ductwork involved).

There are three basic ways in which fans are combined with range hoods:

1. The fan is built right into the hood itself and does not take any of the cabinet space above it.

2. The fan is not in the hood but is instead in-

stalled in the cabinet space directly above the hood.

3. An exhaust fan is simply mounted in the wall above the cooking surface of the range and is vented directly to the outside.

When selecting a ventilating hood and fan, there are two important considerations — noise level and capacity. The latter is measured in CFM (cubic feet per minute) and refers to the volume of air the hood fan or blower removes from the room each minute of operation. Unlike a wall or ceiling exhaust fan, the hood fan's capacity is normally not based on the size of the kitchen; rather, it is determined by the size of the hood. Since the heat, odor, moisture, and smoke are trapped at their source, the fan capacity is independent of the kitchen size.

According to the United States Department of Housing and Urban Development/Federal Housing Administration and the Home Ventilating Institute (HVI) standards, the *minimal* requirement for a range placed against a partition is a hood fan with a capacity of 40 CFM per lineal foot of hood or about 120 CFM for a 36-inch hood. Island or peninsula locations for the same size call for 50 CFM per lineal foot or 150 CFM for a 36-inch hood. The HUD/FHA minimums for range hoods apply when the natural ventilation of the kitchen is below minimum (see page 185) and when ventilation is installed optionally.

While these minimum standards may do the job, most kitchen planners, as well as the Small Homes Council/Building Research Council, recommend that the hood-fan capacity should be 100 CFM for each lineal foot of hood length except for island and peninsula hood lengths. In other words, a 36-inch hood installed against a partition would require a fan with a capacity of 300 CFM and the same size unit in an island or peninsula location should have a capacity of 360 CFM.

For top performance of any indoor barbecue, the HVI suggests hood fans that have at least a 600 CFM rating. The hood should extend at least one inch beyond each edge of the barbecue unit. In the case of an island or peninsula unit where cross-drafts are a factor, it should extend at least 3 inches beyond each edge. The bottom of the hood should be from 16 to 24 inches above the barbecue, with 30 inches the absolute maximum.

In some grill arrangements, the vent is right on the cooking surface, eliminating the need for a hood. Instead, the surface vent pulls heat, odors, smoke, and grease downward, then ducts them outdoors. If the cooking top is on an outside wall, installation of a

vent is simple. If not, ducts can be run under the floor to an outside wall. Incidentally, all CFM ratings on fans bearing the HVI label are certified after independent tests at Texas A & M University and therefore can be compared dependably with one another. CFM ratings can easily be identified either by the manufacturer's literature or by the label on the unit itself.

The kitchen wall or ceiling exhaust fan capacities are determined by the volume of the room and the number of times each hour that this quantity of air is removed from the room. The unit of measure is "cubic feet per minute" (CFM). It is commonly recommended that the fan should be capable of exhausting the room 15 times per hour. This is equivalent to one air change every four minutes. Thus, in a kitchen that is 10 feet wide and 15 feet long with an 8-foot ceiling height, the capacity of the exhaust fan should be:

$$\text{Fan Capacity} = \frac{\text{Volume (cubic feet in kitchen)}}{\text{No. of minutes for each air change}}$$
$$= \frac{10' \times 15' \times 8'}{4 \text{ minutes}} = 1200 \text{ cubic feet}$$
$$= 300 \text{ CFM (cubic feet per minute)}$$

HVI members commonly translate this information as follows on the product tag or in literature for wall and ceiling exhaust fans:

This fan will ventilate a residential:

Kitchen	*80 square feet*
Bathroom	*150 square feet*
Laundry	*200 square feet*

Many vent hoods have two-speed motor controls. Some have three set speeds and a few come with solid-state controls which permit you to dial an almost infinite number of speeds. Most also have built-in lighting, and nearly all feature an aluminum mesh grease filter, removable for cleaning. The latter consideration is very important since the cleanliness of the system will reflect the efficiency of the entire unit.

As mentioned earlier, noise is a very important consideration. Some ratings, a recognized method of measuring loudness in numbers which correspond to the way people hear them, are given to vent hoods and exhaust fans. They help greatly to make accurate comparison of sound levels among different models. Fans rated at 4 sones (the level of conversation speech) make half the sound of those rated at 8 sones. All fans bearing the HVI label are certified for sones ratings as well as for CFM specifications. No certified kitchen exhaust fan or hood (up to 500 CFM capacity) can exceed 9 sones. Every certified fan must be rated for sones at maximum air delivery, but multi-speed fans may also be rated for sones at lower speeds. Dual ratings permit selection of whatever combination of air delivery and quietness is desired in steps of 10 CFM and 0.5 sones. In many cases, the multi-speed fan is a good solution, offering heavy-duty ventilation when needed and low-speed quietness at other times.

Vent Hood Installations

A properly selected vent hood and fan can only do its work if it is correctly installed. The main rules are simple, but important:

1. Follow the manufacturer's instruction sheet to the letter, including the duct size recommended and the corresponding elbows and fitting.

2. If possible, locate the fan across the room from incoming air.

3. Make ducting as short and direct as possible to the outside, with a minimum number of elbows.

4. Do not reduce ducting in size from the fan discharge.

5. Install proper terminal accessories.

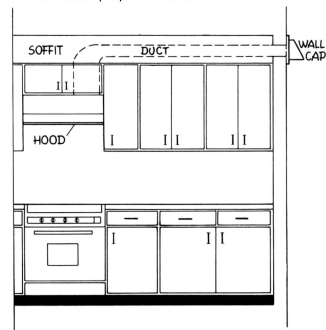

This is generally the best method of installing a vent when the range is located on an inside wall in a two story home.

Wall-mounted hoods should extend at least to the front of the cooktop and 2 inches to 6 inches out on each side. On peninsula or island installations, the hood should overhang the cooktop 3 to 6 inches on all four sides. (Standard widths are usually manufactured from 30 to 48 inch widths, in 6 inch increments; custom sizes are also available, but are more expensive.) The more overhang the better in these wide-open spaces because of air turbulence, which tends to make cooking vapors spread. The factors affecting the depth of a hood are its length, width, and distance from the cooking surface and placement of the exhaust inlet. Cooking vapors should be picked up from the top of the hood where they have concentrated, and the larger the hood the more depth is necessary to hold these vapors. A 5- or 6-inch depth has practically no holding power and allows cross-drafts to spread the vapors. A 9-inch depth holds vapors in a wall-mounted hood that is fairly well closed in on the sides with cabinets. A 14-inch depth is needed where the hood is placed as high as a person's head, and on large island and peninsula installations an 18- or 20-inch depth is desirable. The arrangement of the kitchen sometimes limits hood depth, but it is often possible to change kitchen arrangements when you are aware of the importance of "vapor holding capacity."

When the hood is installed, the bottom of the hood should be placed at least 24 inches from the burners. If the hood gets any closer to the heat source, the cook cannot see into the pots and pans, especially if the hood is wide enough to cover the front burners, as it should be. Twenty-seven to thirty inches is the safe distance for the placement of the hood and generally makes the most attractive installation. Thirty-four inches is the maximum distance and should be used only for wall-mounted hoods, which are better protected from cross-drafts.

It is often desirable to install an exhaust hood over a built-in oven. This is particularly useful when the oven door must be left open during broiling.

ACCESSORY APPLIANCES

A number of small accessory appliances which can be built into the kitchen are now available. For example, built-in toasters are available which can be wired and recessed into the wall, tilting out for use and then pushing back to their flush position. There also are built-in knife sharpeners, can-openers and similar small appliances which can be set in wall recesses.

Another small appliance setup has a small drive motor mounted on the underside of the

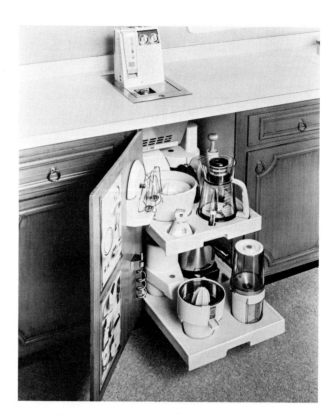

Two popular built-in appliance units that mix, blend, crush ice, sharpen knives, grind food, open cans, squeeze juice, etc.

countertop and it is used to operate such attachments as a mixer, blender, ice crusher, knife sharpener, juicer, can-opener, food grinder, vegetable shredder, etc. On the top of the counter, there is either a small stainless steel plate which is lifted up to expose the drive shaft onto which the various attachments fit or there is a small control panel which protrudes above countertop and holds the appliance attachments. The motor usually has a variable speed selection with six or more settings.

CHAPTER 4

CABINETS, COUNTERTOPS, AND KITCHEN STORAGE

Regardless of the kitchen's size, the arrangement of its work centers, and the variety of its equipment, it will not function properly unless there is an adequate amount of storage space.

Depending on the kind of housing unit being built or remodeled and the location of the work centers, there are various standards and recommendations for the amount and kind of kitchen storage required. Actually, kitchen storage is usually in the form of built-in wood cabinets — base cabinets and wall cabinets. Kitchen cabinets can be built on the job, built in a local cabinet shop, or built as finished prefabricated units by a manufacturer. The units are medium-priced, high-quality furniture units in various popular styles and finishes. They are available in a selection of sizes that permits any kitchen layout using standard components with a minimum of fillers and spacers. Since the number of skilled local cabinetmakers is decreasing, and because it is difficult to get a fine finish on job-built cabinets, most builders, designers, and homeowners rely on prefabricated wood kitchen cabinets. Prefabricated cabinets are manufactured to standard sizes and dimensions, and most cabinet manufacturers do not offer special sizes or shapes. There are cabinet components designed for use with each of the kitchen's work centers and for special requirements. Incidentally, it is a good idea when using ready-made cabinets to check for the round blue certification seal of the National Kitchen Cabinet Association, which guarantees that the cabinet's design meets national standards for quality.

KITCHEN CABINETS

Cabinets come in a variety of period styles, from Early American to French Provincial and Spanish, and in a variety of colors and finishes to suit any decorative scheme. Cabinet door panels may also be decorated with vinyls, brass grilles, cane, spindles, reinforced plastic, fabrics, or colored glass. Some even boast reversible door panels that permit covering with wallpaper or other material for a completely personalized scheme. But it must be remembered that the most permanent part of any kitchen is its cabinets. When a portion or all of the cabinets become obsolete in usefulness or appearance, they cannot be replaced without also disturbing countertops, flooring, wallcoverings, and perhaps the plumbing, wiring, and appliances. The cabinets should therefore be chosen with care for their quality and lasting value. As is the case in the purchase of all furniture, good design coupled with expert workmanship and a durable finish should be the first criterion in selecting kitchen furniture. Styles and colors should be ones that can be "lived with" for many years. The colors that are "in" today can and should be used in the kitchen but should be limited to wall areas and decorative accessories that can be replaced easily and relatively inexpensively tomorrow.

Cabinet Materials

Kitchen cabinets come in a variety of materials. Solid lumber, plywood with fine wood veneer facing over an inner core, prefinished hardboard or laminate of a wood frame, molded polystyrene or polyurethane foam with a plastic laminate covering, steel, and steel with wood fronts are some of the more common ones used.

Wood. Both hardwood and softwood are used in kitchen cabinet manufacture. Softwood species commonly used are ponderosa and sugar pine, Idaho (western) white pine, Douglas fir, and western hemlock. Knotty pine and western red cedar are used for some "rustic" cabinet styles and for units which are sold as unfinished products.

Birch, oak, maple, ash, walnut, and fruitwood are used in cabinets which are prefinished with the natural look — the cabinets are stained and finished with clear lacquer or other plastic finishes which are sprayed on.

Plywood has always had a prominent place as a basic material for cabinets, and hardboard is used to some degree. In recent years the use of particleboard has expanded greatly. Particleboard has proven particularly useful as a base for cabinets finished with wood or plastic laminates.

Plastic. Plastics of various types are employed in cabinet manufacture. Acrylics and polyesters are used in liquid form as finishes; melamines and rigid vinyls are used as laminates for a thin veneer finish. When laminates are used as the finish surface (of a door, for example) it is necessary to use a similar laminate or backer laminate on the back side of the door in order to prevent warping. Particleboard is the predominant core stock for this kind of cabinet, but some companies use plywood while others use a styrene foam board or a honeycomb paper core.

Some companies are now producing molded polystyrene or polyurethene foam plastic cabinetwork using the vacuum-forming process. Available in several wood grain patterns, as well as some novel finishes, these molded cabinets are inexpensive when compared with the other raw materials and are considered the base of *low-cost* cabinetry.

Sometimes different cabinets are combined such as steel base cabinets with wood wall cabinets.

Steel. Steel is used as the basic material for the case work in some cabinets. The doors, drawer fronts, and other exposed elements of the cabinets may be of steel, but steel cabinets may also be finished with wood and plastic laminates. Steel cabinets are often constructed so that doors and drawer front occupy the full front of the cabinet and no stiles or rails are visible on the front of the cabinet. With this design, fillers are always needed to turn corners in an assembly of cabinets.

Cabinet Construction

Wood is still the most popular of kitchen cabinet materials. Of course, wood cabinet construction varies among manufacturers to some extent, but it is fairly well standardized for stock cabinets.

The major components of typical cabinets, regardless of type of construction, are the front frames, end panels, doors, backs, bottoms, shelves, drawers, and hardware.

Case Parts. The front frames usually are made of hardwood, ½ to ¾ inches thick. Rails, stiles, and mullions are doweled (or mortise-and-tenoned),

Three types of material used in the making of kitchen cabinets: wood (top), plastic (center) and steel (bottom).

Wood cabinets come in various grains and finishes.

as well as glued and stapled for rigidity. Lap joints and screw joints are also used.

End or side panels typically consist of ⅛- or ¼-inch plywood or hardboard, glued to ¾-inch frames or of ½-inch and thicker plywood or particleboard, without frames. The end panels frequently are tongue-and-grooved into the front frames. The mortise-and-tenon and butt joints are also used to affix the end panels to the front frame. Furniture-grade plywood and particleboard with veneer facings are the most common materials for end panels.

The backs of cabinets range in thickness from ⅛ to ¼ inch and are of plywood or hardboard construction. The backs are fastened to the side panels by insertion and with glue blocks that are pinned with staples.

The tops and bottoms of cabinets also vary from ⅛ to ½ inch in thickness and they are let into the sides (dadoed) and fastened with glue blocks. Base cabinets generally do not incorporate tops, however, some manufacturers still use the dust caps as cabinet tops on the base units.

Shelving in both the base and wall units vary in material composition from plywood to particleboard with or without wood or plastic-banded edges. Thickness varies from ⅜ to ¾ inches. Shelving in wall cabinets is either fixed or adjustable with the trend toward adjustability, using either plastic or metal adjusting hardware.

Doors. Doors are ¾ to 1¼ inches thick. The construction of doors is of two types: flush and panel. The flush doors may be hollow, or may have a particleboard, wood, high-density-fiber, or foam-plastic core. Veneer overlays may be wood or plastic.

The panel doors consist of stiles (vertical side members), rails (cross pieces), and panel fillers of various types. These flush panels or raised panels, with beveled edges, may be shaped to fit openings that are rectangular or curved.

A number of producers are now using doors and drawer fronts primarily made of plastics. A wood frame with a foam-plastic core and laminated plastic face is a common type. Complete assemblies consisting of vacuum-formed plastic faces assembled over a foam core are increasing in popularity because of the ease of molding grain and trim patterns. Such material is cleaned easily.

Doors may be designed to meet the cabinet

Typical wood styles (left to right, top to bottom): Country, Mission, Colonial, Classic, Applique, Regency, Paneled, Contemporary, Provincial, Traditional, Batten and Old English.

Several other door treatments.

face frame with an overlap contact, a lip front joint, or a flush joint.

Drawers. Drawers frequently have hardwood lumber sides and backs, and plywood bottoms. There is as wide a variation in drawer-front styling as there is in door design. Drawer construction also varies depending on cabinet quality. In some cabinets, the sides are connected to the front and back with multiple dovetail joints. In others, they are connected with lock-shouldered or square-shouldered joints. Drawer bottoms are dadoed into the sides, front, and back for more rigid construction. Some drawer units are one-piece molded polystyrene plastic (except for the front), with rounded inside corners for ease of cleaning.

Cabinet hardware includes pulls or handles, knobs, hinges, catches, and slides. Hardware is

Typical door pulls

available in various materials, finishes, and designs to meet the needs of almost any style of cabinet. Many manufacturer's permit customers to select the design and finishes of knobs and pulls or handles they desire.

Cabinet Finishes

Most natural finishes on wood cabinets consist of a penetrating stain and seal followed by spray-applied clear finishes. Acrylic and polyester have largely replaced nitro-cellulose lacquer for this application. Other manufacturers use curtain coating or immersion finishing systems.

Probably the most durable finish is produced by a plastic laminate, but such a finish is usually limited to slab doors or plain panels, although decorative moldings are sometimes applied over the laminate.

Steel (often called metal) cabinets are usually first treated with a rust-proofing process called bonderizing. Primer is then applied and baked on to the steel parts. To complete the job, a smooth heavy coat of synthetic enamel is sprayed on and the cabinet is baked in an electronically controlled oven. With quality steel and wood cabinet installations, all components of each individual kitchen are finished at the same time.

New materials and finishes are constantly being developed to improve cabinets and gain advantages in material availability. Therefore the specifications for materials and finishes as given above are subject to change at any time.

Cabinet Types

There are three classes or types of kitchen cabinets: base cabinets, wall cabinets, and tall cabinets.

Base Cabinets. Base cabinets are usually installed under all kitchen counters except in those places where the sink and dishwasher are located. Base cabinets are used for storage of cleaning materials, cooking utensils, portable appliances, cutlery, bread and cake storage, dry vegetable storage, tray storage, miscellaneous packaging and preparation materials, linens and table service materials, and built-in appliances usually in specialized cabinets.

The standard base cabinet has a single drawer over a half shelf and a full shelf. The half-depth shelf is above a full-depth shelf at the bottom. The front-to-back dimension is 23 to 24½ inches, with 24 inches being the most common. The unit is 34½ inches high and supports a 1½-inch-thick counter, making the counter surface 36 inches above the floor. Most

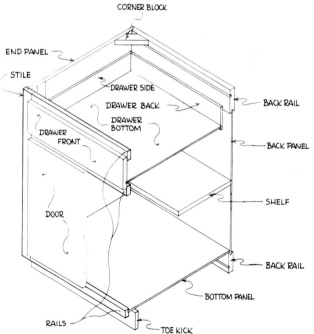

Typical wood base cabinet (left) with its construction and component parts (right).

base cabinets are equipped with built-in toe space. Storage in standard base cabinets is primarily for cooking utensils and other larger or heavier kitchen items, small appliances, and foodstuffs.

Single-door base cabinets are generally available in widths of 9, 12, 15, 18, 21, and 24 inches. (The 9-inch cabinet usually does not have a drawer.) Double-door cabinets are usually available in widths of 24 to 48 inches. They are also available in 3-inch increments, but some manufacturers do not provide 39-inch and 45-inch units. Remember that using few wider cabinets rather than more and narrower-width cabinets reduces the cost of the installation.

Base cabinets provide a major portion of the storage needed in the average kitchen. In planning kitchens, it is convenient to assess the amount of available base-cabinet storage in terms of "accessible frontage." That is, the accessible frontage for the typical base cabinet is equal to the actual width measured across the front of the cabinet. Accordingly, a cabinet that is 24 inches wide has an accessible frontage of 24 inches. Since a cabinet installed below a single built-in oven has a reduced volume, it should be credited with an amount of accessible storage equivalent to only two-thirds of the actual width of the unit.

No accessible frontage credit is given for storage cabinets located under the sink because plumbing lines and traps prevent the installation of drawers and shelves. Furthermore, the space behind the front may be further restricted if a garbage disposer unit is installed. No storage credit can be given for appliances which are 36 inches high or higher and occupy base-cabinet space, even though in some instances a single drawer may be provided in the appliance.

Early studies of storage space in kitchens recommended certain amounts of base-cabinet frontage to accompany each kitchen activity center. However, in actual practice, base-cabinet storage is usually distributed by providing base cabinets in all under-counter space, and then adding additional frontage if necessary to meet the standards selected. When this practice is followed, the distribution of the base-cabinet storage is usually adequate. But, the recommended standards for total base-cabinet frontage are still as follows:

Liberal	10 feet
Medium	8 feet
Minimum	6 feet

Other Forms of Base Cabinets. Other types of base cabinets have several drawers, or pull-out trays, in place of the shelves. For example, the base drawer units have no doors or shelves. They contain only drawers — usually three. While they are used in all kitchens, regardless of size, they are found most frequently in small kitchens in order to comply with HUD/FHA minimum drawer requirements (see page 185). They are available in widths of 12, 15, 18, 21 and 24 inches; the most popular sizes are 15 and 18 inches. Linen drawer units — a four-drawer base cabinet — are usually available in widths of 24, 30, 33 and 36 inches.

Base tray cabinets generally are available in various sizes from 9 to 24 inches. The 12- and 15-inch widths are the most popular ones. Tray cabinets provide convenient storage space for items such as broiler pans, serving trays, cookie sheets, and other large, flat utensils. Below the drawer there is no shelf and the entire height of the storage area is left free

Some of the many available drawer accessories.

Typical base cabinet storage accessories.

for these large, flat items.

Base corner cabinets are employed to turn a corner where another run of cabinets will join at a right angle. They are blank (no drawer or door) in the area where the other cabinets must butt up against them. Base corner cabinets eliminate the use of base fillers since the cabinets can be pulled away to adjust to add dimensions along the wall (see page 77). Base corner cabinets are usually blind corner (reach-in) units or rotating shelf (lazy susan) units. The latter are used in higher-priced kitchens as storage for items of frequent use. Incidentally, the base-cabinet frontage may be supplemented by a corner cabinet with revolving shelves. If equipped with three shelves at least 26 inches in diameter, or two shelves at least 32 inches in diameter, an extra 6 inches of accessible frontage can be credited.

A typical peninsula base cabinet.

Peninsula base cabinets are used in the same manner as standard base units, but this cabinet is generally positioned as a divider between rooms — usually between the kitchen and dining area. These cabinets are also used in island installations. Several widths are available from 18 to 48 inches with finished (panelled) backs or with door access from both sides. Blind island base cabinets are available for "turning corners" into a peninsula.

The primary function of the *sink/range base cabinet* is to support the sink or range. Widths are available from 24 to 48 inches and most with 3-inch increments in between. Drawer fronts are fixed ("dummies") as there are no functional drawers, but ample storage space is provided behind the door area.

Sink fronts, which are basically employed to reduce the overall cost of the kitchen cabinets, are used in conjunction with sink bowls and countertop range installations in much the same way as the sink/range cabinet except they have no floor and back. (Some manufacturers have sink-front floors available). These units can be had in one- or two-door patterns in widths similar to base cabinets. Some fronts are designed to permit trimming so that the cabinet assembly frontage may be adjusted in width.

Some manufacturers build other special base units such as the pantry base, the sliding shelves base, buffet base, and bread-board base cabinets. Desk units 30 inches high are also made by some firms. For sizes available of these speciality units, check the manufacturer's literature.

A sink front unit.

Wall Cabinets. Wall cabinets at each center are important to supplement the base-cabinet storage. They are generally used for storage of dishes, glassware, staples, canned goods, spices, and other small items used in the preparation of meals. To be classified as net accessible frontage, however, a wall cabinet should be at least 30 inches high and have two shelves in addition to the bottom shelf. The top shelf should be within 72 inches of the floor. Wall cabinets that extend higher may be desirable for storage of infrequently used items, but no use can be made of shelves that are higher than 72 inches above the floor. Except in unusual instances, wall cabinets over the refrigerator, oven, sink, or cooking surface should not be included in the readily accessible cabinet frontage for evaluating the kitchen because their shelves are limited and not easily accessible. However, if wall cabinets are pulled forward and positioned over the front of the refrigerator, one-third of the shelf that is 72 inches or less above the floor can be used for storage.

The minimum clearance between the countertop and the bottom of the wall cabinet should be 15 inches. Actually with a clearance of 15 to 18 inches

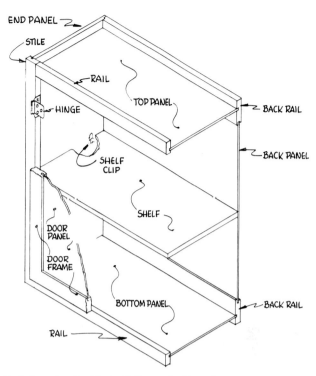

Typical wood wall cabinet with its construction and component parts.

above a 36-inch-high counter, the top shelf of a 30-inch wall cabinet with fixed shelves will not be more than 72 inches above the floor. With adjustable shelves in the wall cabinet, the top shelf can be set at an accessible height even if the cabinet is 18 inches above the counter.

The criteria for wall cabinets are:

Minimum Accessible Frontage 72 inches
Liberal Accessible Frontage 120 inches

The amount of dinnerware is the key to wall-cabinet storage requirements. The recommended criteria provide ample space to accommodate a single set of dinnerware for four people. For the many families that have dinnerware for twelve, an additional 48 inches of wall-cabinet frontage may be recommended.

Wall cabinets should be located over counters, and whenever possible, some wall cabinets should be located at each center. In order to provide a convenient and adequate location for everyday dishes, at least 42 inches of the wall-cabinet frontage should be placed within 72 inches of the center front of the sink. Extra wall-cabinet storage may be provided in tall cabinets if they are located in a direct path from a work center or in a sideboard located in the dining room.

The most commonly used wall units have a front-to-back depth of 12 inches, although some

Typical base-cabinet storage accessories.

Typical heights of kitchen cabinets.

Ways of making wall cabinets more useful and helpful.

cabinets may have greater depths, up to 15 inches. The most popular height is 30 inches. Heights of 12 to 15 inches are commonly used over refrigerator installations. Heights of 15 to 24 inches are sometimes used over ranges. Some manufacturers provide cabinets with heights of 18, 20, and 24 inches. Also, a few companies make cabinets 33, 36, 45, or 48 inches high. The selection of the height depends largely upon the space between the counter surface and the bottom of the cabinet (15 or 18 inches) and upon the height of the top of the door trim or ceiling.

Single-door wall cabinets are usually available in widths of 9, 12, 15, 18, 21, and 24 inches. Double-door cabinets run from 24 to 48 inches in width, in 3-inch increments.

The capacity for the accessibility of small items often can be improved by equipping some wall cabinets with narrow shelves on the back of the cabinet door. The regular shelves must then be reduced to an 8-inch depth. These 8-inch shelves will accommodate most food packages stored with the narrow end out, and the 1½- to 3-inch-deep shelves on the back of the door will hold small items such as spice containers.

Other Forms of Wall Cabinets. Wall cabinets are available in the *blind* corner configuration, and in *corner cabinets with diagonal front.* A few manufacturers make diagonal front cabinets with rotating shelves (24 by 24 inches) or with 90-degree lazy susan arrangements. Check manufacturer's literature for the various sizes of wall corner cabinets available.

Peninsula wall cabinets are used in a peninsula type arrangement and are finished with either paneling on the back side or access doors on both sides. They are usually available in standard wall-cabinet widths and in heights of 24 and 36 inches. Peninsula blind corner wall and peninsula diagonal wall cabinets are also available.

Tall Cabinets. Tall cabinets are generally constant at 84 inches — the height accepted by the kitchen cabinet industry as the standard hanging height of cabinets. Tall cabinets are most commonly made in 12, 15, and 24 inch depths (front-to-back).

A lazy susan unit in a wall corner cabinet.

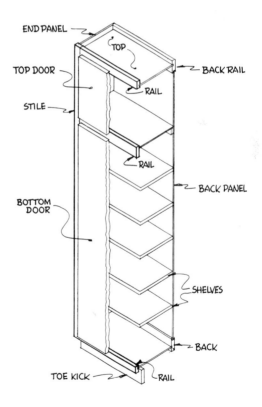

Component parts of a tall wood cabinet.

73

Common frontage widths are 15, 18, and 24 inches. Larger widths are available particularly for oven cabinets.

There are several designs for tall cabinets. For instance, the *utility style cabinet* has one tall door with no shelves in the lower portion of its storage area. Above that, the upper portion has a fixed flat shelf behind a smaller door. Storage, therefore is intended for brooms, mops, and other tall utility items below and small utility items (often used for cleaning) above. Actually the articles which influence the size of this storage space, with their approximate dimensions, are:

	DEPTH	WIDTH	HEIGHT
Upright vacuum cleaner	13"	13"	48"
Ironing board	5"	15"	63"
Broom			56"
Mops			59"
Tank-type vacuum cleaner	24" Max.	24" Max.	24" Max.

A storage space with front-to-back depth of at least 13 inches is necessary for most of this equipment. The storage space within 12- to 14-inch deep "utility-type cabinets" is too shallow for bulky items such as a tank-type vacuum cleaner. Hence the 24-inch deep utility-type tall cabinet is best suited for this need. One storage compartment in this type unit should be at least 64 inches high to accommodate the larger items such as the ironing board or broom. A maximum shelf height of 72 inches above the floor is desirable for convenient accessibility for most people. A unit at least 24 inches wide is desirable to accommodate all cleaning utensils, except the largest tank-type vacuum cleaner which would require a unit at least 29 inches wide.

The utility cabinet should face a traffic path leading to the rest of the house but should be located so as to avoid interfering with access to any kitchen cabinets, counters, or appliances that are used daily.

Adjustable shelf kits can usually be added to utility cabinets thus converting them to other types of multi-shelf tall cabinets such as canned goods storage or linen cabinets.

The *pantry-type tall cabinets* usually combine a stack of sturdy adjustable shelves with some type of swing-out storage shelves. In deeper models, inner as well as outer swing-out shelves may further increase shelf storage capacity. These tall units function like an old-time pantry in providing a large-volume food storage area.

Utility style tall cabinet (left) and pantry type (right).

Tall oven cabinet.

Tall oven cabinets are intended for housing built-in or slide-in ovens. They are available with openings designed to stack one, two, or even three ovens as required. Available in several widths, these cabinets usually come so that the cutouts (openings) can be trimmed to meet the exact requirements of a particular oven. Frequently the oven cabinets are designed for using oven-hood vent fans in conjunction with the built-in ovens. As a money-saving item, some manufacturers make tall oven and utility fronts. A few companies also produce cabinets for built-in type refrigerators.

Accessories. Different manufacturers provide a wide variety of accessories which may be added to cabinets. These items include metal boxes for flour and sugar, sugar dispenser, flour sifter, tray dividers, cutlery drawers, spice shelves, fruit and vegetable bins, canned good racks, towel bars, bread boards, and so on. Other specialties include lazy susan hardware, mixer shelf hardware, pull-out shelves, pantry units, and the like.

Some manufacturers have decorative wall and base shelves, valances that can be used as decorative trim across windows between two cabinets, molding for trim work around cabinet installations, end panels to finish runs of wall and base cabinets, and filler strips. The strips should not be used except to take up, or fill-in odd dimensions, at the end of a given run or in conjunction with corner base cabinets to provide drawer clearance in L-shaped or U-shaped kitchens.

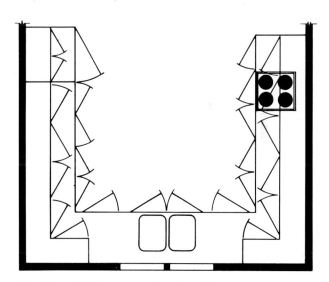

Cabinet doors should open away from the work area.

Other uses for tall cabinets.

Detailing Cabinet Layouts

There are certain considerations that should be kept in mind when laying out cabinets. For example, clearance should be provided in front of cabinets and kitchen equipment to allow room for access to these facilities. This may require room for such activities as walking, reaching, bending, and crouching. Although a homemaker may want to be uninterrupted while preparing meals, room for aid by others is important even though it may occur infrequently. Space for activities other than meal preparation and cleanup, such as dining, should be provided outside of the kitchen activity area. Other special counter clearances for safety and convenience are specified in the section on counters.

The minimum clearance between base cabinet fronts in the food preparation area is 40 inches as recommended by the HUD Minimum Property Standards for One- and Two-Family Dwellings. The same minimum clearance should be provided between base cabinets and a facing wall or a facing tall cabinet. This clearance is adequate for a single worker in the kitchen. If two persons are working, the

clearance should be increased to a minimum of 48 inches. A clearance of 60 inches is a liberal allowance.

A distance of 30 to 38 inches is recommended for the clearance space between the face of one and the side of another cabinet or appliance. This will only allow room for one person to work. A second person can pass only if the working person stands. This narrow clearance is acceptable if located in front of cabinets or counters, including a counter beside a sink. The greater clearance is recommended in front of a sink, range, dishwasher, built-in oven, or refrigerator.

The recommended corner-to-corner clearance between appliances or base cabinets at right angles to each other is 28 to 34 inches. This diagonal

Method used by HUD for measurement of kitchen storage and work space.

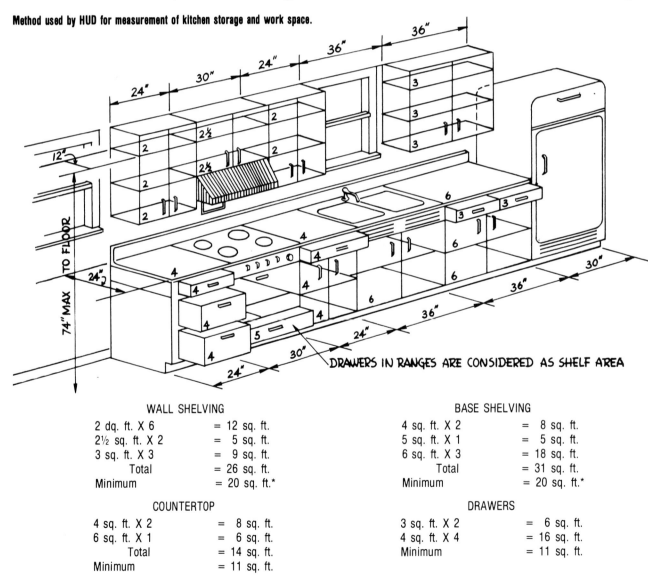

DRAWERS IN RANGES ARE CONSIDERED AS SHELF AREA

WALL SHELVING	
2 dq. ft. X 6	= 12 sq. ft.
2½ sq. ft. X 2	= 5 sq. ft.
3 sq. ft. X 3	= 9 sq. ft.
Total	= 26 sq. ft.
Minimum	= 20 sq. ft.*

COUNTERTOP	
4 sq. ft. X 2	= 8 sq. ft.
6 sq. ft. X 1	= 6 sq. ft.
Total	= 14 sq. ft.
Minimum	= 11 sq. ft.

BASE SHELVING	
4 sq. ft. X 2	= 8 sq. ft.
5 sq. ft. X 1	= 5 sq. ft.
6 sq. ft. X 3	= 18 sq. ft.
Total	= 31 sq. ft.
Minimum	= 20 sq. ft.*

DRAWERS	
3 sq. ft. X 2	= 6 sq. ft.
4 sq. ft. X 4	= 16 sq. ft.
Minimum	= 11 sq. ft.

clearance is important to allow room for a person to carry bulky items, such as packages of food.

Sometimes cabinet assembling problems do occur when planning a kitchen layout. The most common is when a counter surface is to be extended around a corner; great care must be taken to compensate for the corner that is not truly a right angle. This situation frequently arises in remodeling work and it is not uncommon in new construction. This problem is particularly critical when the countertop is to be prefabricated in the factory. In this case, it may be desirable to fabricate an angle template rather than to rely upon measurement alone. This can be done by placing 1- by 4-inch boards along the face of the walls of the corner and fixing them into the position of the angle by fastening a scab in the corner where the two boards meet and by applying a third board along the hypotenuse of the angle.

Turning Corners with Base Cabinets. In L-shaped and U-shaped kitchens, internal corners are created in the base-cabinet assembly. Many base cabinets are built in such a manner that hinges, knobs, drawer pulls, etc., will interfere with each other unless measures are taken to assure adequate

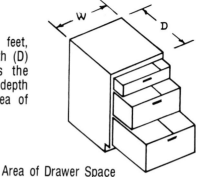

Width (W) in feet, times the depth (D) in feet, times the number of full-depth drawers = area of drawer space.

Area of Drawer Space

Method used by HUD for measurement of shelf and countertop areas.

clearance at the corner. This is particularly the case when the cabinet style is such that doors and drawer fronts extend the full width of the cabinets. There are basically four different units used in turning base corners, as follows:

1. *The base corner filler* is used in making a dead corner, allowing no corner space for storage. It requires 27 inches of wall area on each wall (24 inches of cabinet width plus 3 inches of filler strips or 27 inches in both directions). Using fillers

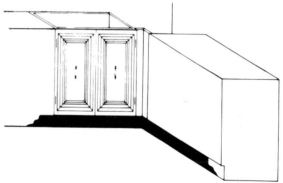

How a wall filler strip is used.

guarantees full operation of adjacent doors and drawers. This method of "blanking out" a corner is the most economical way of turning a corner, but because of the lost storage space is not recommended where storage space is limited.

2. *The blind corner base cabinet* as noted earlier, is built with a door opening in only one side of the face of the cabinet. The remainder of the face is blank or blind. This section of the cabinet is extended under the counter into the corner and the blind face is covered by the adjoining base assembly. Some corner base cabinets can be pulled out from the wall as much as 9 inches. The designer should check cabinet specifications for correct pull-

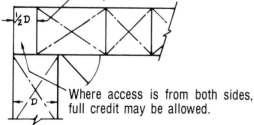

18" MAX
4" MIN
24" MIN - SINK OR RANGE
15" MIN - OTHER
30" MAX
15" MIN
74" MAX
12" MIN
38" MAX
30" MIN
24" MAX

Height, depth and spacing of shelves and countertop.

Area to be included in required space of base shelving where access is from one side only equals ½ depth of corner.

½ D

D

Where access is from both sides, full credit may be allowed.

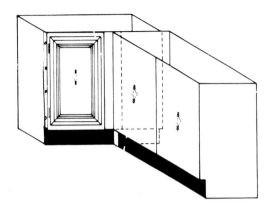

Use of a blind corner base cabinet.

spin shelves affixed to the door, requires 36 inches of space on each wall. It is the most requested cabinet for turning the corner but it can be overused. The storage area is limited, insofar as to type of storage, however it is the most accessible cabinet available.

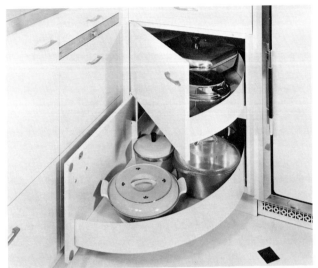

out dimensions. This possibility allows greater flexibility in the adjusting of the base-cabinet assembly to the room dimensions and eliminates the need for one-corner filler strip. Usually a filler strip should be used in attaching the base assembly which abuts the blind cabinet in the perpendicular direction. Blind corner base cabinets permit partial utilization of the corner space beneath the counter, but the space gained should be considered as suitable only for dead storage space. It does not count as accessible frontage. If the room arrangement is such that the corner base cabinet is accessible from the reverse face, peninsula-type base cabinets can be used to utilize the corner space in its entirety.

3. *The base lazy susan cabinet*, utilizing three

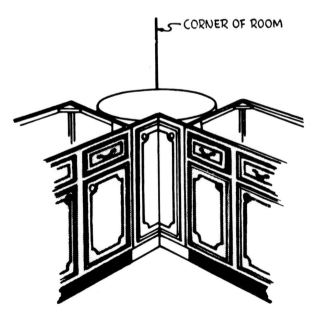

Use of a rotary or lazy susan base cabinet.

Use of lazy susans or revolving shelves for many different storage purposes.

4. *A sink front* for a diagonal sink installation is used when it is desirable to install a sink in the corner of the room. It can be used to create a focal point. The area required on each wall is determined by the size of the sink bowl being used.

Turning Corners with Wall Cabinets. Corners in wall-cabinet installations may be turned in three ways:

1. *A wall corner filler* is used in making a dead corner, allowing no storage space in the corner.

78

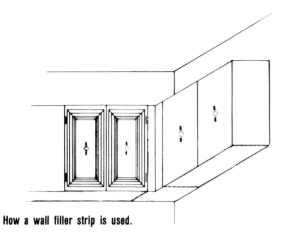

How a wall filler strip is used.

There is a corner filler panel available for corner fillers, which is to be used to close the hole in the bottom between the two adjacent wall cabinets. This method is used only when price is a factor and where adequate storage area permits.

2. *A blind corner wall cabinet* is highly acceptable for turning the corner, utilizing all space for storage by using the "reach into" procedure. Rather than two doors, the blind corner wall unit has one door (hung on a center stile) and a blank face. The blank face is extended behind the abutting cabinet at the corner. Adjustment of up to three inches can be accomplished by pulling the cabinet out from the corner. When a blind corner wall cabinet or a blind corner peninsula cabinet is used, the space requirement is dependent on the size of the cabinet being employed.

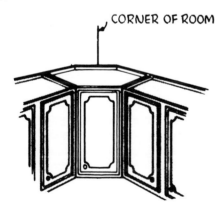

Use of diagonal wall cabinet.

3. *A diagonal-faced wall cabinet* may utilize the space in the corner of a wall cabinet assembly somewhat more effectively with a diagonal (45-degree) front. The typical diagonal-faced corner cabinet occupies 24 inches on each of the two perpendicular walls. (At the line where wall-cabinet frontage is measured, the diagonal cabinet occupies

12 inches on each frontage line.) Fillers are not required where diagonal corner cabinets are used to turn corners in wall-cabinet assemblies. Diagonal cabinets may be equipped with fixed shelves or rotating shelves. Corners may also be turned with 90-degree lazy susan arrangements, again occupying 24 inches on each wall at the corner.

Installing Cabinets and Appliances

Whether the installation of the kitchen equipment will be troublesome or easy depends on good preparation and proper installation techniques. Out-of-square walls, insufficient clearances, and incorrect installation procedures can create costly problems and delays.

Probably the most common installation problem is the out-of-square wall. It is most troublesome at the end of a wall or base cabinet run, and can prevent drawers and sliding shelves from being opened their full length, cabinet doors from being opened a full 90 degrees, and countertops from being properly fitted. If a wall is built out of square with the cabinet wall, a filler strip as shown should be used at that wall. It will move the cabinet door or drawer away from the out-of-square wall enough to allow the full use of the cabinets. Filler strips are available from cabinet manufacturers, and are finished to match cabinet finishes. Since many oven doors are the same width as the oven cabinet, an oven placed against an out-of-square wall at the end of a cabinet run will not leave enough room for the oven door to be opened fully.

Special consideration should be given to cabinets whose design places the hardware in the center of the cabinet doors. To insure that the door with its projecting hardware can be opened when against a wall or to allow a pullout shelf, a wide filler may be required. Cabinets placed close to a door or window jamb should be checked to be certain the jamb's trim will not interfere with the pullout drawers and shelves. Ovens and refrigerators placed at the intersection of base cabinets are not only incorrectly located, but difficult to use. They can create clearance problems for cabinet doors and drawers. In tight kitchens, the dishwasher is frequently placed too close to the cabinet intersection, hindering both the opening of the dishwasher and the cabinet that is at right angles to it. In each of the above cases, filler pieces should be used at the corner intersection.

Ovens placed too close to surface cooking units can be affected by the continuous moisture and grease given off by the surface units. Such areas require constant service. If such an installation is unavoidable, the side of the oven should be protected by plastic laminate or tile. Improper installation can not only create problems in the use of the equipment, but can damage the equipment before it is used. Some of the common mistakes during installation are: the use of nails instead of screws in the cabinet assembly; joining cabinets by screwing through the sides instead of the frame; failing to shim base cabinets on uneven floors and wall cabinets on uneven walls; not aligning base-cabinet fronts and wall-cabinet heights; and using an incorrect sequence in hanging cabinets. It is best to start with the corner units and work out in both direction.

Manufactured kitchen cabinets are available already assembled and in knocked-down form. The latter are less costly and come finished or unfinished. Most pre-assembled cabinets are finished at the factory. To assemble the knocked-down cabinets, follow the manufaclurer's instructions to the letter.

Cabinets are fastened to the walls either by the hanger method or directly to studs. With the former, the cabinet manufacturer usually supplies steel hanger brackets that are fastened to wall studs by means of wood screws. The cabinets are then hung on the hangers. A somewhat less complicated method consists of screwing the cabinets directly to the wall studs. The screws should be long enough to go through the wall material and penetrate will into the studs.

Regardless of how the cabinets are fastened to the walls, they must be installed perfectly level, from a standpoint of function as well as appearance. Find the highest point of the floor with the use of a level. Also, using a level or straightedge, find the high spots on the wall on which the cabinets are to be hung. Some high spots can be removed by sanding. Otherwise, it will be necessary to shim the low spots to provide a level and plumb installation. Using the highest point on the floor, measure up the wall to a height of 84 inches. This height, 84 inches, is the top height of the wall cabinets and oven and utility cabinets. On the walls where cabinets are to be installed, remove the baseboard and chair rail. This is required for a flush fit.

Start your installation in one corner. First assemble the base corner unit, then add a unit on each side of the corner unit. This, as a unit, can then be installed in position. Additional cabinets are added to each side as required. C-clamps should be used to connect cabinets together to obtain proper alignment. Drill two or three holes through the end panels. Holes should be drilled through to the adjoining cabinet. Secure a T-nut and draw up the two cabinets snugly with a bolt. It is also possible to drill through the side of the front frame and drill a "lead hole" into the abutting cabinet, insert the screws, and draw them up snugly.

Each cabinet, as it is installed on the wall, should be checked front to back and also across the front edge with a level. Be certain that the front frame is plumb. If necessary, use filler strips or shims to level the cabinets. The base cabinet should be attached with screws into the wall studs. For additional support and to prevent the back rail from "blowing," insert a block between the cabinet back and the wall. After the bases are installed, cover the toe-kick area with the material that is provided by the cabinet-maker.

Once the base units are fastened in place, attach the countertop to the cabinets. This countertop may be purchased with the kitchen cabinets, or it may be built on the job.

The wall cabinets should then be installed beginning with a corner unit, in the same way the base units were. Screw through the hanging strips built into the backs of the cabinets at both the top and bottom. Place them about ¾ inch below the top and ¾ inch above the bottom shelf from inside of the cabinet. Adjust the screws only loosely at first so that the final adjustments can be made after the cabinets have been checked with a level. The wall cabinets should be checked with a level on the cabinet front, sides, and bottom to insure that the cabinets are plumb and level. It might be necessary to shim at the wall and between the cabinets to correct for uneven walls or floors. After the cabinets and doors are perfectly aligned, tighten all screws.

To close the gap between the tops of the wall cabinets at the ceiling, soffits are frequently employed. A ceiling plate is spiked to the joists above, and the wall cleat is spiked to the studs. The short 2 by 6s between the main members are toenailed in place. Afterward, the face of the soffit is covered with wallboard or any convenient sheet material. When the cabinets are hung, gaps remaining between the bottom of the soffit and the tops of the cabinets will be hidden by a cove molding that is the last item to be affixed.

Remember that proper installation means better performance of equipment, less costly installation, and few service complaints.

COUNTERTOPS

The most used "equipment" in the kitchen is the countertop. It is used in conjunction with every work center as a general work surface and as a storage area. The material used to surface the countertop must therefore fill a variety of requirements. Additionally, since it is one of the most prominent of the kitchen's design elements, it must be attractive, colorful, and compatible with the kitchen's decorative theme.

Let us first consider the decorative aspect. The countertop should blend with the cabinets, yet add its own note of beauty, texture, and pattern to the kitchen. At the same time, it must harmonize with the floor and wall colors.

Now for the functional aspects of the countertop. Remember one important fact: The countertop will take almost as much wear and abuse as the floor, so above all it has to be rugged and easy to clean. When selecting the countertop material, the additional factors that should be considered are resistance to moisture, heat, sharp blows, knife cuts, scratching, staining, and fading. The intended use of the counter area will determine which of these factors are most important. In fact, today there is a trend towards variety in countertops. That is, more than one type of material is used in the same kitchen. In this way, different areas of the kitchen can utilize different types of surfaces — heat-resistant ones near the cooking area, a cutting surface near the baking/mixing center, and so on.

Countertop Materials

There are several materials that can be used for countertops. The most common are as follows:

Laminated Plastic Tops. Laminated plastic is the most popular countertop material since it is easy to care for, wears well, and offers the widest possible range of color and design choices. New methods of texturing now make it possible to obtain dimensional finishes with the look and feel of slate, wood, and leather. The most popular finishes for kitchen countertops are satin and velvet. The standard countertop grade is 1/16 inch thick.

Laminated plastics are hard, long lasting, tough, and easily cleaned. They are not affected by soaps, detergents, or hot water. They resist stains, fading, heat abrasions, and moisture and therefore

are ideal for use in most areas of the kitchen. However, a sharp knife blade will scratch them and they should not be used for a cutting surface, nor should they be subject to direct contact with hot metal surfaces over 275 degrees F (135 degrees C).

The core stock of most kitchen countertops is either ¾-inch exterior plywood or particleboard (also known as flakeboard). Laminated plastics usually are available in sheets a few inches larger than standard 4- by 8-foot (or 4 by 10 or 4 by 12, etc.) panels, to allow for the edge trimming that is necessary. When figuring the amount of material needed, remember to avoid joints as much as possible by using the longest lengths available. For example, if a countertop is to be built 9½ feet long, buy a 10-foot length of base core and laminate rather than joining an 8-foot piece with a 1½ footer. If the countertop has to turn a corner, it is probably best to join pieces.

There are two basic types of laminated plastic countertops — self-edged and post-formed. Self-edged tops offer a straight line effect achieved by 90-degree corners at the backsplash and the front edge. Post-formed countertops are one continuous sheet rolled at the backsplash and front edge. Both types can be had with a standard 4-inch backsplash or with a full-fixed backsplash. Of course, both are available as a flat top with no fixed backsplash. Where the backsplash is not an integral part of the countertop, many of the wall materials described in Chapter 6 can be used in its place.

Another popular plastic countertop is flexible vinyl. Because it has a higher resiliency than laminated plastic, it is gentler to dropped dishes. It resists stains, moisture, abrasion and alcohol, and is not hurt by heavy impact. This material should not be used as a cutting surface, hot utensils or small appliances should never be set directly upon it, and hot water should not be put directly on it.

The following materials can also be used as complete countertops, but will probably be more efficient and useful if used as small inserts in countertops of some other materials, such as laminated plastic.

Ceramic Glass Tops. A recent innovation, ceramic glass is primarily used as inserts for sections of counter. It is resistant to damage from heat changes or scratching, can be easily cleaned, and is suitable next to a range or oven or at a sandwich-making center. Ceramic glass comes in a range of sizes. It cannot be cut on the job.

Ceramic Tile Tops. Ceramic tile, either glazed or quarry tile, is durable and heat resistant, but

Popular countertop materials: Laminated plastic with laminated hardwood on the island (left); laminated plastic with ceramic glass insert (center); and ceramic tile (right).

noisy. Also, more care is needed when working to avoid breakage of glasses and china. It offers great design flexibility since ceramic tiles are available in a wide variety of sizes, colors, and shapes. But, when selecting tiles, keep in mind that glazed tile should have a matte finish for better resistance to scratching. Quarry tile, a hard-wearing surface, has a warm earthy look, but it sometimes is too porous and thus it may have to be sealed.

Marble Tops. An insert of marble can be used in the same way as ceramic glass, but it is more likely to break, needs more care, and has a greater tendency to stain. However, marble is a handsome natural counter material for kitchens decorated in traditional styles.

A new solid plastic that looks like marble is becoming popular as kitchen countertop material. This imitation marble (methyl methacrylate plastic) has the good stain and heat resistance that is most desirable plus the characteristics of wood (it can be sawed, shaped, and sanded) for maximum adaptability. These solid plastic countertops are now being offered in patterns other than marble.

Stainless-Steel Tops. Stainless Steel is heat and moisture resistant, but because of its cost, it is seldom employed for an entire countertop. As an insert material, stainless steel wears very well and will not crack, chip, or break. It may, however, show cuts, scratches, and water spots.

Laminated Hardwood Tops. The good old chopping block is still the gourmet cook's favorite for slicing or chopping. Hot pans should not be set directly upon it, and prolonged moisture should be avoided. However, if the wood is oiled occasionally, it will serve faithfully for years, and the surface can always be sanded down if it gets too chopped up.

Laminated hardwood countertops are available in a wide range of standard sizes from 12 to 120 inches. They are usually a full 1½ inches thick and 25 inches deep, and come with or without a 1-inch-thick backsplash. They come ready for installation on top of the base cabinets. Follow the manufacturer's instructions carefully for best results. Hardwood block inserts are available that come with a standard stainless-steel sink frame. They are also available in the drop-in type that can fit in a hole cut into the countertop.

Criteria for Counter Surfaces

Just as important as the proper countertop material is sufficient counter space. While some mention was made of desirable counter surfaces in Chapter 2, it is now time to take a better look into the criteria of this important subject. For instance, counters are normally placed at the standard height of 36 inches above the floor. The height was selected on the basis that it provided a convenient level for the average person to perform normal kitchen work while standing. The 36-inch height also coordinates with the height of kitchen base cabinets and most appliances. Under special circumstances, counter heights may be varied. Counters should be raised for taller people and lowered for shorter people as well as for people in wheelchairs. Occasionally, counter heights may be varied for specific kitchen activities. For example, counters are sometimes placed at a lower level for baking and mixing operations, or they may be placed at a 30-inch height for working while seated. Since most counters are installed above base cabinets, the usual front-to-back dimension of the counter is 25 inches or thereabouts. This provides an overhang in front of the base cabinet.

Counter surface should be distributed so as to provide a working surface at each work center. More specifically, counter space should be located on both sides of the sink and of the range (or cooktop) and on one side of the refrigerator and of a separate oven. A counter is most effective when it is continuous between appliances.

For isolated centers, the following counter frontages (in inches) are recommended*:

Center	Minimum	Good	Better
Mix and Preparation	30	36	42
Sink (one side)	24	30	36
Sink (other side)	18	24	30
Range or Surface Cooking Unit (one side)	15	24	30
Range or Surface Cooking Unit (other side)	12	15	24
Separate Built-In Oven	15	18	24
Refrigerator	15	18	24

* See page 185 for HUD's Minimum Property Standards.

Although Minimum Property Standards do not have a specific total number of inches in their regulations, the Small Homes Council at the University of Illinois recommends the following total counter frontage:

Minimum counter frontage 72
Liberal counter frontage 109

An upper limit of 180 inches is suggested for the kitchen area proper, as expansion over this amount would probably result in excess walking between appliances.

When counters are turned around a corner, as in the case of a U-shaped or L-shaped kitchen assembly, counters should be arranged so that there is a certain amount of counter frontage between the internal corner and the range, the sink, and/or any tall appliance, such as a refrigerator. These clearances are necessary in order that the counter and/or the appliance may be used with safety and greater convenience. Recommended corner clearances are:

1. *Between range or cooktop and corner:* 12 inches (9 inches*). This clearance is necessary to avoid a possible burn injury to a person who might inadvertently extend an arm or an elbow over a burner while working at the adjacent counter.

2. *Between sink and corner:* 12 inches. This clearance makes it possible to use the sink more easily, particularly when two people are working at the sink.

3. *Between a tall appliance (refrigerator or built-in wall oven) and corner:* 15 inches.* This clearance is necessary to make the counter surface more accessible.

*These clearances are required by HUD's Minimum Property Standards.

PLAN FOR ADEQUATE STORAGE

Cabinets are, of course, the most common storage area, but there are many possibilities for imaginative and practical storage in the kitchen. Here are a few suggestions:

1. *Use the walls.* The space between wall studs is great for storage of many varied common household items — ironing board, shelves for canned goods, cleaning materials, etc. Leave open or closed with bifold doors, curtains, or window shades. A full 24-inch depth is not necessary for pantry and broom closets.

2. *Plan around obstacles.* Do not let the chimney, clothes chute, heating ducts, or pipes interfere with storage plans. Locate a cabinet to house these necessary things, but let it also be just a bit larger for valuable additional storage — a broom closet, tray rack, or liquor cabinet.

3. *Add an in-between cabinet.* The space between wall and base cabinets is often wasted. Shallow cabinets with sliding doors are available from several sources. Many of these fine units have lights built into them for even better value.

4. *Vary the cabinets.* Wall cabinets do not *have* to be hung on the wall or from the ceiling. These useful shallow units can be arranged as a room divider at the sink or range. They cut off the clutter of the kitchen and allow complete visibility from the kitchen to the family room or breakfast nook.

5. *Use wall cabinets as bases.* This is a most useful idea especially when space is important. And do not forget about some open shelves. They can be most useful as auxiliary storage. Remember though, dust will collect on open shelves.

6. *Use roll-around carts.* Such carts can slide

Here is a summary of popular kitchen accessories (A) plate rack; (B) subshelf for cups; (C) cup hooks or slide-out cup rack; (D) recipe rack; (E) dispenser for Baggies, waxed paper, foil, etc.; (F) general shelf space; (G) inside cupboard spice rack; (H) door hung spice rack; (J) glass sliding doors; (K) cutting board; (L) silverware drawer; (M) flour bin; (N) waste can; (O) single action faucet; (P) vegetable and fruit bins; (Q) bag rack; (R) pan rack; (S) lazy susan; (T) utensil and accessory stand; (U) tray cabinet; and (V) canned goods and cake rack.

under a counter and provide extra storage space, as well as an additional work surface.

7. *Add a pantry*. There is much to be said for the old-style walk-in pantry or a wall of floor-to-ceiling cabinets for storage of canned and packaged foods, small appliances, dishes, and glassware. When wall space is limited, plot the pantry with a pull-out unit that uses the full height and depth of the line of cabinets and brings all the stored items within easy reach. Pantry units mentioned earlier in the chapter can also be cleverly designed with hinged shelf sections on both sides, opening like leaves of a book to make everything accessible. Some manufacturers offer ready-made ones. Slanting shelves, supermarket style, can also be used for

canned goods storage, with cans lying on their sides so that a replacement slides into position as a can is removed.

8. *Use sliding doors*. Cabinets with sliding doors may be installed between the underside of the wall cabinets and the countertops, to store the appliances close at hand. A heavy appliance, like a mixer, may be set on a rolling stand, easy to pull out and use.

9. *Use display shelves*. Open shelves can be used to display attractive dishware. Use walls to hang utensils, a spice rack or cutting board. Pegboard hung on the wall can store a variety of items conveniently and it can be rearranged later on if desired.

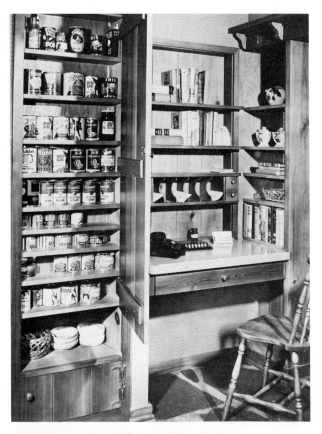

Pantry storage unit can be tied into kitchen office area.

Roll-out cabinet type cart.

10. *Add an island center.* An island activity center can be used as a work surface (cooking, mixing/baking, preparation/clean-up, or serving) and as an area for storage. Ideally, the island should contain everything needed in that activity — work surfaces, appliances, and storage for foods, utensils, and supplies. For instance, if the island is to be a real "cook's table," by all means design a ceiling rack above it with hooks to hold pans and large cooking tools. Add storage facilities for other basic utensils

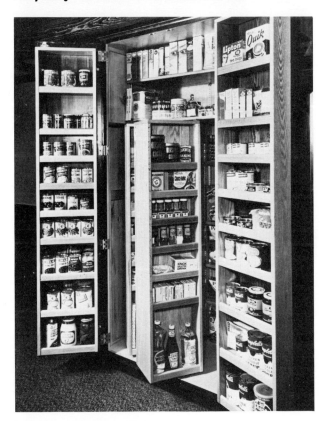

Fold-out type tall pantry cabinet.

Under-counter pantry cabinet.

and supplies and perhaps a wooden, marble or ceramic glass top section.

11. *Put in a drink cabinet.* Entertaining is fun, and much more convenient when the drink ingredients, glasses, and the rest of the necessary supplies are all right at hand in a single storage unit. This would also be a nice place to put a wine rack.

12. *Add a linen closet.* With all the linens that are used in the kitchen, everything from napkins and tablecloths to dish towels and cleaning and dusting utility rags, the life of the homemaker can be made easier if the linens are all concentrated in one convenient space.

Small things can often increase storage. For instance, hooks or slides for cups to hang inside the cabinets are still good storage space savers. Racks can be set up in the cabinet for different size glassware and china. The storage of "small" or portable appliances is often a major problem in some kitchens. Many a gift appliance is tucked away in a hall closet when it could be at work in the kitchen. Therefore, plan a "small-appliance center" that includes counter space or storage space and enough circuits and outlets for the proper operation of the appliances. When there is ample counter space, it is a great labor-saver to keep the frequently used portable appliances out and ready. If it is desirable to screen them from view, cupboards can be created from countertop corners by building doors diagonally under the wall cabinets. A stand mixer can be mounted on a typewriter-style shelf that swings up from a base cabinet, and many portable appliances and appliance heads can be mounted on the wall. Another desirable small-appliance center is a roll-around utility cart or portable island.

It is useful to have two circuits for the use of portable appliances, with outlets to serve each section of the counter. The homemaker may want to use an electric fry pan, toaster, and coffeemaker at the same time. Heating appliances draw more current than motor appliances. Check wattages and avoid overloading the circuits. (see page 102). Put in enough outlets for appliances that will stay plugged in, such as a can opener or rechargeable battery for a knife, and still leave some free for other uses.

In a large kitchen it may be better to store appliances according to use: a coffeemaker near the sink because it takes water as the first step in its use, a toaster near the breakfast table, a mixer at the baking center, and an automatic fry pan near the range or barbecue hood.

While the amounts of storage space mentioned earlier in the chapter are a good general suggestion, the best way to judge the storage requirements for your kitchen is to refer to the activity list described in Chapter 1 and make a list of the supplies, foods, and utensils used in each activity. Actually, every family's storage needs are a little different. These needs stem directly from the activities and interests of each member of the family. Awareness of those activities will help anticipate ways to solve the storage problems they create. If possible, take an inventory of the items you are presently storing, noting where items are stored, what is stored inconveniently, and what items you would like to add to the new kitchen.

List the items under the work center category in which they will be used in three groups: (1) used every day; (2) used once a week; and (3) used once a month or less. Measure the space they will take, and, if possible, add one-fifth additional space for future needs. Plan storage for each work center. Everyday items should be close at hand. The area between one's waist and eye level is most efficient for storage. Seldom-used items can be placed in areas where a person has to bend or stretch to reach them. However, try to avoid using "dead" storage high above the head or in deep corners except for items used only a few times a year. Once the general layout is set up, the storage suited for each individual item can be allotted. With a little planning, it is possible to customize the storage facilities to handle every item conveniently.

CHAPTER 5

ELECTRICITY IN THE MODERN KITCHEN

In the previous chapters, the basic principles of planning a kitchen layout, as well as of selecting appliances and cabinets were covered. There is another aspect of the kitchen that is of equal importance to its dual role as a work and living area — adequate electrical provision with particular emphasis on lighting and convenience.

Because of all that can be done with electricity in a kitchen, the biggest part of a house's electrical load — up to 80 percent of the total house wattage — is drawn by kitchen appliances and lighting. Because electricity offers such convenient power (and appliance makers are so inventive) there will be more and more power being used to make the storage, preparation, and cooking of foods and the cleanup after meals more convenient and time saving. But, before going into how to wire for these kitchen conveniences, the important subject of kitchen lighting will be discussed.

KITCHEN LIGHTING

No kitchen is complete without adequate lighting. Daylight or electric light must provide illumination where it is needed and when it is needed. In the field of kitchen design, it is amazing how often the subject of lighting is treated casually. After all, lighting is a part of decorating, and decorating is a part of lighting.

In a purely technical sense, whenever you look at an object, you do not see the object itself but rather the light reflected from it. So every surface in the kitchen becomes a part of the lighting design. Reflected light is always tinted with the color of the reflecting surface. That is why the paint on the wall may look far more intense in color than the paint swatches from which you selected it. Colors live in light. People actually become color blind in the dark. Colors literally become gray and lifeless in poor illumination. That is why you must ask certain questions. 1. Is the lighting level adequate over the range? 2. Is a fixture located to eliminate shadows and glares? 3. Does the window over the sink allow a blinding afternoon sun to make the clean-up center an unbearable place to work?

Most kitchens have four basic kinds of lighting: natural daylight resulting from windows and skylights; general lighting that gives overall illumination; local or task lighting that provides proper illumination at specific work centers; and decorative lighting that emphasizes the color and decorative theme of the kitchen.

A skylight gives light to a kitchen.

Windows

Windows furnish the natural light to brighten working areas and supplement the artificial light. Minimum property standards of the HUD/FHA specify a window area totaling, in square feet, 10 percent of the floor area. (Good kitchens should have at least 15 percent — an area equal to 20 to 30 percent of the room's area is still better.) Whenever possible, two window areas should be planned. Glass panels in outside doors and skylights count as part of the total window area. Incidentally, the latter gives a great deal of natural light without cutting down on wall cabinet space. A skylight can also help avoid that claustrophobic feeling in kitchens by opening up spaces to the outdoors where there are no windows. Obviously, skylights cannot be put in every kitchen, but a feeling of soaring freedom can be experienced in a kitchen that has one.

A window is not just a hole in a wall. It is far more. Because it is a part of the wall, it demands serious consideration. Windows can permit you to make the outdoors an integral part of the room decor or to shut out an unsightly brick wall (as in the case of some apartment kitchens). Windows can be used to invite the world into the home or to make it a cloistered retreat.

Windows can also be used to play an important part in the overall kitchen decorating plan. A paned window fits into many traditional kitchens, but would be an unusual choice for some contemporary rooms. Decide on the type of window, then on the window treatment that is desired. That is, start window planning by thinking about the exposure of the kitchen to sunlight. Consider the view from the window, the need for privacy, possible glare from uncovered windows at night, and the proximity of the window to spatter from the sink or range.

A good north window usually provides a nice view while it keeps the sun from shining directly into the homemaker's eyes while he or she works. East windows are not too bad because the morning sun does not seem to have quite the intensity of the hot afternoon sun. South and west windows begin to allow the glare of the sun into the kitchen about 1 p.m. and continue to do so for as long as seven hours. This may be more sunshine than desired. Windows facing south can be shielded from the sun's direct rays by a roof overhang. Those on the north are not bothered by sun. If the windows face east or west, a roof overhang will not provide protection from the sun because the sun shines into windows on these sides of the house from a low angle. Tall shrubbery, fences, and louvers can be used to keep the low sun's rays away from windows.

Before decorating a kitchen window, decide on its purpose. Is it to hide a view or to enhance one? Is it to accent the kitchen theme, to help shade a too-sunny kitchen, or to provide added privacy? A window can do any of these things depending on its decoration. Cafe curtains, casement cloth curtains, window shades laminated to match wallpaper, Roman shades (fabric curtains that are pulled up venetian-blind style into horizontal folds), beaded curtains, and shutters are among the decorator possibilities.

Curtains are, of course, the traditional kitchen window covering. They soften a room, and help deaden noise. Fabrics may be specially treated to guard against soil, sun, and humidity. Also, there are almost unlimited window curtain materials. Investigate dress materials, Indian cloth, bedsheets, cotton bandannas, and so on. Curtain material can be matched to a tablecloth, to wallpaper patterns, or to a fabric "painting"' on the wall. Or a coordinated look can be achieved by matching the dishwasher front panel to the curtains.

Shades no longer mean just the plain white variety. Window shades now come in wild colors and patterns. In addition, shades can be decorated by

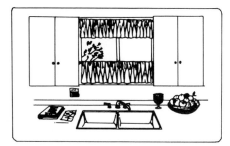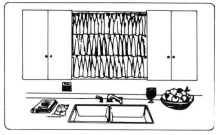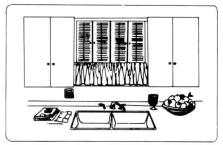

Three ideas for a typical over-the-sink kitchen window designed to offer both privacy and daylight plus that all important view of the children at play, or a relaxing out-of-doors scene.

Blinds offer both light and privacy.

adding trim, fringe or fabric to match the wallpaper or paint. Designs can be painted or stenciled on shades to match another pattern in the room. One new shade material is laminated so that any fabric can be ironed on bonding it to the shade. These shades may be translucent to let in light, while at the same time cutting down on glare.

Blinds are available in new colors, too, with new trims and styles. They help control and direct light and maintain privacy. Shutters and screens also give privacy without shutting out the light. They may fold or slide open, or remain stationary.

Stained-glass windows (which have made a great comeback in home construction in the last few years) and window graphics are great if the view from them leaves something to be desired. Some householders like to have glass shelves across the window to hold plants. Others like to frame the window with fabric or a decorative wooden valance

across the top and down the sides. The window can also be used to hang something like wooden utensils or cooking items. To do this, simply start with a spring tension rod at the top of the window opening, then string up anything that appeals to the homemakers, such as wooden spoons, rolling pins and slotted forks.

General Lighting

General lighting is the "fill-in" lighting that provides the soft glow throughout the room, enhancing its decoration and making it more livable. General lighting also provides the lighting that is needed to carry on work in the kitchen.

General lighting can come from hanging fixtures, fixtures mounted on the ceiling, or recessed fixtures mounted in the ceiling. It also can come from a "luminous ceiling" where light floods through an entire translucent suspended ceiling or it can come from valance lighting or illuminated soffits.

How much general light is needed in the kitchen? It is difficult to tell in terms of light bulb wattages, because wattages are not accurate measures of light intensity. However, the following system will serve a rough guide. Measure the kitchen to find how many square feet of floor space is there. Then simply apply the following minimums. If you feel more comfortable with more light, do not hesitate to move up from the minimums.

For ceiling-mounted or suspended fixtures in the kitchen, you should have 2 watts per square foot for incandescent and 1 watt per square foot for fluorescent fixtures. For valance, cornice, or wall bracket

Window shapes (top) or an added window decoration (right) can make for an interesting kitchen.

types of indirect lighting, you will need 5 to 6 watts of fluorescent lighting per square foot of floor space.

For non-directional recessed lighting (fixtures mounted in the ceiling), the minimums are 3 watts per square foot for incandescent and 1½ watts per square foot for fluorescent fixtures.

It is important to know the general characteristics of both incandescent and fluorescent light sources in order to choose types appropriate to contour, light output, wattage, color quality, and directional control for each kitchen application. By knowing how to work successfully with either type or with both in combination, it is possible to achieve lighting results that are visually comfortable, functional, and beautiful.

The light from incandescent-filament bulbs — the oldest of our light sources — is warm in color quality and imparts a friendly, homelike feeling to interiors. Under this light source the warm colors (oranges, reds, brown, etc.) are enhanced while the cool colors (blues and greens) are subdued. Generally, when the overall atmosphere of a room is on the warm side, the full values of the warm colors will be acceptable when lighted with filament bulbs. Under such light, many of the blues and greens in fabrics, flooring, countertops, wallcoverings, and paint will be muted or slightly changed in color, but there will not be a general consciousness of these shifts.

In designing kitchen lighting, inside-frosted standard-service incandescent bulbs ranging in wattages from 15 to 300 are the most commonly used types. Some of these wattages are available in other finishes. Today the white-coated bulbs that produce a softer quality of light and less harsh shadows are used in portable lamps and fixtures where greater diffusion is desired. Due to a fine white inner coating in these bulbs, light is distributed over the entire surface, eliminating the previously apparent bright spot near the center.

There are also tinted incandescent bulbs in yellow, pink, aqua, green, and blue from 40 to 150 watts. They are recommended for locations where the specific effect of a warm or cool mood or atmosphere is desired. In general, tinted light subtly accents like colors and subdues complementary colors. Yellow and pink bulbs produce a warm color tint of light that intensifies warm coloring in home furnishings. Aqua, green, and blue bulbs give emphasis to cool colors in a decorative scheme. If desired, the appearance of a color scheme may be changed by using yellow and pink bulbs to subdue cool colors and aqua, green, and blue bulbs to tone down warm colors.

Seasonal changes can be made without resorting to complex or expensive methods to achieve the color appearance of coolness in summer and warmth for the winter. In rooms that have neutral color schemes, tinted bulbs can subtly create quite different atmospheres. The addition of color to incandescent bulbs will, however, reduce the light output compared to that obtainable with either the inside-frosted or white-coated bulbs. It is suggested that to compensate for the reduced light output, tinted bulbs of the next higher wattage be used if approximately equal lighting results are desired.

Incandescent reflector (R-type) and projector bulbs (PAR-type) can be used where a very definite application of either a moderately concentrated spotlight or a more widespread floodlight beam is desired. But, remember that all incandescent bulbs, for the best light results and the most economical operation, should have the same voltage rating as that of the power supply line.

Fluorescent tubular sources offer a higher light efficiency, cooler operation temperatures, and longer life than incandescent bulbs of comparable wattage. The average fluorescent tube will deliver 3 times as much light as an incandescent for the same wattage and will last 20 times longer. For these reasons they are most adaptable to and very commonly used in kitchen custom-designed built-in installations, as well as in surface-mounted and recessed fixtures.

Fluorescent light sources commonly used in the home range in size from the 4-watt, T-5, 6-inch length to the 40-watt, T-12, 48-inch length. ("T" means tubular and the number equals the diameter in eighths of an inch.) The length of the tube given in all cases is the overall nominal length including the required sockets. All fluorescent light sources require a current-limiting and control device called a ballast, which is located in a metal enclosure. For the operation of some fluorescent tubes an automatic switch known as a starter is required in addition to the normal wall switch. The starter is a small metal can inserted into the fixture body or channel and is a replaceable part. There are several methods of fluorescent tube operation commonly used in residences. Listed below are the sizes, lengths, bases, and types of operation of fluorescent tubes suggested for residential kitchen use. Also included are circular fluorescent tubes.

With the various fluorescent "whites" available,

Wattage	Designation	TUBES Diameter (inches)	Length (inches)	Type of Base
4	T-5	⅝	6	Miniature bipin
6	T-5	⅝	9	Miniature bipin
8	T-5	⅝	12	Miniature bipin
14	T-12	1½	15	Medium bipin
15	T-8	1	18	Medium bipin
15	T-12	1½	18	Medium bipin
20	T-12	1½	24	Medium bipin
25	T-12	1½	33	Medium bipin
30	T-8	1	36	Medium bipin
30	T-12	1½	36	Medium bipin
40	T-12	1½	48	Medium bipin
		Circular		
22	T-9	1⅛	8¼ *	
32	T-10	1¼	12 *	
40	T-10	1¼	15 *	

*outside diameter

light can be produced ranging from a very cool blue-white to a warm pinkish-white. Today the skilled kitchen designer can work successfully with a palette of seven "whites" to create the desired atmosphere. Listed below are the seven "whites" used most in kitchen work, with a description of the color characteristics of each.

1. *Deluxe warm white (WWX)* creates a warm atmosphere and blends well with incandescent bulbs. It enhances complexions, foods, and warm tones in countertops, appliances, furniture, fabric, and paint. For kitchen use where warm colors predominate, color appearance is important and warm atmosphere is desired.

2. *Deluxe cool white (CWX)* flatters all colors and creates a cool atmosphere. This fluorescent color gives the most accurate color rendition of all fluorescent tubes but its cool light is quite different in appearance from the mellow, yellowish incandescent lighting usually found in the home. For kitchen use where cool colors predominate in the decoration and where a cool atmosphere is desired.

3. *Warm white* is a light which will blend with incandescent lighting but somewhat adversely affects both warm and cool colors.

4. *Cool white* is a light which produces a cool atmosphere, but dulls warm colors and intensifies cool colors.

5. *White* is a compromise between warm white and cool white; slightly dulls the appearance of warm colors.

6. *Daylight* is a very blue-white light seldom used in homes because it grays complexions, dulls warm colors, and creates a very cold atmosphere.

7. *Soft white* is a pinkish white light that emphasizes reds and pinks but has a tendency to gray cool colors.

The choice of fluorescent tubes is simply a matter of deciding first whether a warm or a cool atmosphere is desired for the kitchen. Therefore, when the kitchen atmosphere and color rendition are of prime importance, the corresponding warm or cool tube would be chosen. Otherwise, warm white or cool white tubes will serve if light output is the more important requirement. More on the selection of color schemes for the kitchen can be found in Chapter 9.

All white fluorescent tubes look alike when unlighted. The name of the color white (which varies among manufacturers), as well as the wattage of the tube, is printed on the glass tube at one end. Fluorescent tubes in colors — red, pink, blue, and gold — may be used for a decorative accent or combined to produce a desired blending of colors.

Ceiling and Recessed Fixtures. The easiest way to obtain good general lighting is by using one or more ceiling-mounted fixtures. Today there is a wide range of well-designed ceiling fixtures of the surface-mounted or pendant type on the market. When selecting a fixture for the kitchen keep the following points in mind to assure the most lighting effectiveness and comfort.

1. *Type of Shielding Material.* For visual comfort, completely diffusing materials such as opal or ceramic-enameled glass or diffusing plastic are

Ceiling light box over cooking area.

Kitchen lighting fixtures range from decorative hanging chandeliers to simple ceiling globes.

preferred as shielding materials. (Clear glass and frosted glass are suitable only for decorative fixtures using very low wattage or controlled by a dimmer switch.)

2. *Size of Shielding Material.* With a given wattage in diffusing enclosures such as spheres, cylinders, or other unusual shapes, the larger the diameter of the enclosure, the lower its brightness and the softer the shadows cast by it.

3. *Position of Fixture* (relative to viewing angles of occupant). Ceiling-mounted fixtures in the kitchen are more readily seen within one's field of view and consequently should have only half the surface brightness of similar fixtures in utility areas. Similarly, pendant fixtures (directly in the line of sight) should have half the surface brightness of ceiling-mounted fixtures. Most luminous small-diameter pendant fixtures should use 25 watts or less as they serve only for decorative accent. However, pendant fixtures of very dense or opaque materials may use much higher wattage without causing discomfort.

4. *Light Distribution.* A well-shielded fixture distributing light up, down, and to the sides will (by itself) create a much more pleasing atmosphere in a room than one which produces only downward light. When the latter types are used there should always be several per room. Fixtures suspended from the ceiling and reflecting all or nearly all of their light to the ceiling for redistribution produce very comfortable (though bland) general lighting.

Recessed fixtures provide no light on the ceiling. Because most of the light is directed downward, the wattage and the number of fixtures needed should be at least double the number of surface-mounted or pendant fixtures used to light the same area. To avoid glare at the ceiling, select a fixture having one of the following (listed in order from lowest to highest brightness):

1. Special low-brightness louvers (parabolic wedge).

2. Reflector and lens for control of light direction. When used in conjunction with a so-called adjustable "eyeball" fixture, the light direction can be set for good visibility of contents inside cabinets.

Recessed lighting over eating area.

3. Metal or plastic louvers.

4. Flat opal glass (not below the ceiling line).

Recessed fixtures may be used for fluorescent tubes or incandescent bulbs. Keep in mind that while any downlighting done in recessed fixtures holding R- or PAR-type bulbs may be most decorative in the light patterns and shadows they cast, it is not suitable for general lighting because it is not diffused enough for comfortable visibility throughout the kitchen.

Luminous Panels and Ceilings. A luminous ceiling can be fully illuminated. Or it can have just one panel of light. In the latter case, a panel of louvered or diffusing material — usually about 4 by 6 feet in size — is mounted on the ceiling or suspended from it, with the light source concealed behind it. Most of the major fixture manufacturers offer "kits," consisting of: (1) plastic diffusers in pans, sheets, or rolls; (2) a suspension system with a gridwork of wood, metal, or plastic; and (3) fluorescent fixtures to mount above the suspended luminous panel.

While more than one luminous panel may be

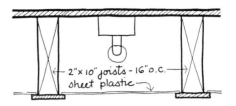

One method of installing a luminous ceiling.

used in a kitchen, a single unit is best where it is to be employed as an architectural feature, for example suspended over an island work center. When used in this manner, the luminous panel should be the same size as the island and about 6 inches deep. If it is hung at least a foot from the ceiling, it will provide good general illumination as well as providing shadowless light for the work center island.

For shadow-free general lighting throughout the kitchen, the luminous ceiling is the answer. But such a lighting plan is usually only possible where there is a cavity of at least 10 inches above the desired ceiling line. (Frequently the cavities between

Two luminous panel arrangements.

93

the ceiling joints are used as a part of or the whole space needed for the luminous ceiling fixtures.) For uniform lighting, use a minimum of one 40-watt fluorescent tube for every 12 square feet of room area, or one 60-watt incandescent bulb for every 4 square feet of panel. For proper light diffusion, all surfaces of the cavity must be of high reflectance and must have a matte texture. White lampholders for incandescent bulbs or white-finished channel strips for fluorescent tubes are also needed. In addition, any other materials within the cavity, such as joists, conduits, pipes, etc., should be painted white. The ceiling panels themselves are usually made of translucent plastic, with decorative metal gridwork providing the necessary support. Manufacturers of luminous ceilings can provide design and installation instructions for their particular products.

Curved luminous panels add interest to the work area.

Valance and Soffit Lighting. A valance board installed between the cabinet tops and ceiling is an easy and effective way to obtain general kitchen light. The valance faceboards which shield a continuous row of fluorescent tubes running the full length of the cabinets can be simple and unobtrusive, or they can be as decorative and stylish as the imagination will allow. A wide variety of faceboard materials are available that can be trimmed, scalloped, notched, perforated, papered, or painted. Faceboards should have a minimum width of 5 inches and seldom should be wider than 10 inches. They should not interfere with the opening and closing of cabinet doors. To obtain proper upward diffusion of the light, the top of the fluorescent fixtures and the top of the faceboard should be at least

10 inches from the ceiling. The faceboard should also be mounted a minimum of 6 inches from the wall or soffit face to permit air to circulate freely around the fluorescent tubes. It is a good idea to tilt the faceboard in 15 to 20 degrees as this will shield the light source from anyone sitting in the kitchen. The inside of the valance board should always be painted flat white.

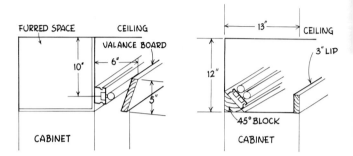

Two methods of soffit lighting.

Where the space above the wall cabinets is not enclosed and there is at least 12 inches between them and the ceiling, the bare fluorescent channels can be mounted on the top of the cabinets at the rear. The channel should be tilted on 45-degree blocks for upward diffusion of light. If the fluorescent tubes can be seen from across the room, a 3- to 5-inch board can be fastened on top of the cabinets at the front. This faceboard can be finished to match the wall cabinets.

If the soffit area above the cabinet is at least 12 inches high, it is possible to illuminate the perimeter of the entire kitchen. The continuous two-tube fluorescent fixtures are fastened to the wall at the back of the cavity and the soffit is faced with either translucent plastic or glass. The inside of the cavity should be painted flat white or lined with a reflecting material. To be most effective, the ceiling itself should be white or a very light color.

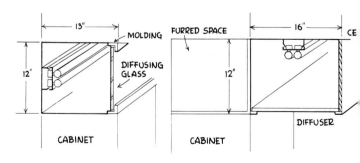

Two methods of valance lighting.

94

Soffit lights are excellent for lighting work areas.

Another way to have an illuminated soffit is to extend it out from the cabinets 16 to 24 inches and on the ceiling of this extension, install continuous, two-tube fluorescent fixtures. The bottom of the extension is then covered with either translucent plastic or glass. The result is a soft, intimate light all around the cabinet walls. This extended soffit method is very similar to the cornice lighting that is used often in other rooms of the house to dramatize wall textures and wall coverings.

Before leaving the subject of general lighting, it should be pointed out that ceiling color scheme and height can modify some of the suggestions already made. That is, the guidelines given thus far are based on light colors and average ceiling height (8 feet). A light color on the ceiling reflects 60 to 80 percent of the light. Light reflection is reduced when dark colors are used. A kitchen with a high ceiling and dark counters, cabinets and/or walls needs higher wattage light sources.

A "bullet" fixture spot-lights a work area.

Task Lighting

Once the general illumination has been planned, the next step in designing the overall lighting plan is to lay out the local illumination needed for the special task areas of the kitchen. Among the things that must be planned for are lighting level, lighting color (most people find warm colors more acceptable), and location.

Task lighting should be provided over the work surfaces (counters) and over the cook and sink/cleanup work centers. If an informal dining area is planned for the kitchen, lighting for this area must be considered too. The lighting fixtures for task areas may be mounted under cabinets, on the ceiling, on the walls, or in soffits. But regardless of where the source is located, it must fall on the area in front of you to prevent you from working in your own shadow. With well-lighted work areas, time is saved and the possibility of accidents is greatly reduced. Remember to provide shielding for each light, so no one ever has to look directly at a bare bulb or fluorescent tube.

Under-Cabinet Lighting. When overhead cabinets are present, the best method of lighting the counter surfaces below is to fasten fluorescents channels either to the bottom of cabinets at the front (preferable) or directly under the cabinet on the back wall. The channels may be painted to match the wall if desired. An opaque shield is recommended. It may be of metal, wood, or laminated plastic to match the cabinets or countertops. The wattage used depends on the total length of counter areas as follows:

15W (18") for counters less than 24"
20W (24") for counters less than 36"
30W (36") for counters less than 48"
40W (48") for counters less than 72"

A continuous under-cabinet arrangement.

Plug-in under-cabinet fixture.

Built-in under-cabinet fixture.

Use the longest tube that will fit, and fill at least two-thirds of the counter length. These wattages are good for up to 22 inches above the countertop, a height for wall cabinets that is rather uncomfortable for most householders, but sometimes found in cost-cutting kitchens. A 2-socket incandescent bracket with 60 watts in each socket is the equivalent for each three feet of countertop, but incandescent light is not as popular for under-cabinet applications as fluorescents.

For a right-angle counter with cabinets above, use a fluorescent channel mounted lengthwise under the center of the upper cabinets, with an opaque shielding on both sides of the tube. The tube length and wattage needed are the same as given for other under-cabinet installations.

For a right-angle counter with no cabinets above, use either louvered, surface-mounted, or semi-recessed cylinders or recessed, louvered "high-hats" with 75-watt R-30 floodlights, spaced 20 inches from center to center. If the counter doubles as an informal dining area, a pulley fixture or several pendants could be used as described later in the chapter.

Cook and Sink/Cleanup Centers. The cooking and sink/cleanup work centers need special lighting. The sink/cleanup center is best lighted by a hanging fixture, soffit lighting over the sink, or valance or cornice lighting that utilizes fluorescent strips. If there are cabinets above the sink, the area can be illuminated in the same manner as already described

Under-cabinet lighting for a serving area.

for under-cabinet lighting. If the sink has wall cabinets on either side of it, the light source can be mounted in or on the soffit as mentioned earlier. If the sink is not located under a soffit, wall brackets mounted from 14 to 22 inches above the sink will provide some general upward light as well as the necessary task lighting. The minimum for such a bracket unit is one 30-watt fluorescent tube or a multiple-socket incandescent in a box at least 18 inches long with 60 or 75 watts in each socket. A surface ceiling-mounted fixture or recessed downlights can also be used. When using a fluorescent surface-mounted fixture, it is usually a good idea to shield it with a faceboard at least 8 inches deep, installed between the cabinets. Recessed downlights should have lenses or louvers to provide the necessary shielding.

Modern ranges usually have their own lighting and ventilating hoods that provide task lighting for cooking surfaces. If the vent hood does not have its own lighting fixtures, one or two sockets can usually be mounted inside it to hold one 100-watt or two 60-watt incandescent bulbs. (To obtain optimum reflectance of light, the inside of the hood should be painted flat white.) Some larger vent hoods contain fluorescent tubes, shielded by plastic lenses. The number of tubes and their wattage (generally anywhere from 15 to 40 watts) will depend on size of the hood.

Should additional illumination be needed, the cook/work area can be lighted in many of the same ways as the sink/cleanup center — soffit lighting, a ceiling-mounted fixture, under-cabinet lighting, recessed lighting, or hanging fixtures. When using the latter, it is an interesting touch to drop a heat lamp from the ceiling over the cutting board. This provides both illumination and warmth to keep foods piping hot while they are being readied for serving.

If the task lighting over the work surface is in the ceiling or soffit, sufficient illumination can be provided by 75-watt incandescent bulbs in fixtures located two feet on center or equivalent fluorescent tubes. An equivalent amount of lighting could also be provided by recessed 100-watt incandescent fixtures with inner reflectors or pendant or bullet-shaped fixtures equipped with 75-watt reflector flood lamps. If wall-mounted fixtures are preferred over the sink or range they should be mounted 14 to 22 inches above the surface with at least one 30-watt fluorescent tube.

Light for Informal Dining. While the kitchen is seldom used for the "candlelight and wine" romance

Range hood and under-cabinet lighting are ideal for cooking areas.

Soffit and under-cabinet lighting are a good combination.

97

Still the most popular way to light an area is with a hanging fixture. They may be either modern or traditional.

of more formal dining, many people like to eat snacks, brunches, and lunches there. These occasions are often filled with the warmth of gay laughter and friendliness, and the lighting for this area should provide the appropriate atmosphere. Usually, it is best to provide some kind of fixture over the center of the table (or snack bar) to provide downlight that is shadowless, yet relatively low in intensity. The fixture can be hung from the ceiling or from a swinging bracket mounted on the wall. When several pendant fixtures are employed over an island work counter or projecting "L" dining bar, they may help to serve as a room divider. While the fixtures may be mounted 16 to 20 inches apart at the same or varying heights, the bottom of the lowest fixture should be a minimum of 72 inches from the floor.

A pulley lamp can be utilized to allow for adjusting the light level over the table. Be careful, though, in locating the fixture on the ceiling. The furniture arrangement of such things as hutches or buffets can necessitate the placing of the table off center, but make sure the light is centered over the table. The softness and warmth of incandescent lighting are usually thought to be more comfortable for dining than the brighter illumination of fluorescent lighting.

The lighting levels of the kitchen can be controlled by both switching and dimming. As a bare minimum, the general illumination, the task lighting and dining area should have their own separate switches. It is always best, of course, to have each lighting arrangement on its own switch.

Inside the cabinet lighting can be a big bonus.

For special lighting effects in the kitchen, dimmer controls can be used on both incandescent and fluorescent light sources. This type of control would be especially desirable in combination family-kitchen rooms where variable lighting levels would be useful for creating different moods. There are several sizes and varieties of dimmer controls available for incandescent bulbs. The smaller-sized controls can be used in place of a standard type switch which makes installation extremely simple. For larger-sized dimmers a double box may be needed. It is also possible to obtain a switch that has "hi-lo" positions. The "hi" position gives full light output while the "lo" position gives 30 percent of full light output. Dimmers are also available to control fluorescent light. However, it is necessary to have special ballasts installed in the fixtures. For uniform dimming all tubes controlled by one dimmer should be of the same size.

The following is a summary of kitchen lighting suggestions already made:

TASK LIGHTING

Location	Type	Light Sources	Installation
Above sink	Fluorescent or	Fluorescent tubes	Behind 8-inch faceboard or in recessed or surface-mounted fixture, well shielded.
	Incandescent	75-watt reflector flood lights	Spaced 15-inches apart in recessed high hats or surface-mounted fixtures.
Above range with hood With no hood Above food preparation centers	Incandescent	60-watt soft white bulb min. same as sink	Use longest tube that will fit and fill at least 2/3 of counter length. Install
With cabinets above	Fluorescent	15-watt 18" tube 20-watt 24" tube 40-watt 48" tube	beneath cabinet attached to bottom of cabinet at front, or in fixture mounted at back wall; shielded.
No cabinets above	Incandescent	75-watt reflector flood lights or 100-watt standard bulb	Space lights 32-inches apart over length of counter, either recessed downlights or surface-mounted cylinders.
Above dining area Counter without cabinets above	Incandescent	75-watt reflector flood lights	See above
Table and Chairs	Incandescent or	150-watt or 50/ 150-watt 3-way soft white bulb	Single shade suspended fixture directing light up and down, 15-inch min. diameter shade; diffusing bowl or disc.
	Incandescent	40 or 60-watt soft white bulbs	Multiple arm suspended fixture, 18-inch min. spread, shielded.

GENERAL LIGHTING

Small kitchen (under 75 sq. ft.)	Incandescent or Fluorescent	150 watts min. 60 watts min.	
Average kitchen (75-120 sq. ft.)	Incandescent or Fluorescent	150-200 watts total 60-80 watts, min.	Ceiling-mounted or suspended; double number of fixtures when using recessed equipment.
Large kitchen (over 120 sq. ft.)	Incandescent or Fluorescent	2 watts/sq. ft. 1 watt/sq. ft.	

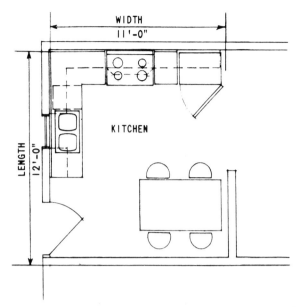

When the eating area is located within the confined space of the working area, it should be considered part of the kitchen. From the Power Budget Table, the allowable lighting power for an 11- by 12-foot kitchen is 400 watts.

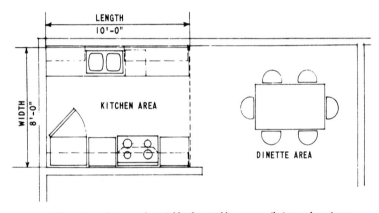

When the eating area is outside the working space, that area is not considered part of the kitchen. From the Power Budget Table, the allowable lighting power for an 8- by 10-foot kitchen is 360 watts.

With some states and communities now providing energy conserving guidelines in their building codes, the Illuminating Engineering Society (IES) has developed a residential lighting power budget or limit formula, which is based on well-organized task lighting and the use of energy efficient lighting equipment. The wattage tables for residential kitchens given here have been prepared in accordance with procedures outlined by the National Conference of States on Building Codes and Standards (NCSBCS) in the lighting power budget (limit) determination procedure. Calculations were based on levels of illumination for specific tasks and for normal vision requirements listed in the *IES Lighting Handbook* which was the basis of many of the kitchen lighting suggestions given in this book. The tables provide an upper limit of power for the budget proposed and should be used as such for developing the actual lighting design. In using the power budget tables, if dimensions of a kitchen fall in between two categories, then take the next higher category. The length of a kitchen is defined as the longer dimension of the room.

POWER BUDGET TABLE

KITCHEN DIMENSIONS (feet)		POWER BUDGET (watts)
Width	**Length**	
4	4-12	280
5	5-11	280
	12 & over	320
	6-9	280
6	10-12	320
	13 & over	360
	7-8	280
7	9-10	320
	11-14	360
	15 & over	400
	8-9	320
8	10-11	360
	12 & over	400
9	9-11	360
	12 & over	400
10 & over	10-11	360
	12 & over	400

Decorative Lighting

While general lighting and task lighting provide required illumination for the work areas of the kitchen, decorative lighting provides the soft glow throughout the room that enhances its decor and makes it more livable. A well chosen fixture can decorate a kitchen with a minimum of cost. Today, fixtures are available from manufacturers for every possible decorating theme or budget.

KITCHEN WIRING

Modern kitchens require an adequate supply of electricity. Of course, adequate wiring in a kitchen includes general purpose circuits for lighting, branch circuits for small appliances, and individual major appliance branch circuits. The recommen-

Proper fixture can set the mood of a kitchen.

dations may vary from city to city, depending on standards and codes. Since every community has its own set of wiring standards, consult local authorities for the standards of the locale concerned. Some electric utility companies offer free analysis of home wiring needs as part of their consumer service programs.

To wire a kitchen for convenience, each of the major work centers as well as the various supplementary ones makes its own electrical demands as follows:

1. *Storage centers* should have separate 120-volt circuits for each freezer and refrigerator. The separate circuit is a must because if other appliances are operated from the same circuit as the freezer they might inadvertently trip the breaker without the knowledge of the homeowner. This could leave the freezer without power for a long period of time with resultant food spoilage. Also, it is a good idea when installing the freezer outlet to use a locking type receptacle to prevent accidental disconnection.

2. *Cook centers* alone can use enough watts to heat a house. A double oven and a high-speed cooktop can add up to 16,000 watts. This calls for a minimum of a separate 3-wire No. 6 circuit fused to handle 50 amperes. While most electric ranges are designed to operate on 240 volts, a house wired for 208-volt service can obtain better cooking results if the selected range (and oven, if separate) is rated for 208 volts rather than for 240 volts. If a gas range is used rather than the electric type, it needs a convenient 120-volt wall outlet for its clocks, lights, and rotisserie.

3. *The cleanup center* creates a second major load. Heating water may take up to 4,500 watts and operating a dishwasher, disposer, and compactor will take at least another 2,600 more. Dishwashers and disposer compactors usually run on 120-volt circuits, and can be supplied, if convenient, by the second side of the refrigerator loop. A water heater takes 240 volts and requires a separate circuit.

4. *The laundry center* forms the third major load. A dryer needs about 4,500 watts, a washer 700 watts, and a hand iron draws approximately another 1500 watts. The dryer needs a three-wire No. 6 circuit fused for 30 amperes. The other appliances can be taken off one side of a three-wire No. 12 circuit.

5. *The mix center* works off the convenience outlet loop. Motor-driven power appliances like mixers, blenders, knife sharpeners, can-openers, etc., draw relatively light loads — 100 to 200 watts — but small cooking appliances draw up to 1,500 watts. Two cooking appliances in use at the same time may overload one 120-volt circuit. The National Electric Code requires that every kitchen be provided with two 20-ampere 120-volt circuits for the operation of kitchen appliances. The circuits may extend into dining areas and laundry areas if they are immediately adjacent to the kitchen. While two 20-ampere circuits are generally sufficient, some thought should be given to providing one or even two additional 20-ampere appliance circuits. Each year the number of portable or small kitchen appliances increases, making increased demands on the electrical capacity of the kitchen. In more elaborate kitchens, where a small appliance center is planned in, provide hidden outlets in the cabinetry itself so that appliances remain plugged in while being stored. Over-the-counter power sources should be about two to four feet apart, unless a continuous strip system is used. Over-the-counter wall outlets should be installed 44 inches from the floor. The National Electrical Code requires that grounding outlet receptacles be installed on all 15- and 20-ampere circuits. Most new small appliances have grounded three-prong plugs. This helps eliminate shock hazards from a faulty appliance.

6. *A planning center* has the lightest draw. It is usually a well-lighted desk area, close to the telephone, intercom master station, and climate

center (with heating, cooling, filtering, and humidity controls). The area is served by part of one convenience outlet circuit and by the low-voltage wiring for the intercom and climate center.

A kitchen needs more artificial light than any other room in the house. It is usually in use for several hours every day. Wiring should provide for special area lighting, either from adequate ceiling fixtures or a luminous ceiling. A 1,000 watts of lighting is not too much to figure on. It can be supplied by one side of a three-wire No. 12 loop.

Areas in the kitchen other than the work area should not be neglected. Provide ample outlets around eating spaces for toasters and other small table-top appliances. While these outlets are often placed 44 inches from the floor, it is a better idea to drop them to standard over-the-baseboard height so that the eating area is not strung with cords.

Here are typical wattages needed for typical kitchen uses:

Major Appliances	Wattage		Circuit (volts)
Range and oven	14,000	3-wire No. 6, 50-amp,	120-240
Dishwasher	13,300		
Disposer	800	3-wire No. 12, 20 amp,	120-240
Trash compactor	500		
Refrigerator	400	2-wire No. 12, 20-amp,	120
Freezer	400	2-wire No. 12, 20-amp,	120
Washer	700		
Hand iron	1,500	2-wire No. 12, 20-amp,	120
Sewing machine	75		
Dryer (std speed)	4,500	3-wire No. 10, 30-amp,	240
Water heater	2,500-4,500	consult your utility	

Small Appliances	Wattage		Circuit (volts)
Can opener	110		
Mixer	120		
Blender	300		
Toaster	750	2-wire No. 12, 20-amp,	120
Waffle iron	1,100		
Coffeepot	900		
Intercom-radio	100		
Vent hood	150		
Microwave unit	1,500		
Rotisserie	1,500		
Deep-fat fryer	1,300	2-wire No. 12, 20-amp,	120
Electric frying pan	1,100		
Broiler	1,500		

Kitchen carpeting gives maximum underfoot comfort as well as a beautiful appearance.

Because of today's multiple needs, 150-ampere service is minimal in normal kitchen installations. (The service ampere rating is obtained by adding together the current required for general lighting, major appliances, motors, appliance circuits, and other special circuits.) Circuit breakers, which should be used in place of a fuse box, should be placed in an easy-to-reach location in or near the kitchen, so the homemaker does not have to hunt for it in a dark basement or garage.

CHAPTER 6

FLOORS, WALLS, AND CEILINGS

There has been a revolution in kitchen furnishings and materials, with a wider-than-ever selection and a new emphasis on easy-care materials. "No-wax" vinyl floors, improved kitchen carpeting, and washable wallpaper all come in an amazing variety of patterns and colors. Coordinated fabrics, wall-coverings, and flooring are now offered by several major manufacturers.

In choosing kitchen components and furnishings, consideration should be given to evaluating their cost, durability, resistance to heat, dirt, and grease, and their cleanability. But just surveying the marketplace can be overwhelming, so in this chapter a listing of many of the available materials and some of their advantages and disadvantages is given.

Most kitchen designers find it easiest to pick one major component first — perhaps a vinyl floor pattern or wallpaper design that is especially liked. Then build the rest of the decorating scheme around that first item, choosing colors, materials and patterns that complement floors.

FLOORS

What kinds of floors should be used in the kitchen? There are many factors that should be considered before making any selection. For example, the durability desired, amount of moisture present, amount of resistance to alkali and grease wanted, traffic expected, and degree of quietness wanted should all be determined when selecting the type of flooring material for a kitchen. Another important consideration is the fact that the kitchen floor helps coordinate the color scheme. The floor is usually one of the most important design features in tying the kitchen design together. It correlates the rich warmth of the cabinets to the colors of the walls, appliances, countertops, and drapes.

With these thoughts in mind, let us look at what a good kitchen floor should do. First, the floor should provide a measure of safety. That means it should be smooth (nothing to trip over) without being slippery, and it should be level.

A second consideration, because the homemaker spends a lot of time in the kitchen, is that the floor should provide some comfort. This means the floor should have resiliency. It should absorb the shock of one's footsteps, and it should be easy to stand on.

People who work on solid floors (concrete, for example) find them extremely tiring to stand on hour after hour. On the other hand, a floor that is too soft can also be tiring. The luxury of deep pile carpeting and extra thick sponge padding might enhance the living room, but it can be a deterrent to comfort in the kitchen.

Cleanability is something else that should be considered in selecting a kitchen floor. The easier to clean, the better. That is the reason why many people prefer firm-surfaced floor coverings.

Beauty is also something that is wanted in a kitchen floor, in the form of design, color, pattern, texture, or a combination of these. The floor selected should be carefully coordinated with the basic design of the kitchen.

These are some of the factors that must be balanced out carefully when selecting a kitchen floor material. There is, of course, an almost infinite variety of materials, colors, textures, and patterns. But they can be sorted into three major classifications and some minor ones before the final choice of the exact flooring material is made.

First, kitchen floor coverings are classified by hardness, then by basic material. After deciding on hardness and basic material desired, then the appearance — texture, pattern, and color — is considered. Keep in mind that this is merely a brief overview of the floor coverings available for kitchen use.

Resilient Surfaces

Resilient surfaces are ones that most people think of when they think of kitchen floor coverings. They have been designed to include the advantages that most householders like in a kitchen floor — practicality, convenience, and long wear. With the tremendous variety of materials, designs, and colors available, it is possible to create just about any floor scheme that strikes one's fancy. For example, it is possible to install a floor of all one color, or combine it with different coloring into a custom floor design that matches the kitchen's requirements and individual taste. If the homemaker's decorating taste leans to the natural look, he or she will find countless resilient materials that closely resemble the appearance of slate, brick, wood, terrazzo, marble, or stone. Many of these floors feature an embossed surface texture that adds a striking note to the design.

Resilient floors are manufactured in two basic

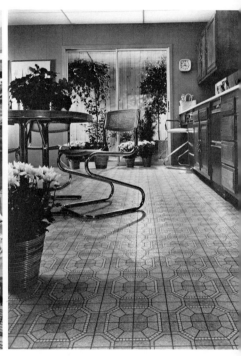

Resilient floor surfaces — in either sheet material or tiles — are available to fit into any kitchen design or style.

types — sheet materials and tiles. The latter are cemented into place to serve as a permanent floor. Sheet materials are also cemented into place, but in some cases can be installed loosely like rugs. Tiles generally come in 9- or 12-inch squares. Sheet materials are available in continuous rolls up to 12 feet wide.

Tiles. Made of vinyl, asbestos fibers, and other components, resilient tiles are exceptionally durable and easy to keep clean. They lend themselves to a variety of customizing effects, since tiles of different colors and styles may be easily combined.

What kind of tile should be selected for the kitchen? Asphalt tile, the first resilient tile, is the least expensive and can be installed at any grade level. It offers good durability, but compared to other types of resilient floors, it ranks low in resistance to grease and soil. For this reason, it is not recommended for kitchens.

Vinyl-asbestos tile is the most popular of all resilient tiles. It is inexpensive and can be installed anywhere, above, on, or below grade. Vinyl-asbestos tiles have exceptional durability and are easy to clean. They do not require waxing; they can be given a low sheen by buffing after the floor is mopped.

Wear resistance in the kitchen is generally rated very good. These tiles are available in thicknesses of 1/16, 3/32, and 1/8 inch.

Solid (or homogeneous) vinyl tiles that have a backing are the ultimate in the tile type of kitchen flooring. They rank as excellent in durability and have a surface that is smooth and nonporous. This makes upkeep easy and economical. These tiles can be used on any grade level, and solid vinyl is available in many colors and patterns, and ranging in thickness from .080 gauge (thin) to 1/16 and 1/8 inch.

Rubber tile is one of the most resilient of all flooring materials, and it offers a great deal of comfort underfoot. Wear and soil resistance and upkeep maintenance are good. Today's rubber tile can be used on any level, but for some unknown reason, it has never become popular for kitchens.

Cork, possibly the quietest of all floorings, is available as pure natural cork or combined with vinyl. The latter combination retains the beauty and warmth of cork while providing an added degree of cleaning ease. Vinyl cork has a higher degree of durability than natural cork and should be the only one used in a kitchen.

Guide to Resilient Flooring

Material	Backing	How Installed	Where to Install	Ease of Installation	Ease of Maintenance in Kitchen	Resilience and Durability	Sound-proofing
Tile Materials							
Asphalt	None	Adhesive	Anywhere	Fair	Difficult	Good	Very poor
Vinyl-asbestos	None	Adhesive	Anywhere	Easy	Very easy	Excellent	Poor
Vinyl	None	Adhesive	Anywhere	Easy	Easy	Good-excellent	Fair
Rubber	None	Adhesive	Anywhere	Fair	Easy	Good	Good
Cork	None	Adhesive	On or above	Fair	Poor (with vinyl, good)	Good	Excellent
Sheet Materials							
Inlaid Vinyl	Felt	Adhesive	Above grade	Fair	Easy	Good	Fair
	Foam and Felt	Adhesive	Above grade	Difficult	Easy	Good	Good
	Asbestos	Adhesive	Anywhere	Very Difficult	Easy	Excellent	Fair
	Foam	Adhesive	Anywhere	Very Difficult	Easy	Excellent	Good
Printed Vinyl	Felt	Loose-lay	Above grade	Easy	Fair	Poor	Poor
	Felt	Adhesive	Above grade	Fair	Easy	Fair	Poor
	Foam and felt	Loose-lay	Above grade	Easy	Easy	Fair	Good
	Foam and asbestos	Adhesive or loose-lay	Anywhere	Fair-easy	Easy	Good	Good
	Foam	Loose-lay	Anywhere	Easy	Easy	Good	Good

Resilient flooring can be designed to emphasize the kitchen layout as was done with this octagon-shaped island unit. All cabinets and appliances follow the same plan.

Sheet Flooring. The principal advantage of sheet flooring in the kitchen is seamlessness. Since it is installed in wide rolls, there are few seams in the finished floor. The result is a beautiful wall-to-wall sweep of color and design, a perfect setting for room furnishings. Some sheet floors can also be customized by combining two or more colors or styles. Sheet vinyls are resilient, therefore comfortable underfoot, and resistant to grease and alkalis as well. With special backing they can be used below, on, or above grade.

Sheet vinyl may be inlaid, meaning the design element extends throughout the entire vinyl layer. A less durable variety of vinyl has the design printed on a vinyl sheet, which is then coated with a transparent vinyl layer. This type, known as rotovinyl,

Tiles are used under cabinets as kick- or toe-strips.

is more economical, offers a wider variety of patterns, and is more flexible. The gauge or thickness of the vinyl will probably affect its cost. Other options in vinyl floor coverings are foam cushioning, which gives added warmth, quiet, and comfort, and the new "no-wax" floor finishes, which can extend the time between waxings or eliminate waxing altogether.

Linoleum, the oldest resilient flooring, is no longer with us. The last of this popular kitchen flooring was made in America in the mid-1970's.

Kitchen carpeting gives maximum underfoot comfort as well as a beautiful appearance.

Soft Floors

Soft floors are growing in popularity, with the new versatility in kitchen carpeting. Carpeting can provide the maximum comfort underfoot. It absorbs shocks of walking and cushions footsteps like no other covering can. It reduces noise, and also absorbs spilled liquids and often holds them against the underflooring. (If the underflooring is not water resistant, this could be a problem.)

Kitchen carpeting now is available in regular carpet widths and in tiles. Carpet tiles have the advantage of being replaceable if they become stained or burned. They can be removed for easier cleaning. But in high traffic areas, they are likely to pull up, especially around the kitchen table and chair.

Kitchen carpeting is improving in stain-resistance and cleanability each year. Make sure the carpeting selected is recommended for kitchen use. Jute-backed carpeting, for example, is not moisture resistant. While polyester, acrylic, and wood fibers are used for kitchen carpeting, the most often used are nylon and propylene. Nylon is resistant to abrasion and most stains. It is also resilient and easy to

Characteristics of Kitchen Carpet Fibers

Performance Characteristics	Acrylic	Polyester	Nylon	Polypropylene	Wood
Wear Life	High	High	Extra high	Extra high	High
Texture Retention	Good	Good to Medium	Exceptional	Good	Good
Abrasion Resistance	Good	Very Good	Exceptional	Exceptional	Good
Soil Resistance	High	Medium	Medium	High	High
Stain Resistance	High	Medium	Medium	Exceptional	Medium
Static Buildup	Little	Only in low Humidity	Very much	Very little	Only in Low Humidity
Moisture Absorbency	Little	Little	Some	Lowest	Highest
Mildew	Resists	Resists	Resists	Resists	Subject to Mildew
Need for Moth Protection	No Effect	No Effect	No Effect	No Effect	Needs Treatment
Non-allergenic	Completely	Completely	Completely	Completely	Minor
Appearance Characteristics					
Appearance	Warm, Soft, Luxurious	Soft, Luxurious	Dull to Lustrous	Subdued Luster	Soft, Warm, Luxurious
Dyeability	Good	Good, but Brilliance Limits	Good	Medium	Good
Crush Resistance	Medium	Medium	Good	Low	Medium
Resilience	High	Medium	High	Medium	High
Fade Resistance	Good	Good	Medium	Good	Medium

clean. Static electricity can be a problem with nylon, although newer, specially treated nylons minimize this problem.

Polypropylene (olefin) offers good moisture and stain resistance, and resists fading and shrinking. Polypropylene is not as resilient as nylon. Rayon is also sometimes used in kitchen carpet, but has poor stain resistance and is not recommended for kitchen use.

In any material, tweed patterns, tone-on-tone patterns, and textured designs will tend to disguise dirt better than plain one-colored carpets. Subdued or dark colors will also hide dirt better than light, bright tones.

Area rugs can offer accents of color to certain spots and provide a measure of standing comfort in some areas — by the range, or sink, for example. These rugs really serve more as decorative elements than as floor coverings. They, however, should be the non-skid variety and should not be too shaggy, or they may be easy to trip over.

Hard Floors

Hard flooring such as ceramic tile, slate, flagstone, terrazzo, wood, and brick, offers beautiful textures, durability, and a luxury look. But hard floors can be uncomfortable to stand on for long periods of time and are heavier than other types of flooring.

Slate tiles and flagstone are available in random shapes or can be purchased in geometric shapes, usually squares and rectangles. They may be had in green, red, purple, gray, and black. Both materials give a very permanent flooring with beautiful texture and a random pattern that is intriguing. The disadvantage of flagstone and slate is their heaviness. The floor must have adequate support and, while flagstone and slate are hard and close-grained, they can still be stained. Also, long hours of standing on a flagstone slate floor can be uncomfortable.

Brick floors also have a weight problem. But, brick provides a striking floor that will wear longer than any other in the home, plus it has the advantage of being able to work out some truly unusual patterns. Staining can definitely be a problem with brick. The discomfort of standing can also be a drawback.

Ceramic tile is a hard surface that overcomes the major disadvantages of the previously mentioned hard-floor materials. It is scratch-resistant, fireproof, waterproof, and never needs waxing. The weight is no problem and cleaning is easy. Actually, there are three types of ceramic tiles in common kitchen floor use today — quarry tiles, ceramic mosaics, and glazed tiles. The last are usually a little thinner than glazed wall tiles, but are made in various sizes and shapes and a variety of designs and colors. Some are so perfectly glazed that they form a monochromatic surface. Others have a softer,

Brick and ceramic tile will give a luxurious look to any kitchen or dinette.

natural shade variation within each unit and from tile to tile. In addition, ceramic floors can be bright-glazed, matte-glazed, or unglazed. There are also extra-duty glazed floor tiles suitable for heavy-traffic areas.

Ceramic mosaics are available in 1-by-1 and 2-by-2-inch squares, and come with or without a glaze. In addition to the standard units, they may be had in a large assortment of colorful shapes. Mosaics are usually sold mounted in 1-by-1- and 1-by-2-foot sheets for easy installation.

Quarry tiles, which are also made from natural ceramic materials, are available in a variety of colors; the most common types are in shades of red, chocolate, and buff. They come in shapes ranging from square tiles to Spanish forms. Some quarry tiles, however, require special sealing to prevent staining.

Marble tile, made in sizes of 8 by 8, 8 by 12, and 12 by 12 inches, is available in a wide variety of types and colors. Extremely durable, it provides a touch of elegance.

For handsome appearance and rugged durability, terrazzo floors are hard to beat. But they are tiring to walk or stand on for any length of time and noise is more of a problem. Terrazzo like the other hard floor materials, except wood, needs no waxing.

For years, wood was the number one flooring, even for a kitchen floor. But wood is sensitive to water and staining so it went out of style. Now, new finishes — penetrating seals and plastic varnishes — have encouraged some designers to bring back the warmth and beauty of real wood to kitchen floors. There really is no substitute for its appearance, especially in the dining areas of the kitchen.

Another material — seamless plastic flooring — is worth mentioning for the kitchen, especially in remodeling projects. Seamless flooring systems are colorful, decorative, and durable. There are a number of seamless systems on the market, and most contain three basic elements; (1) a liquid plastic background base, (2) plastic color chips; and (3) a clear liquid plastic wear surface. The background and base coat is applied first, then alternate layers of the clear liquid and color chips. The chips become embedded in the clear plastic as several layers are built up, and then several more layers of the plastic are applied to seal the floor and give gloss to the surface. All the coats are applied in a continuous flow without seams, leaving a sanitary, smooth, and easy-to-maintain finished surface.

Unlike other floor coverings, seamless flooring becomes a permanent part of the substrate. Most systems can be applied over existing worn floors such as wood, linoleum, concrete, ceramic tile, or vinyl. The condition of the existing floor and care in surface preparation are often more critical, however, than for an application over a new floor surface or subfloor of plywood and similar materials.

Seamless flooring is formulated to withstand extreme wear and abuse. Wear is normally limited to the top coat, which is easily retouched or restored simply by sanding the area and applying another glaze or wear coat. Since their introduction into the commercial and residential flooring field, seamless systems have proven highly satisfactory. Unsatisfactory installations usually can be traced directly to poor substrate preparation or failure to use a single manufacturer's complete system. The latter is extremely important since each component of the various systems — sealers, base coats, colored chips, or other decorative materials and wear coats — is formulated for compatibility with the others to give top performance.

WALLS

Not too many years ago a wall was made of wood, covered with plaster, finished with either paint or wallpaper, and that was that. Now, an almost infinite variety of materials exist for use on kitchen walls, and more are being developed every day. Uniformity of material or finish need not be maintained throughout the kitchen; function can and should dictate form.

Paint

Paint is still the most popular of kitchen wall finishes, but today it offers an almost unlimited variety of colors and hues. It can be mixed to the precise shade and color selected, though it does not offer the variety of texture and pattern found in other wall coverings. An interesting decorating idea with paint, however, is "supergraphics" — super-scale designs on walls, floors, ceilings, cabinets, and even across furnishings. Bold bands of color sweep across a wall, plunge down to the floor, or swoop up and across the ceiling, changing the dimensions of a room and providing a feeling of movement.

There are, of course, some disadvantages to paint. In areas where there is high wear, such as around light switches, paint can wear off in a year. Keep in mind that paint for a kitchen should be either semi-gloss or gloss. This improves its cleanability and helps to increase its "fair" lifespan.

Wallpaper

As employed in this book, the word wallpaper is used in a general sense. Wallpaper can be paper, plastic-coated paper, foil, coated paper, cloth, or plastic-coated cloth. Each kind has its advantages and disadvantages.

For kitchen use, a plain paper style of wallpaper is not recommended. Dirt builds up on it fast. Grease is absorbed into the paper. Plastic-coated papers

and cloths tend to overcome this drawback. The plastic is cleanable with a damp rag. Also, plastic-coated coverings seem to have a higher resistance to sun fading.

Wallpaper used as a wainscoting is also applied on the cabinet fronts. This makes a most attractive finish.

Ceramic tile is excellent wall material for a kitchen. It is impervious to grease and also fireproof.

There are many variations in the quality of papers and coatings. The better ones naturally cost more money. But they are usually worth the difference in their resistance to dirt and their easy cleanability. Then, there are the straight cloths. These are often specialty wall coverings used for their unique texture. Among the most popular of these are burlap. Japanese grasscloth, and other new vinyl wallcoverings come in rolls like wallpaper. They add interesting texture to a wall. Some, like the vinyl, are easy to clean. Others like burlap or grasscloth are neither dirt-resistant nor easy to clean. Since they are hard to clean, they should be used out of the main work centers.

Tile

Tile for the kitchen walls may be ceramic, plastic, or metal. Ceramic tile has some truly outstanding features for use in a kitchen. It is highly resistant to food acids, impervious to grease, and almost completely scratch-proof. It is also fireproof and waterproof. It never needs waxing or painting. Cleaning can be done with a damp cloth, and most cleaning agents can be used on it. An extensive selection of colors and shapes of tiles offers infinite possibilities in pattern design on the wall. Actually, wall tiles range in size from small 1-inch-square mosaics to impressive 12-inch squares, and are available in high- or low-relief designs with colorful glazes or multicolored patterns. There are also handsome contoured tiles. Along with hexagons, octagons, and rectangles, there are curvilinear shapes inspired by historic Moorish designs, houses in Normandy, and villas in Florence. Many of these are quarry tiles which are now offered in a large range of natural colors as well as in durable glazes.

Plastic tiles had a period of popularity. However, in recent years, they have seldom been used in kitchen installations. They do not offer as broad a selection of shapes and sizes as the ceramic type and they may be damaged by heat. On the other hand, metal tiles — copper, stainless steel, and aluminum — do have beauty, but their high cost usually limits their use to the grease-catching walls of kitchens.

Paneling

The various types of paneling suitable for kitchen use include wood (prefinished and unfinished), hardboard (with baked-on finishes, plastic laminates, and lacquer finishes), particleboard (with all kinds of surface finishes), and other types of

Metal tile used in cook work space.

wallboard (with all kinds of finishes). What is the best? It depends on what the homemaker wants. Most paneling never needs painting, is easy to clean, and has a good resistance to dirt. The smoother the surface of the paneling, the higher the resistance.

Various types and patterns of solid woods are available for application on kitchen walls to obtain the desired decorative effects. For informal treatment, knotty pine, redwood, whitepocket Douglas fir, sound wormy chestnut, and pecky cypress, finished natural or stained and varnished, may be used to cover one or more sides of a room. In addition, there are such desirable hardwoods as red oak, pecan, elm, walnut, white oak, and cherry also available for wall paneling. Most types of paneling come in thicknesses from ⅜ to ¾ inch; widths vary from 4 to 8 inches, lengths from 3 to 10 feet.

When planning a wood-paneled room remember that when the wall is to be accented, use boards of random widths. Subdue it by the use of equal-width boards. Small rooms can be given the illusion of increased size by applying the paneling horizontally. Of course, paneling can be applied vertically, horizontally, diagonally, or in combined directions. Solid wood paneling must be finished with a good wood sealer and finished to prevent staining.

Plywood paneling is more popular in kitchens than solid wood. It comes in finishes ranging from richly figured oak, mahogany, birch, and walnut to fir and pine, allowing a choice of decorative material to meet every taste and budget. It can be applied effectively to either traditional or modern interiors. A great many plywoods come prefinished and will resist staining to a degree.

Hardboard manufactured for use as prefinished paneling is specifically treated for resistance to stains, scrubbing, and moisture. It is also highly resistant to dents, mars, and scuffs. In most cases, the material is prefinished in wood grains such as walnut, cherry, birch, oak, teak, and pecan, and in a variety of shades. It may be smooth surfaced or random grooved. In addition there are the decorative and work-saving plastic-surfaced hardboards which resist water, stains, and household chemicals exceptionally well. A typical surface consists of baked-on plastic. Most hardboard is sufficiently dense and moisture-resistant for use in kitchens and laundry rooms. The variety of laminated plastic finishes and sizes is extensive. Finishes include rich-looking wood grains, exceptional marble reproductions, plain colors, speckled colors, simulated tile, lace prints, wallpaper textures, and murals. Vinyl-clad panels are also available in decorative and wood-grain finishes. In addition, the same sheet-plastic laminates described in Chapter 4 for countertops can be employed as wallcoverings. Their use opens many decorating avenues.

Perforated hardboard is a very versatile material. In addition to being a most attractive wall material, perforated hardboard may be a permanent solution to the problem of using walls for more than just places to hang pretty pictures. There are a wide variety of fixtures available at most hardware stores that make it possible to use walls for many different purposes, including storage.

Wood paneling is becoming increasingly popular in kitchens.

Floor tiles are used to decorate the kitchen walls.

Real or imitation bricks and stones are used in kitchens. Many imitation bricks and stones are fireproof.

Brick and Stone

These materials can provide a wonderful feeling of warmth and create an outstanding highlight wall in a kitchen. Real brick and stone have a permanence matched only by ceramic tile. But real bricks and stones do have certain disadvantages. They are porous and grease will sink right in, as will dirt of any kind. In addition, bricks and stones add enormous weight to a wall, so the wall may have to have extra support.

These disadvantages have led manufacturers to develop imitations. Imitation bricks and stones are made of various plastic materials. Styrene, urethane, and rigid vinyl are the most common. Some are fire resistant and may be used near ranges and ovens. All false bricks and stones are highly durable and come in a wide variety of colors and styles. Some are sold in sheet form, while others are installed individually.

So far, we have covered the important groups of wallcovering materials. There are others that might be considered. For certain highlights, the use of plastic sheets — plexiglass and reinforced plastic — and glass blocks can be most interesting. Careful use of mirrored walls can give "size" and "richness" to a small kitchen. Of course, a decoupage wall can be a conversation piece, sparking up a dining area wall. Colorful posters, interesting matchbook covers, old sheet music, children's art, etc., can be posted on the wall and varnished to preserve the collection.

CEILINGS

Almost everything that has been mentioned for use on walls can be applied to the kitchen's ceiling — paint, wallpaper, tile, or paneling — to give the broadest possible spectrum of colors, textures, and patterns. But it is important to remember that most experts agree that ceilings should be relatively light in color, especially in a kitchen. This maximizes the reflection of light to provide more even lighting in the kitchen.

In addition to using wallcoverings on ceilings, there are ceiling tiles and panels available. There are three popular ways to tile or panel a ceiling: (1) fasten the tiles directly to the ceiling or to furring strips nailed directly across it; (2) install a grid system directly to the exposed beams; and (3) suspend the new ceiling from a grid which will drop it below the existing one. The first is the one most often employed for installing a new ceiling in an existing

A little imagination makes a kitchen theme. A good example is this Turkish-feeling kitchen.

room. If the old ceiling is in fairly good condition, the new ceiling can be fastened directly to it with adhesive. But if the ceiling is in poor shape, furring must be used. The use of grids, either fastened directly to the beams or suspended below them, offers many interesting ceiling treatments including the so-called invisible seam arrangement.

The materials available for ceiling coverages generally range in size from 12-by-12-inch tiles all the way up to large 4-by-10-foot panels. However, the most popular sizes for direct application are the 12-by-12-inch and 12-by-24-inch varieties. For suspended ceilings, the 2-by-2-foot and 2-by-4-foot units are usually used.

Most ceiling tiles and panels deaden noise, but acoustical tiles are specially designed to absorb more sound — usually more than half the sound in a room. Tiles now come in many designs and textures, as well as in panels that fit together for a one-piece ceiling look. They can be painted, but painting sharply reduces its sound-deadening ability. Therefore, other ceiling finishes are better. Keep in mind that new developments in acoustical tiles occur from time to time. Some manufacturers now have vinyl-coated ceiling tiles that have sound-deadening properties along with better cleanability.

Kitchen ceilings can be made very interesting and can be made to fit most any design or style of decoration.

As described in Chapter 5, a luminous or light ceiling can be used in a kitchen and it will spread the light uniformly and shadowlessly throughout the room.

The ceiling can be made most interesting with a beam arrangement as shown above. Real beams are employed in the kitchen below, while man-made ones are used at right.

Beams

While beams are not a part of the ceiling, they often add to the beauty of it. What would an Early American kitchen be without a beamed ceiling? Today, ready-made, ready-to-install beams are available at most lumber dealers for this purpose. They are made of solid lumber, plywood, polyurethane plastic foam, or metal. The number of beams and patterns employed depends on the size of the room and personal preference. Some room ceilings will appear best with the beams running in one direction only, while others look fine with crossing beams. The beams themselves can be finished or painted to match any color scheme.

In floors, wallcoverings, and ceilings, as we have seen, there is almost unlimited choice of materials, textures, colors, and patterns. Remember, in choosing, select ones that not only match the decor but are also easy to care for in the years the kitchen is being used.

CHAPTER 7

PLAN A KITCHEN PLUS

As stated in Chapter 2, a kitchen should always be designed to give some "extras." Sometimes it is necessary to do a great deal of planning to obtain the necessary space in which to put these extras. Remodeling a roomy old kitchen may help, of course, to condense the work area, allowing extra space for other kitchen activities. Adding on a new kitchen automatically leaves the old kitchen to be transformed into a family room, playroom, laundry room, or dining area. The result: a kitchen plus!

DINING AREA

Dining areas are the most popular kitchen extra — whether a table and chairs, a snack bar or counter, or a complete home party center. The size of the table or counter, as well as the space for seats, will determine the eating capacity. This informal dining space should be of a size sufficient to accommodate the family, but not necessarily any guests.

Ideally, the informal area will be separated from the working kitchen by a decorative divider that allows transfer of light, but screens unavoidable kitchen clutter. This divider may be a freestanding serving unit, with two-way doors for easy access to

dishes, serving platters, table linens, or glassware from either side. Where there is no room for a table and chairs, careful planning can often find space for a snack bar or dining counter.

A snack bar or counter can be many things to the careful planner. It can be a homemaker's dream of convenience, combining snacks, buffet dining, and pass-through to nook or dining room. It can even include the family message center. Plan enough space to serve the family adequately, from breakfast through school lunches to a quiet candlelight supper when all the day's work is done. A dining counter, as mentioned in Chapter 2, should usually be 29 inches high for chairs and no higher than 40 inches for stools. The minimum counter depth of 15 inches (30 inches, if both sides of the counter are used) is adequate for family breakfasts or for quick snacks. But, it is better to allow a 24-inch depth or more if the counter is extended for serving dinner or for a line-up of buffet foods. This depth provides space for the casseroles, large platters, and accessories that are employed for dinners and special parties.

The dining area — either table or counter — should be located for convenient serving. The

Various seating arrangements for eat-in kitchens.

Two table and chair sets that are popular for kitchen use.

homemaker does not want to have to walk across the room a half-dozen times every time a snack or lunch is served. Also the amount of space available is important when planning the family's dining area. A too-small or cramped eating area is a major annoyance that will haunt the family every time food is served. For comfortable dining, the desirable minimum spacing for persons seated side by side at a table or counter is 24 inches. This spacing will usually provide ample elbow room for dining and will accommodate the usual armless dining chair. Chairs with arms are sometimes wide enough that the 24-inch spacing must be increased. In this case the spacing should be equivalent to the width of the chair plus 2 inches.

The recommended clearances for access to dining table or counter are as follows: To allow room to pull out and return the chair when sitting or rising — 26 to 36 inches; for additional space for a second person to walk behind one who is seated — 36 to 44 inches. If the table faces a closet, the clearance should be at least 2 inches more than the door swing. A greater clearance will be required if the chairs at the table cannot be pushed under the table and out of the way.

If the space is to serve 4 people, a 30-inch table is sufficient. If 6 people will use it then a 36-inch table will be required. A 48-inch table will seat eight. An area 6 feet 6 inches by 6 feet 6 inches is a minimum for four people, and there should be, as already mentioned, 24 inches of clearance on all sides of the table.

The amount of space necessary to accommodate dining can be reduced considerably by using a longer table, by eliminating seating at the ends of the table, and by placing the table in a "nook." This latter boothlike arrangement has the same disadvantage of a typical restaurant booth — people

seated on the inside chairs cannot leave the booth without causing other persons to move. However, the arrangement is superior to the fixed booth in that the chairs may be brought up to the table in a comfortable position once each person is located in a chair. The minimum serving clearance of 36 inches allows the server to edge behind the people seated in their chairs. The liberal serving clearance permits the server to walk behind the chairs. If serving clearance in back of the seating is not needed, the width of the booth can be reduced an additional 20 inches. In this case the diners may have to bend their knees and enter the booth in a slightly crouched position.

When planning built-in seating and a table in the kitchen, be sure to set aside a space no less than 4 by 5½ feet. This space is designed to serve four people in comfort.

Dining facilities are often provided in the same space with the kitchen working area. In this case the table and chairs should be located so that when they are occupied, the kitchen working area can be used

Kitchen and dining room all in one.

Pass-ways such as shown here save many steps between the kitchen and dining room.

A pull-out eating counter.

by at least one person. This means that the table should be placed a minimum of 50 inches from the counter, or preferably 58 inches from an appliance such as a dishwasher, range, etc. These dimensions include 20 inches of space for an occupied chair.

Different clearances are recommended for the space beside a dining table that does not face a counter or appliance. If there is no passageway, the clearance from the table to a wall or counter back should be 36 inches (liberal), 30 inches (medium), or 26 inches (minimum). Liberal clearance allows a person to leave the table without disturbing others.

If there is a passageway along one side of the table, the clearance to a wall or counter back should

be 44 inches (liberal), 36 inches (medium), or 30 inches (minimum). The liberal clearance alows room for a person to walk past a seated person.

It is frequently possible to get the necessary space for a dining area by changing the floor only slightly. In the L-shaped illustrated on page 137, for example, the relocation of the rear door and the dividing of the window allowed for the desired eating space. In the other drawing of the two-wall corridor kitchen on the same page, the relocation of the utility closet changed the shape of kitchen to an "L" and provided the necessary dining area.

Before leaving the subject of eating, it would be wise to mention pass-through counters between

Pass-ways such as shown here save many steps between the kitchen and dining room, plus they double as eating counters.

117

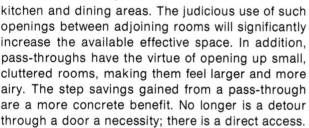

Another pass-through idea.

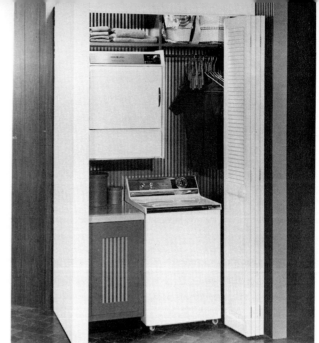

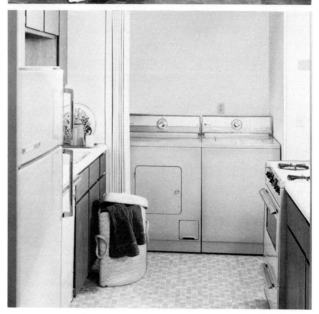

Laundry area need not be too big to be effective.

kitchen and dining areas. The judicious use of such openings between adjoining rooms will significantly increase the available effective space. In addition, pass-throughs have the virtue of opening up small, cluttered rooms, making them feel larger and more airy. The step savings gained from a pass-through are a more concrete benefit. No longer is a detour through a door a necessity; there is a direct access.

LAUNDRY CENTER

A second suggestion for a "kitchen plus" room is a laundry center. This, too, should be separated from the kitchen, so dirty clothes do not end up on kitchen counters. Place laundry equipment around a corner or on the other side of a divider, or in any area of the home that allows easy access to water and drain connections, and permits the dryer to exhaust to the outside.

A laundry area must be planned as logically as the kitchen. Activity centers in the laundry include: (1) soiled clothes storage; (2) sorting and preparation area; (3) washing and drying centers; and (4) ironing center and clean clothes storage. Each center should contain the appliances, storage space and work surfaces needed for that task. The basic kitchen can also be used to organize laundry activity centers into a work triangle. But even if space for the

laundry center is extremely limited, there are certain basics necessary for even a minimum installation. They are: the appliances (washer and dryer); storage for soiled clothes (preferably at least three bins); counter space for sorting, pre-treating (nearby water supply necessary), and folding; and storage for laundry aids.

An optimum laundry center would include the following:

1. Laundry equipment consisting of an automatic washer and dryer. Because of floor space or preference, a combination washer-dryer may be chosen. Remember to inquire about load capacities of the appliance selected. Frequently, in the case of a big family, a large-capacity washer and dryer will save time and money.

118

Various laundry room arrangements (right)

2. Space to pre-sort and store soiled clothes. Changing laundering habits and the variety of washable fabrics now being used have intensified the need for pre-sorted storage. Providing storage for each of the categories into which the laundry is sorted makes it easy to know when a washer load of each has accumulated. A minimum of three storage units is required for adequate pre-sorting by laundry procedure. Five or six are desirable, particularly if the family laundry includes large amounts of delicate items or washable woolens. Types of storage containers can vary. Tilt bins or large rollout drawers built in under a counter are convenient. The bins or drawers can be labeled, and the family can put laundry in the proper bin as it is soiled.

3. Storage for laundry aids and stain removal supplies. Adequate space must be provided near the washer for all detergents, bleaches, and other laundry aids used. To eliminate stooping, and to keep these items out of reach of small children, overhead storage is best. However, it may be necessary to set aside some under-the-counter storage for extra-large boxes of detergent and heavy bleach bottles. The most frequently used items should be easiest to reach. Stain-removal supplies can be stored in a drawer, or on the shelf with other laundry aids.

4. Sink for pre-treating and other laundering needs. This sink should be located between the sorting bins and the washer. However, if the kitchen sink is located nearby, it can be used instead.

5. Space to fold clothes and store those that require ironing. It is most practical to remove items from the dryer one at a time, hang or fold them immediately, and sort them according to where the clean clothes are to go. A counter is most desirable for folding, but if the space is inadequate, the tops of the appliances can be used. A shelf over the appliances is useful for the temporary storage of folded items. However, if the washer is the top-loading type, the shelf should be high enough to allow the top to open without interference.

6. Place to hang permanent press items. A full-length hanging closet next to the dryer is especially desirable for hanging permanent press items as they are removed from the dryer. A clothes rack can also be used for this purpose or, if no room is available, a wall hook can be installed.

7. Provision for sewing supplies. Mending should be done before clothes are washed, so tears do not get larger. Mending supplies — needles, thread, and scissors may be all that are needed — can be stored in a small drawer or in one of the cup-

A laundry is a good spot for plants.

boards. However, if much garment making is done, a full sewing center will be needed. A shelf that pulls up and out from under the counter (similar to a typewriter shelf in a desk) is especially handy for a portable sewing machine, because it eliminates the need to lift the machine. Perforated board on the inside of a cupboard door is convenient for hanging scissors, thread, and other sewing accessories.

The space required for the laundry center will vary with the type of appliances selected, and the other activities planned for the area. A washer and dryer require a space of from 4 feet 6 inches up to 5 feet 3 inches wide, and 30 inches deep, depending upon the widths of the appliances chosen. The amount of space needed for a washer and a portable dryer depends on whether the dryer is wall-hung, set on a counter, or equipped with casters and rolled out of storage only when needed. If the dryer is wall-hung over a narrow sorting counter next to the washer, for example, only 3 feet 6 inches would be required. But adequate work space should either be provided or be accessible nearby.

A University of Illinois study of home laundry operations shows that the amount of work space needed for most people is relatively constant. The following recommendations are the minimum to permit freedom of action. These measurements are in addition to space for the appliances.

Washer and dryer: 5 feet 6 inches wide by 3 feet

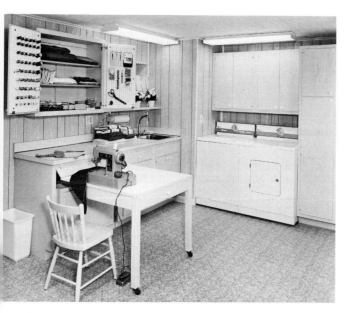

Sewing equipment in the laundry makes good sense.

6 inches deep in front of the appliances.

Washer or dryer alone: 3 feet 8 inches wide by 3 feet 6 inches deep in front of the appliance.

If the appliances are located in a traffic area, or if the washer and dryer are opposite each other, the work space should be increased to at least 4 feet deep.

Ironing: A space at least 5 feet 10 inches wide by 4 feet 3 inches deep will be required for an ironing board, a chair, and a laundry cart or basket. If a clothes rack is used, 2 feet 4 inches of working space should be allowed in addition to the rack measurements.

To help justify the space needed for an adequate laundry center, consider additional uses for the space. Many of the facilities required for the laundry can be used for other purposes, depending on the location in your home and the amount of space available. Ironing is a part of sewing, as well as of laundering. Thus, the laundry center may be combined with a sewing room. The laundry sink can also be used for arranging flowers or as a place to wash up. Using the space as a family hobby center is another possibility.

Laundry Appliances

Some modern washers offer many time and work-saving conveniences, such as multi-wash cycles, wash and rinse temperatures and wash and spin speeds. Other handy features on some models include permanent press cycle, soak cycle for pre-washing, variable water level control, and programmed automatic controls. One of the newest washer features is an automatic detergent, bleach, and fabric softener dispenser. Some models offer mini-baskets for small loads.

Capacity of the washer, of course, is very important, but do not be misled by claims that a washer will hold so many pounds of clothes. Because there is such a wide variation in fabrics, pounds are a meaningless gauge of washer capacity. Five pounds of nylon curtains take up much more space than five pounds of bath towels. Regardless of the weight of the load, the volume should be such that all items circulate freely in the washer tub during agitation. Instead, select a model with a tub large enough to hold the loads the householder normally washes, but engineered to handle all size loads — small, medium, and large.

Economy of operation is also important. It is a good idea to compare the number of gallons used by each washer being considered. A washer should use only the amount of water and electricity necessary for the load size selected. Controls should be easy to understand, yet provide the range of flexibility that is needed for proper laundering of the many fabric blends in today's washload.

If low or fluctuating water pressure is present in the home, be sure the washer selected has metered fill. With metered (or pressure) fill, a pressure switch controls the electrical circuits so the washer cannot begin operation until it has filled to the proper level.

Loading and unloading should be easy, without lint filters or other obstructions. A perforated washtub that spins as it drains is preferable as it allows for the removal of sand, grit, and heavier-than-water soil without straining the wash water back through the clothes. A safety lid that stops washer action a few seconds after the lid is opened, during washing as well as spinning, is an important feature. Important, too, are a lint filter, fabric softener dispenser, and unbalance shutoff.

Once a luxury, the automatic clothes dryer today is essential to care properly for modern easy-care fabrics. A dryer enables the homemaker to realize the full benefits of wrinkle-free characteristics of acrylics, nylons, and polyester fabrics. Articles with permanent press finish must be tumble-dried to achieve the best results. And with the increasing variety of such apparel and home furnishings, much ironing of present and future purchases will be eliminated. A dryer also saves time and effort re-

121

quired for putting up and taking down clotheslines, or cleaning existing ones; carrying laundry to and from the lines; and hanging laundry and taking it down. Thus a dryer saves the energy of lifting, stretching, bending, and carrying. Because drying the laundry can be done regardless of weather or time of day, flexibility is added to the homemaker's schedule. In addition, a dryer reduces the family inventory of clothes and household furnishings needed since, with a dryer, items can be washed, dried, and returned to use quickly.

Both gas and electric dryers operate equally well. A good yardstick for making a choice is to compare the cost of each fuel in the local area. Consider also the present use of each in the home (type of range, furnace, water heater).

Controls should offer flexibility to dry the wide variety of today's fabrics, as well as be easy to understand and to operate. Three types of controls are available: (1) a manual control that is set for the desired drying time; (2) an auto-dry control that can be set for the degree of dryness desired; and (3) an electronic control that shuts off the dryer when the load has been properly dried. Since loads vary and numerous factors affect drying time, it is difficult to guess the precise time required. An electronic control dryer literally "feels" the clothes and automatically shuts off when the clothes are dried properly and ready to be removed. This saves energy as well.

For safety sake, the dryer should automatically stop if the dryer door is opened during use. If the cycle has been interrupted, it should be necessary to reactivate the start control in order for the dryer to start again.

If the family is small or space is limited, compact laundry appliances are available. There are units about half the size of standard washers and dryers, combination washer-dryers, portable models and over-under or stack-on types.

An automatic washer requires a drain and plumbing lines for both hot and cold water. To minimize installation costs, try to locate the laundry equipment near existing plumbing (ideally, it should share a wall with a bath or the kitchen.) Location near the water heater is added assurance of adequately hot water. The washer needs a 120-volt, 60-hertz electrical outlet and it should have its own circuit. An electric dryer requires its own 240-volt, 60-hertz three-wire circuit (the portable dryer is an exception). A gas dryer needs ready access for connections to either natural or LP gas. A gas supply line of rigid pipe or flexible copper tubing is standard, depending on local codes. A gas dryer also requires a 120-volt, 60-hertz connection for the motor (this outlet should be on a separate circuit from the washer).

If other activities are planned for the laundry area, be sure to include additional convenience outlets, such as a separate circuit for the iron or a nearby outlet for the sewing machine.

All standard-size air-flow type automatic clothes dryers, gas or electric, should be vented to the outside air. Non-vented standard dryers inevitably add to dust accumulation through small particles of lint that are not caught by the filter. In addition, the high moisture content of the exhaust air creates problems in humidity control throughout the house and can result in blistered paint or peeling wallpaper on the surfaces near the exhaust. Venting is an important consideration in planning the location of your laundry center. Too long a venting line or too many elbows (turns) reduces the efficiency of the dryer and prolongs drying time. It is best to follow the dryer manufacturer's recommendations for venting. (Rigid aluminum vent tubing is recommended.)

As a general rule, venting distance should not exceed 30 feet (minus 5 feet for each elbow) and should not include more than two elbows. Some dryers can be vented through either side, through the back or straight down. And since fine dust can accumulate outside the exhaust, its location should be as inconspicuous as possible. It should not, however, terminate either under the house or a porch, nor in a chimney, since an accumulation of lint could create a fire hazard under such conditions.

The farther the water heater is from the washer, the more loss there is in the water temperature. It is wise, therefore, to consider installing the water heater in the laundry center, if it is practical.

A mechanical water softener may also be desirable if the water has a high mineral content.

Planning A Laundry Center

When planning the laundry center arrangement, consider the homemaker's height and build. Working surfaces should be at a comfortable level. A counter is at the correct work height when the homemaker can stand and rest his or her hands on the counter with arms comfortably relaxed from the shoulder. Hands should not have to be raised above the level of the elbows while folding clothes. People of average height maintain good posture and avoid

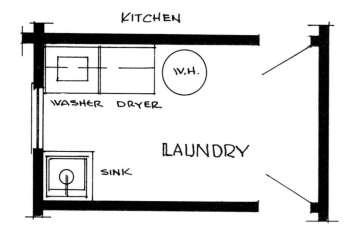

(Top) Laundry area including water and laundry tub. (Bottom) Rearranged to include sewing center, built-in ironing board and additional work counter by using an under-counter water heater.

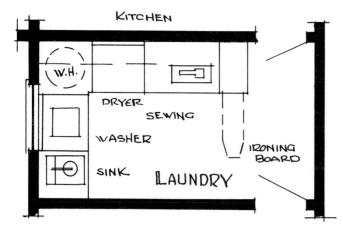

average person this is about 72 inches from the floor. Shelves should be adjustable. Upper shelves, which cannot be reached easily, can be used for seasonal storage of bedding or other items that are not used frequently. When a wall cabinet is to be directly above the washer, allow for clearance of the washer lid when open. Hamper type cabinets are very popular in a laundry, especially when located near the washer.

Placing the dryer on a riser to prevent stooping is often convenient, especially for the older homemaker. The riser can be a solid base, or it can contain a drawer.

Because one of the purposes of a laundry center is to ease the homemaker's workload it should also be easy to keep clean. Wall cabinets built to the ceiling or soffit, and flush drawers and doors without paneling prevent dust from accumulating. Wallcoverings or paint should be washable. Durable, stain-resistant countertops make cleaning simpler.

A pleasant decor can do a great deal to make work more pleasant. Therefore, choose cheerful colors and patterns that agree or complement those of the kitchen. Follow the suggestions given earlier in Chapters 4 and 6 for kitchen countertops, floors, walls, and ceilings, since the problems these surfaces pose are about the same for both areas. The laundry area also needs good general lighting, plus specific illumination for the pre-treating, mending, and ironing centers (see Chapter 5).

There are areas in the home other than the kitchen area where the laundry center can be located. Many architects and designers contend that the laundry belongs in the bedroom area since that is where the soiled laundry accumulates. In tight

fatigue when working at a counter 36 inches above the floor. The depth of the counter depends on the length of the homemaker's arms, and his or her build and physical agility.

Wall cabinets should be low enough so that the homemaker can reach the top shelf easily. For the

A complete housekeeping room.   A great utility-sewing-hobby room.   Laundry with a freezer center.

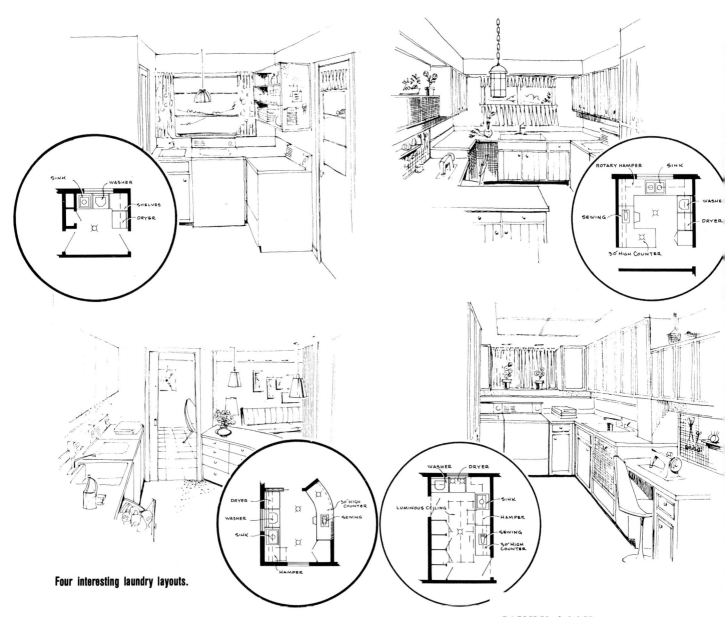

Four interesting laundry layouts.

floor plans, where space is at a premium, a good location for the laundry is in the bath. And, if the bath size is minimal, the use of stack-on units is ideal. By using stack-on units (illustrated earlier) a floor space of only 24 by 24 inches is required. The two stack-on units (washer on the bottom, dryer on top) also have the advantage that a standard wall cabinet can be placed over them to serve as a storage area. Because of the laundry's proximity to the bath plumbing is another savings effected. In this laundry, there are two additional advantages — the use of the tub as a drip-dry closet, and the use of the washer as a bathroom hamper for the storage of soiled laundry. Other prospective laundry center locations include the utility room and the basement.

FAMILY ROOM

A family room and kitchen are a perfect combination for several reasons. A parent can keep an eye on the children and be readily available in a crisis. In addition, children, especially young ones, like to know that a parent is nearby. Being close to the kitchen also simplifies the serving of food and refreshments that would otherwise require a trip through the house for delivery. A location on the opposite side of the kitchen from the living or dining room can be particularly effective. The kitchen serves as a buffer between adults in the living or dining room and the noise of children in the family room. At the same time the kitchen can serve both areas.

A family room as part of the kitchen.

The decorative theme of the kitchen is usually carried over into the family room. And most of the materials — floor, walls, and ceiling — may be used in the family room. There should be plenty of storage for the activities that will be carried out there. It should be kept in mind that the family room is for informal everyday living and entertaining, for television, reading, children's play, sewing, records, hobbies, card games, coffee with neighbors, or just plain informal talk and conversation. In short, it neatly handles those overflow activities that often occur by default in a crowded kitchen or formal living room, neither of these rooms being satisfactory as a genuine family room.

U-shaped and L-shaped kitchens adapt particularly well to kitchen-family room plans. If the kitchen is not close to the family room, a small, one-wall snack and entertainment kitchen may be built at one end of the family room.

DESK/MENU-PLANNING AREA

A planning center need not take up much of the kitchen's area, is a real convenience, and if standard furniture-like kitchen cabinet components are used, need not include costly built-ins or special cabinetry. A kitchen desk is a perfect place for paying the household bills, writing a letter while a meal is cooking, or planning menus for the week. If it is built around the telephone and intercom service, it is possible to create a small business office right in the kitchen.

In a U-shaped or in an L-shaped kitchen, the planning desk can be placed at either end of the principal work areas. The desk can also be placed along the free wall that is opposite the cabinet-appliance line-up. In the one-wall and the corridor kitchens, try to fit your desk along the end of the kitchen, just outside of the traffic path. That is, locate the desk, which should be about 29 or 30 inches high out of a traffic lane, both so that the homemaker can work at it without interruption and so that passersby will not be dropping baseball mitts and other clutter. Be sure it is not near the spatter of a sink or range. It may be wise to provide space above the desk for recipe and/or reference books. A file drawer can be used for business supplies and material if the space is used as an office, or to keep children's medical

Two desk/menu-planning areas.

Using a cabinet drawer for filing (top), while desk and storage are combined (right).

and school records, appliance instruction books, and the family's business and social records organized. A typewriter can be located on a spring-up platform that lifts out and up to the correct working height.

KITCHEN GREENHOUSE

In recent years plants have become a vital part of our lifestyle. They are found not only outdoors, but in most every room of the house. Kitchens are natural habitats for plants and the growing of herbs since this room usually includes plenty of light and humidity. Such plant growing areas help make a "kitchen plus."

In new construction the plant growing center can be figured in the kitchen layout. The remodeling of a kitchen usually involves either bumping out a wall or a window. The latter simply involves extending the window out from the wall into a bay-window type frame. There are also three-sided window greenhouses manufactured that will fit most window-size openings. These window units usually come complete with glass shelves and hanging basket attachments.

It is often possible to stretch a portion of the kitchen out to the very edge of the roof overhang. In most cases a foundation is not usually necessary and no change in the heating or plumbing system is

Open glass area creates a greenhouse effect.

Sometimes it is possible to build a greenhouse/hobby room just off the kitchen.

A cutting board (top) and mixing stand base (bottom) that lifts up into use.

needed. If the floor cannot be cantilevered by tying the extension into existing floor joists, pour a couple of concrete piers one for each end of the new area. The actual extension should be made, following conventional construction methods, but once completed, it will offer a greenhouse center for the kitchen.

OTHER "PLUS" IDEAS

Here are a few additional inspired touches to consider that will help to give any kitchen that "plus" feeling:

* Snack and sandwich center near the refrigerator with ceramic glass or chopping block insert, bread box, sandwich bags, canisters for corn chips, and so forth

* Pull-out racks for soft drinks near the refrigerator

* Turntables in the cabinet over refrigerator

* A hospitality sink with pass-through above it on the wall adjacent to the family room

* Children's corner for high chair and drawer or cabinet for toys

* Cabinet for baby foods and utensils used in preparing bottles and feeding the baby

* Built-in warming grill and rotisserie with exhaust fan and hood

* Undersink heater to serve a tap with instant near-boiling water for coffee, dehydrated soups, gelatin desserts, and the like

* Vertical dividers in a deep drawer or cabinet for baking pans

A slide-out serving cart.

Shelves in their many forms solve a lot of kitchen storage problems.

* A pull-out lid rack in a cabinet near the range
* Cork board on the side of a cabinet or inside a cabinet door on which a recipe can be pinned
* Decorative clip near the oven for pot holders
* Step stool
* Outlet for electric wall clock
* Wall telephone with chair and note pad nearby
* A decorative but readable wall calendar
* Tall utility cabinet for cleaning supplies to be used in and near the kitchen

* In cold and wet climates a mud room for wiping feet, leaving boots and hanging jackets
* A chimney divider between kitchen and family room, fireplace on family room side, charcoal-cooking hearth on kitchen side
* Changeable door panels (framing kits for some appliances so you can have front panels made to match the cabinetry
* Space away from the major work areas for the family pet to eat and/or sleep

CHAPTER 8

COMMON PROBLEMS AND THEIR SOLUTIONS

When a kitchen is being assembled in a new house, structural problems should not arise. But, whenever it is planned to remodel an old kitchen, some problems commonly arise. Even if the home is only a few years old, it seems that the windows are never quite where they ought to be. Or the chimney flue forms a jutting corner right where a cabinet is desired. And just about as common as things that jut out are problems that are already in the wall. That is, doors, wiring, and plumbing lines never seem to be where they should be. Electrical lines and outlets can be added or moved without too much trouble, but use existing piping and ductwork wherever possible — taking out and putting in new fixtures can cost a lot of money.

KITCHEN PLUMBING

The plumbing system of the home provides a means of bringing water to an outlet and a means of taking used water away. In today's kitchen, water is needed at many places in addition to the kitchen sink. Water must be supplied to the dishwasher, icemaker, and special preparation or service areas such as a bar or vegetable sink and salad-making

A vegetable sink is a handy feature in a kitchen.

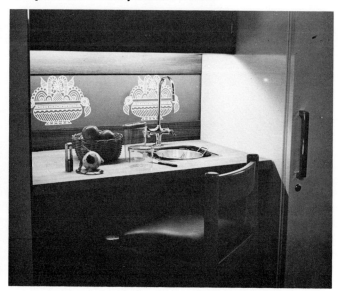

work areas. It is also necessary to provide a means of draining waste water away from each of these sinks and appliances (with the exception of icemakers). Once installed, the plumbing system is relatively permanent. Changes to existing systems are usually expensive because they require walls to be opened and holes to be cut in floors and ceilings. The effect changes may have on rooms located below or above the kitchen, or both, can also increase costs considerably.

Water-Supply System

The water-supply system should deliver water to the sink and appliances in the quantity and rate needed. The size of pipe, number of fittings, the length of pipe from the main, the pressure available, and the number of other fixtures in use at the time will determine the rate at which water will flow from the faucet.

The service from the main or well should be underground to avoid freezing or mechanical damage. A 1¼-inch galvanized iron pipe or a 1-inch copper pipe is usually sufficient for most residences. A valve to control the water (main shut-off) should be located inside the house near the entrance of the water-service pipe. The water meter (if installed) is usually located at this point.

The size of the water piping from the main to the individual fixtures is determined by the number and

Typical sink water-supply system.

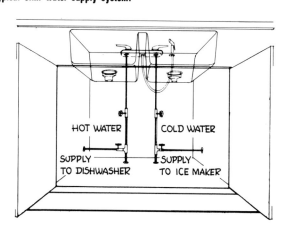

type of fixtures served by the pipe. The following relationship can be used as a general "rule-of-thumb":

For service to 3 or more fixtures, use ¾-inch pipe.

For service to 2 or less fixtures, use ½-inch pipe.

Each fixture is supplied by a fixture-supply pipe. The following table can be used as a guide:

Fixture	Supply Pipe
Bathtub	½ inch
Dishwasher	½ inch
Kitchen sink	½ inch
Lavatory	⅜ inch
Shower	½ inch
Water closet	⅜ inch

Each supply pipe should be equipped with a valve or "stop" so that repairs can be made to an individual fixture without interrupting service to other fixtures in the house.

Water Heaters

New dishwashers and laundries will add to the hot-water draw. Make sure the equipment has the capacity to handle them or replace it. The tank size and recovery capacity of the water heater is determined by the number of people in the family, the number of baths available, and the type of laundry equipment used in the house. For example, an automatic clothes washer may use from 25 to 40 gallons of hot water per load, a shower can use up to 30 gallons per hour (g.p.h.), and an automatic dishwasher may use up to 15 gallons of hot water. The required storage capacity of the water heater will be affected by the recovery capacity of the equipment. Generally a larger storage tank will be needed with electric water heating equipment than with gas or oil heating equipment. The following table can be used as a guide for selecting the proper size water heater for single-family residences. For luxury houses or for families with additional hot water requirements, the next larger size heater should be selected.

In some houses the distance from the water heater to the point of use may be quite far and may result in long waiting periods for hot water. A circulation line can be installed so that hot water is always available at each fixture. As an alternative to the circulating system, a separate water heater should be considered for the remote area. Or, in some instances it may be convenient to install a small hot water booster in the kitchen or laundry if the primary source of hot water is too small in storage or recovery capacity to provide sufficient hot water.

Sizing Water Heaters

Baths		1		2		3
Bedrooms	Storage Gallons	R	Storage Gallons	R	Storage Gallons	R
2 gas	40	30	50	35	50	45
2 elec.	66	18	66	28	82	28
3 gas	40	35	40	45	50	63
3 elec.	82	18	82	28	82	28
4 gas	50	35	50	45	50	63
4 elec.	66	28	82	28	2/66	18
5 gas	40	45	50	63	75	63
5 elec.	82	28	82	28	2/66	18

NOTE: R = recovery — 100 degrees F (38 degrees C) temperature rise in one hour. Storage capacity and recovery rate based on supplying enough hot water for three automatic washer loads of clothing (@ 25 gallons each) over a two-hour peak period. An additional 9 g.p.h. in either storage capacity, recovery rate as a combination thereof has been added for each additional bath or two bedrooms.

Water Softeners

In some areas of the country it is necessary to make hard water soft by piping the domestic water supply through a device called a water softener. Most water softeners have few moving parts and consume little power. The water is treated as it flows through a special chemical that removes the objectionable minerals which make the water hard. Depending on the hardness of the water, the rate of consumption, and the unit's capacity, there comes a time when the chemical must be regenerated, or cleaned and renewed. Different types of chemicals and equipment may be required to treat a specific water hardness problem. For this reason, an analysis of the water should be made. This may be performed by various local agencies or by making a test with a kit that can be obtained from a plumbing supplier.

Drainage System

When water is delivered to an outlet, some provision must be made to drain away waste or excess water. The drainage system differs from the water supply in one very important respect. In the supply lines the water flows under pressure. In the drainage lines flow is entirely by gravity and the pipes must be designed and installed carefully to insure flow at a velocity adequate to keep the pipes clean. The drainage system is also more complex than the supply system in that it consists of three parts all of which are needed in every installation, even if only one fixture is served. These parts are as follows:

1. Traps are water seals that prevent the backflow of air or sewer gas into the house. These should be accessible and as close as possible to each fixture. Sometimes they are part of the fixture.

2. Drainage lines are pipes, either vertical, called "Stacks," or horizontal, called "branches," that carry the discharge from the fixtures to the house sewer. They are usually concealed in walls or floors. The pipes receiving the discharge from the water closet are known as soil lines. Those receiving the discharge from other fixtures are known as waste lines. Some plumbing codes require a grease trap in the waste line from the kitchen sink. Others specifically prohibit them. This trap, which is designed to prevent grease and oil from entering the sewer, must be cleaned frequently for efficient operation.

3. Vent lines are pipes extending upward through the roof. They allow air to flow into or out of the drainage pipes, thus equalizing air pressure in the drainage system and protecting the water seal in the traps.

The relationship between the trap, the drainage line, and the vent line is very important and will have a great influence on the location of plumbing fixtures, particularly in remodeling work where the relocation of fixtures is desired. The maximum distance from the trap to the vent is given on page 43. Actually, the required maximum distance from a trap to a vent does not usually present any problems in residences except when island sinks are used. This can usually be solved by using a drainage line large enough for the distance to the nearest vent. Remember that some plumbing code regulations do not permit sinks or other water-using appliances except along a wall.

All vents must terminate outside the house. The vent terminal must be carried through the roof fullsize. It must be at least 3 inches in diameter to prevent clogging by frost. The minimum extension above the roof is 6 inches.

Each trap installed in a drainage system must be vented. Traps may be provided with individual vents (sometimes referred to as back-vents or continuous vents) or a common vent. The latter is useful when sinks are located side by side or when a new fixture is to be added to an existing drainage system. A new fixture could be added below or above an existing fixture as long as the lower fixture is the one with the greater flow.

The waste lines from each fixture or group of fixtures are connected to the building drain. The building drain takes the waste material to the sewer system or other disposal system. The building drain must be installed with the proper slope ($\frac{1}{8}$ to $\frac{1}{4}$ inch per foot). The steeper slopes will provide higher velocities and will increase the carrying capacity of the pipe and will tend to keep the drain pipe clean.

All plumbing work when installing a kitchen must be done in accordance with local plumbing codes. The primary purpose of a plumbing code, as well as of a building code, is to protect the health and safety of the homeowner. A properly written plumbing code should protect against the following:

1. Contamination of the water supply

2. Contamination of the air and undesirable odor due to escape of sewage gas

3. Excessive maintenance cost

Standardization of plumbing codes is now possible with the recent introduction by the Housing and

Home Finance Agency of a Uniform Plumbing Code for Housing. The scientific testing for this code was done by the National Bureau of Standards. If plumbing work is done in accordance with the Uniform Plumbing Code for Housing, the homeowner is protected against improper fixtures, materials, and installation.

Checking Plumbing

The American Institute of Kitchen Dealers suggests to its members that in checking a kitchen remodeling job the following procedure be undertaken to evaluate the present plumbing system:
Kitchen checklist:
1. Run water in present sink. Check for proper flow.
2. Is water rusty or clear?
3. Does water drain away rapidly?
If negative to any of the above questions, check for:
    a. Restricted supply lines, usually due to accumulation of limestone or mineral build-up.
    b. Rusty pipes, usually due to an old installation.
    c. Restricted or improper drain.
4. Check location of vent stack.
5. Check possible locations of sink arrangements with vent stack and soil pipe locations.
6. Check sizing of drain and supply lines.
Bath checklist:
1. Fill lavatory and bathtub with water. Is water rusty or clear?
2. Do fixtures empty promptly and quietly?
3. Flush water closet, first dropping a cigarette in the bowl. Does it flush completely?
4. Does it fill quietly?
5. With water running full in kitchen, does it run full in the bathroom?
If negative to any of the above questions, check for:
    a. Restricted supply lines.
    b. Rusty pipes.
    c. Restricted or improper drain.
6. Check for location of vent stack.

After completing the plumbing evaluation procedure, accurate assessments can be made on the condition of plumbing systems and how the problems can be corrected.

Unsightly Pipes. When remodeling a kitchen in an older home, unsightly pipes running up the walls can be a problem. There are two relatively simple solutions.

1. Enclose the pipes in the wall. This means that you must cut the pipe and install elbows to move the pipe into the wall itself. And that means cutting a slot in the wall for the pipe, then patching the wall afterward. This is a lot of work, but it is the most satisfactory solution.

2. Box in the pipes. This is an easier solution. Simply build the wall out around the pipes using a simple wooden box construction. Then paint or paper the addition to match the rest of the wall. This is more of a compromise solution, and it does leave a corner jutting into the room.

Pipes can be boxed in false columns and beams.

HEATING AND COOLING

Probably the most difficult task in providing heating and/or cooling for a kitchen is finding a suitable location for the terminal device of the heating/cooling system. Generally the outside walls of the kitchen are lined with cabinets, making it almost impossible to locate air registers, hydronic baseboards or electric resistance baseboards on the wall. The various heating systems used in a home will not be discussed fully here. However, suggestions as to how they can be employed and installed in a kitchen — new or remodeled — are given here.

Warm-Air Systems

Registers for warm-air systems and small electric resistance blower-operated units can be located in the toe space beneath lower cabinets. These units are acceptable for heating but registers in the toe space present problems of proper air distribution for cooling applications. If they are used they should be considered for heating use only and provision should be made so that they may be blocked or turned off in summer when the cooling system is in operation.

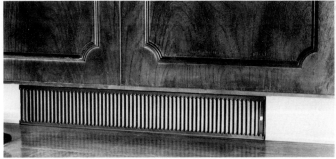

High outlet for cooling (top) and toe-space register for heating (bottom).

In new construction, provision can be made for using toe-space registers for heating and auxiliary registers located on the side walls for cooling if the installed system is one that will provide both heating and cooling. For remodeling work, the relocation of ductwork can sometimes present serious difficulties. This is particularly true if the house is built on a slab or if there is a finished ceiling in the basement below the kitchen. If the "new" kitchen is located in an addition to the house, it is possible to extend the ductwork to provide for heating and cooling the addition. Before this is done the existing furnace should be checked to see that there is sufficient heating and/or cooling capacity for the addition. The blower unit must also be checked to see that it is capable of delivering the additional air needed in the new room. It may be necessary to replace the blower assembly or the blower motor in order to increase the air-handling capability of the system even though the furnace burner has sufficient heating capacity. It is also possible to increase the air-handling capacity of the system by speeding up the blower. In general, this is not a good practice since the increased blower speed will normally increase the noise level from the furnace.

Hydronic (Hot-Water) Systems

In small kitchens or in corridor or U-shaped kitchens, the walls are lined with cabinets making it difficult to locate baseboard units. A valance unit can be used or the radiation necessary to offset the heat loss of the kitchen can be located in an adjoining breakfast area or other space immediately adjacent to and open to the kitchen. In extreme cases where the equipment cannot be located in an adjacent space, part of the wall space must be left free for the installation of a convector with or without an integral fan unit to help distribute the warmed air. When adding to a hydronic system, be sure the new radiator units are made of the same metal as the old or it is a sure invitation to corrosion.

Generally, hydronic systems are not designed as combination heating/cooling systems. Chilled water pumped through the system can be used for cooling if valance units are installed throughout the house. This is *not* a typical installation, however. When a separate cooling system is installed, the registers may be located in the ceiling and no difficulty will arise.

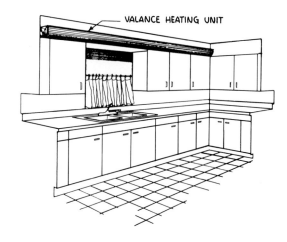

Typical hydronic valance unit.

133

Electric Heat

If electric ceiling cables or panels are used in a kitchen, there is no particular problem except interference from the soffit work over the upper cabinets. Other electric resistance-type heaters are available in the following forms: panels of glass or metal that are mounted on the wall; units that have a small fan which circulates the heated air; and hot-water baseboards in which the water is heated in the baseboard by electrically heated elements similar to those used in a water heater. Also available are resistance units that may be inserted in the branch supply ducts of a central air duct system.

For kitchen installations a small unit or units may be installed in the toe space of the base cabinets that resemble warm-air system registers. These units are equipped with small blowers to provide air circulation over the resistance elements.

If wall space is not available for baseboard units and a toe-space installation is also not practical, electric cable can be stapled to the ceiling. It is also possible to install electric resistance panels on the ceiling. These are rectangular in shape and resemble acoustical tile in their appearance.

With electric resistance heating a separate cooling system must be installed.

Cooling Systems

As already mentioned, it is possible to combine heating and cooling in a central system. It is also possible to have a separate central cooling system. In addition window air-conditioning units or through-the-wall units may be used to cool the kitchen.

Window units fit into the opening of a double-hung window, and special units are available for installation in casement windows. The units vary in cooling capacity from as small as 5,000 Btuh to 35,-000 Btuh. Room air is circulated through the unit, where it is cooled, dehumidified, and filtered. A condensate drain is not necessary since the moisture condensed from the air is evaporated into the outdoor air. The units are electrically operated, and many of the small ones can be plugged into existing electrical outlets. The larger units require 220-240 volts and use up to 200 amperes of electricity. These require a separate circuit that is installed particularly for the air-conditioning unit.

Through-the-wall units are simply window units that have been provided with a metal sleeve built into the wall, which makes the installation more permanent. The chief advantage of the through-the-wall unit is that the window is not obstructed by the air-conditioning unit, and the unit may be placed high on the wall so that the distribution of the cooled air is more efficient. The chief disadvantage of the through-the-wall unit is that when the unit must be replaced after some years of service it may be difficult to find another unit that will fit the sleeve. Some manufacturers have standardized the size of the sleeves, but there are still many non-standard units.

Radiators

While radiators provide a good form of heating and are often found in older homes, they are a real problem when one of them sits right where new cabinets are desired. What can be done? Here are three basic solutions to solving the problem of a radiator in the kitchen.

1. Cover it. Build a cover that matches or complements the rest of the new kitchen design. But make sure this cover allows proper circulation to heat the kitchen adequately.

2. Move it. Is there another location in the kitchen for the radiator? Perhaps moving it to another wall might improve the kitchen design and the heating, although this can be costly. If a radiator is moved it probably will still have to be covered (see No. 1 above).

3. Replace it. The old-style radiator can often be replaced with a new baseboard unit that gives more versatility in decorating the walls. These old radiators are generally of cast iron and are of the column, large-tube, or small-tube design as shown opposite. The output of these units is expressed in Btu per hour (Btuh), 1000 Btu per hour (MBTU) or in square feet equivalent direct radiators (EDR). Columns and large-tube radiators are no longer manufactured but small-tube radiators are still available. The tables opposite give typical ratings for some of the more common sizes of radiators that are likely to be encountered in older residences. When they are replaced by modern equipment such as convectors, finned tubes, or baseboard radiators the replacement must be sized to supply a similar amount of heating. The tables also give some typical outputs for finned-tube and cast-iron baseboard for comparison purposes. It is always best to consult the literature published by the manufacturer of the equipment for the exact amount of heat input of the unit.

Typical Ratings per Section of Cast Iron Radiators

Column-Type	Height	Columns	Btuh per Section	*EDR
	22	2	540	2 1/4
	22	4	960	4
	26	2	640	2 2/3
	26	4	1200	5
	26	5	1680	7
Large Tube	26	3	560	2 1/3
	26	4	660	2 3/4
	26	6	960	4
	38	3	840	3 1/2
	38	4	1020	4 1/4
	38	6	1440	6
Small Tube	25	3	384	1.6
	25	4	432	2.0
	25	6	720	3.0
	32	6	888	3.7

4-COLUMN

3-COLUMN

LARGE TUBE

SMALL TUBE

*Ratings based on steam at 215 degrees F (102 degrees C).

Typical Ratings for Baseboard Heating Elements

Length	Finned Tube Mbh*	Cast Iron Mbh*
2	1.8	
4	3.7	2.6
6	5.5	3.9
8	7.4	5.2
10	9.2	6.5

*Based on an average water temperature of 220 degrees F (104 degrees C).

Flues

Sometimes the chimney flue seems to run right through the kitchen. If lucky, it is already in the wall. If not, there is a problem. A chimney flue cannot be readily moved and enclosed in the wall, whereas a heating duct can. A chimney flue, however, can be boxed in the same manner as pipes.

Another solution is to accept the limitations of the flue location and design around it. It can be wallboarded and hidden. Or it can be dramatized and highlighted. Try adding brick (imitation or otherwise) to it to make it more dramatic. Or put cookbook shelves up the wall.

NOISE ABATEMENT

Noise can be a problem in both a new and a remodeled kitchen. Appliances tend to be noisy while doing their job. Noise can be kept at reasonable levels even in a motorized kitchen, if the following anti-noise steps are taken.

1. Level the refrigerator and/or freezer to eliminate annoying vibrations. Either appliance is properly balanced if the door closes automatically from a half-open position.

2. Dishwashers are very noisy because of the tremendous water activity. Choose a dishwasher that has more insulation and other sound-deadening features built into it or wrap the sides with insulating material to prevent transmission of sound to cabinets and countertops.

3. Mount the dishwasher, food waste disposer, compactor, and other similar appliances on springs or pads to prevent vibrations from being transmitted through the floor, walls, and countertops.

4. Use rubber isolation gaskets at the mount of food waste disposers to prevent the sink bowl from amplifying the grinding noise. The better quality disposers have sound-deadening jackets of insulation.

5. Heavy-gauge stainless-steel sinks vibrate less than thinner ones; porcelain on cast iron is still quieter. Wooden cabinets reflect less noise than metal ones.

6. Place rubber bushings behind cabinet door to stop banging. Check the drawer slides, and if they are noisy, replace with quiet ones.

7. Hum of a fluorescent light often annoys. Use rubber mounts combined with ballast to eliminate hum.

8. Make sure room air conditioners and vent fans are properly mounted to avoid excess vibration. Ductwork should be designed without reduction in size and with a minimum of turns.

9. Install air chambers or pneumatic anti-hammer devices in the water lines to stop any hammering noises.

10. Long runs of hot water supply creak or snap as they expand or contract. Differences up to 100 degrees can exist in piping and can cause expansion up to ⅛ inch in 10 feet. To eliminate, use a swing arm to allow movement and use collars of fiberglass insulation in straps.

11. Holes cut through common walls for plumbing or heating may leak noise. Seal all holes with a resilient material to isolate noise and seal against air leaks, vertical or horizontal.

12. Remember that acoustical ceiling panels or tile, carpeting and fabrics used for curtains and tablecloths absorb most of the sound that reaches them.

OTHER PROBLEM AREAS

More than in any room in the house, the remodeler of a kitchen must watch out for design and structural booby traps. For example, work put in by amateurs is often overengineered (and hard to remove) and often ignores codes (and makes it harder to get the job accepted) and standard practices (so studs, pipes, and wires may not be where one would expect them). Other problem areas are discussed below.

Walls

Frequently, there is the problem of a wall not being where it should be in the new plan. Perhaps the wall needs to be removed. But, before doing so, check the wall most carefully. It may be a load-bearing one. Any nonbearing wall can simply be ripped out. Any bearing wall can be replaced with a beam at ceiling level supported at the side walls.

Sometimes it might be necessary to add a wall. This is simpler and can be accomplished by following standard construction procedures.

As mentioned in Chapter 4, out-of-plumb walls can be a serious problem when installing the cabinets. Actually, nothing can cause more cutting and fitting. A counter cannot be set flush if the wall is out more than ¼ inch. A postformed counter cannot be installed if the wall bows more than ½ inch across its length; nor can an appliance be neatly placed in an out-of-square corner.

It is usually cheaper to work around an obstruction than to remove it. A jutting column can be enclosed in a cabinet made big enough to be useful.

In a kitchen with a high ceiling it is frequently possible to use a second set of wall cabinets.

Pegboard or corkboard can be hung on the column. Shelves can be built next to it, designed to hold glasses, canned goods, small appliances, or an ironing board if the space is not deep enough for a standard cabinet.

Doors

The problems with a door might be that: (1) it is not where it is supposed to be; (2) it should not be there at all; or (3) it will bang into the cabinets or appliances every time it swings open. Recognize the type of problem, and a solution can be found.

1. Move the door. If it is in the wrong location, the door, doorway, and moldings can be removed and the hole can be filled in. Then a new opening can be cut in another wall and the door can be placed where it belongs.

2. Remove the door. If it swings into furniture, cabinets, or appliances, simply take the door out of

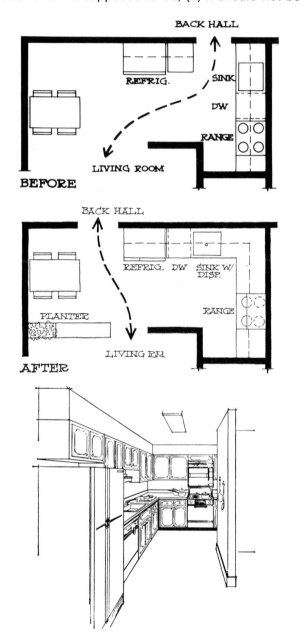

The proper location of the door can make the difference between a good and bad design.

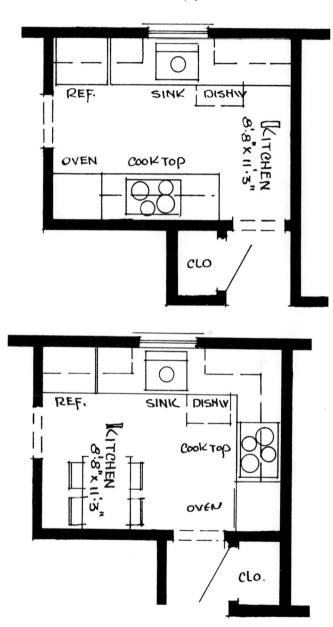

(Top) Two wall kitchen with no provision for breakfast area.
(Bottom) Relocation of utility closet provides for breakfast area.

137

Stained-glass windows are a good way to block off an undesirable view.

the doorway. The doorway can then be changed into an archway if desired, or a curtain of beads can be hung in its place.

3. Replace the door. For instance, it is possible to solve a swinging door problem with a new type of door, swinging cafe doors, bifold doors, or pocket doors. (A pocket door is a sliding door; the pocket is the part of the wall it slides into). A pocket door may require major structural changes in the wall.

Windows

Redesign a kitchen, and the windows will pop up in the wrong places with amazing frequency. The following are some ideas that can be employed to overcome window problems.

1. Move the window. Remove the window and block or fill in the wall. Then cut in a new window where the design shows it should be. A header must be installed when adding a new door or window.

2. Replace the window. Maybe a smaller one would fit the plan and still let enough light in. Or maybe glass bricks would work better where the window was. A very common window problem in an old house is a sill that is too low. Since the standard countertops are 36 inches above the floor, the window sills must be at least 36½ inches high to accommodate them.

3. Make the window into a light box. When building a new room up against the window, it is not necessary to remove it. Instead, add a picturesque scene and some interesting lighting, so you can still look out the "window" to a synthetic outdoors. This approach would help keep a small kitchen from appearing even smaller.

In most cases, remember that a door can be turned into a window or a window into a door without too much difficulty.

CHAPTER 9

COLOR AND THE DECORATING OF THE KITCHEN

Once the kitchen plan has been set, the work triangle established and the general materials agreed on, then it is just a matter of "putting the kitchen together." This means the details of choosing colors, selecting the proper style or theme, finding the right accessories, and assembling the various components into a finished kitchen. Of course, good design and decorating belong in every kitchen. A small, compact kitchen in a small apartment can have as much flair and as much efficiency as a large family kitchen in a big, custom house. While an imaginative decorating scheme will not cure the faults of a poorly planned kitchen, it can turn an uninteresting, straightforward one into an exciting room.

Successfully decorated kitchens are never accidents. Usually they reflect the careful planning and attention to detail by builders and owners who insist on pleasant livability. Such kitchens begin with efficient arrangements of the work centers. Then the color, styling, textures, and accessories are added. The equipment, cabinets, flooring, lighting, and treatment of walls, ceilings, and windows can make a big impact in the final presentation.

In planning a kitchen decorative scheme, select the style before selecting colors and materials. Keep the style of the kitchen consistent with the architectural style of the house or apartment — it takes a very talented interior designer to successfully mix styles, especially in smaller living units. But today, there is no one style for a kitchen. It can be designed with the look of the Orient or of Spain — with the spirit of 1776 or 2076. Actually, the kitchen's decorating style or theme is determined by the choice of the basic materials, colors and accessories. Color, for example, adds life and sets the mood — cool greens to soothe a busy homemaker, or appetite-provoking oranges for the other members of the family. Accessories, of course, supply the touch of individuality. The basic materials — floor coverings, ceilings, walls, light fixtures — have been discussed fully in the previous chapters. Remember though, that much of the equipment and materials used in a kitchen is of a permanent nature and cannot easily be changed or removed. Once the cabinets, countertop, flooring, built-in appliances, lighting, sink, paneling, and other fixed items are installed, it is difficult and costly to change them. So, while currently popular decorating fads might seem the thing to do in the kitchen, remember that the next

A kitchen may be arranged in many decorative schemes, but cabinets play a most important part.

buyer or renter might not agree.

COLOR

Because it has been mentioned so often, it is no longer a trade secret that color can do more to change the look of a room than almost any other single factor. Color in a kitchen is particularly important. Modern technology and materials have made all-white kitchens unnecessary, and today's homemakers are responding enthusiastically to the availability of color.

When planning the kitchen's color scheme, consider the sources of color. The walls, floor, ceiling, cabinets, and countertop offer the largest areas of color. The appliances, sink and dining furniture provide smaller but still important color sources, and the window curtains, chair cushions, canisters, towels, and even utensils contribute still more color. After deciding on a color theme, it is good to translate the selected colors into swatches of material, paint, flooring, countertop, etc. Include all the colors that will be used in the kitchen and arrange the swatches in sizes that approximate the amount of color used in the room. If the swatch-board is pleasing, chances are the finished kitchen will be.

Fundamentals of Color

Learning to work with color is not nearly as difficult as it might seem. And since color is unquestionably the biggest single variable in the design of a new kitchen, it is worth taking a little time and trouble to understand. It offers unlimited potential for freedom of expression and, if handled properly, it can be a wonderful ally and friend. It should be remembered that color can be a mood-maker, an attention-getter, a disguiser, a warmer, and a dazzler.

The key to confidence in planning color schemes is to understand the make-up and use of a color wheel. While the use of a color wheel may seem rudimentary, do not underestimate its simplicity. There are invaluable lessons to be learned in a study of how a wheel is made up and in the use of it for planning initial color schemes. Once a clear mental picture of all the facets inherent in a color wheel is obtained, you can improvise your own combinations with confidence. A closer look at the color wheel will reveal that there are the following:

1. *Three Primary Colors.* Everything starts here with just three colors: red, yellow, and blue. Every other color is made by mixing parts of one or more of these primary colors.

2. *Three Secondary Colors.* By mixing equal parts of one primary color with another we produce a secondary color. And since there are three primary colors, there are three secondary colors: orange, violet, and green.

3. *Six Intermediate Colors.* By mixing the primary colors and the secondary colors, we come up with the six intermediate or tertiary colors. And from there the sky is the limit. You can go on mixing colors indefinitely, producing an infinite number of hues and creating an absolutely unlimited palette with which to decorate.

But, before going any further, it might be wise to point out that any discussion of color requires use of terminology that may be confusing because of different interpretations by various professions. The terms used are those of most common usage and acceptance. For instance, the word *color* is all encompassing and includes the neutrals white, gray, and black.

Hue means the particular name of a pure color. Green is a hue. So are red and orange and every other color.

Value relates to the color's lightness or darkness. White is the lightest color, and the values of all other colors range from white through gradations of gray to black. Colors that are closest to white in value are called *tints*. Colors that are closer to black are called *shades*. If it is light, it is a tint. If it is dark, it is a shade.

Intensity, sometimes also called *tone*, refers to the brightness or dullness of a color. Peacock feathers usually contain a bright, clear green while peas are more of a dull, grayish green. So the green in peacock feathers is described as an intense green. If you like the color of peas better than the color of peacock feathers, you just add gray to the color to make it duller.

Every color has chameleon qualities. All hues, values, and intensities can appear to change when used together. Two or more light values combined afford little contrast. Darker values in combination also provide little interest. But when a light value is used with a dark, the light appears lighter while the dark appears darker.

Intensities also have similar effects. A group of bright-colored cabinets will appear brighter and will stand out when used with walls of dull color, since it will produce a spot of interest. In contrast, dull-colored cabinets will sink into the background if the kitchen contains brighter colored floors, walls and appliances.

Contrasting or opposite hues will emphasize one another. Red with green will make the red look redder and the green appear greener; while similar hues together will seem to change the hues. For example, if a red is used with red-purple, the red will appear more orange while the red-purple will take on a bluish tone.

Color Creativity

Colors today are exciting and vibrant. New processes are giving us all the colors of the rainbow, in a thousand subtle variations. No longer is it necessary to play safe with color, sticking to beige floor or plain white walls. But, while colors can be combined in an infinite number of ways, there are only three *basic* color schemes — monochromatic, analogous, and complementary.

Monochromatic color schemes use only one color and that color appears in various shades, ranging from very light to very dark. For example, in a monochromatic scheme of yellow, the range could be from the dark shades of gold, graduating to clear yellows, and to light, pale yellow tints. A monochromatic color scheme can be restful, and may provide a good background for art objects, collections, or gourmet cooking utensils.

Analogous color schemes use three related colors — colors that appear side-by-side on the color wheel. A scheme using red-orange, orange, and yellow would be one. Also a color scheme using blue, blue-green, and green would be analogous. This kind of color scheme is also restful and refreshing, and the colors are more interesting because of their variations in intensity and value. It is the kind of color scheme that is easily changed. A slight shift of emphasis here and there is all that is necessary to completely change the character of the kitchen.

Complementary schemes use colors that are opposite each other on the color wheel — blue and orange, red and green, yellow and violet. One color is usually a primary color and the other a secondary color. Using such contrasting colors will give a lively and vibrant kitchen, but it is a color scheme that must be used with caution. One color should always dominate, with the others being primarily dramatic accents.

Colors also have temperature. For example, the

cool colors are the evening colors — blues, greens, violets. They are basically soothing and restful colors. The *warm* colors, on the other hand, are the sun colors — reds, oranges, yellows. They come straight from nature and give a room the energy and vibrancy of the earth and sun. The *neutral* colors are the blacks, whites, and grays. They will become either cool or warm depending on the colors used with them.

Generally, cool colors are best for kitchens which get warm light from the south or west. Warm colors are more appropriate in kitchens which face north or east. Warm colors are best for manual tasks, and cool colors for relaxation and concentration. It does not follow however, that because kitchens are work areas they should not have blue or green color schemes. It does mean, though, that if a blue or green color scheme is used, the kitchen will need ample light — preferably a warm light.

Furthermore, colors can be "large" or "small," and thus can be used to shape a kitchen. Warm colors seem large; cool and neutral colors appear smaller. A spot of yellow will seem larger than a spot of blue the identical size. A narrow room can be widened by using an intense, warm color on each end wall, and a lighter color on side walls. Narrow, corridor kitchens can benefit from this color hint.

A ceiling can be raised or lowered visually in the same manner. A dark ceiling will seem lower, a light-colored one will seem higher. Also a strong, contrasting color can draw attention to the kitchen's best feature — an attractive dinette table or a favorite collection. Conversely, painting an ugly radiator or water pipe the same color as the wall will help to disguise it.

Colors are versatile too and can be used to create almost any mood or appearance. Pink looks different depending on the colors used with it. Combined with blue-green, pink gives a cool, restful look; used with cherry-red, it becomes vibrant and exciting. Yellow used with moss-green and orange-red is dramatic; but, combined with pink becomes delicate and muted. A charcoal black used with blue, white, or red gives a sophisticated scheme for a modern styled kitchen. The same charcoal black used with copper cooking utensils and small print wallpaper creates a mellow, Early American kitchen. Colors, properly combined, can create many moods — these are just a few. Others are shown throughout the book and mix a variety of colors, textures, and finishes to create highly attractive kitchens.

When it comes to the actual business of choosing the color scheme, start with some kind of a guide. It can be a color wheel, a color chart, a handful of color chips, or any other source of color. Bear in mind the kind of character the finished kitchen is to have — restful or exciting, placid or vibrant, peaceful or stimulating. Then pick the one basic color that seems to best convey that mood.

The next step is simply to select several companion colors, several additional colors that will help to create the desired mood of the area. Limit this additional selection to a total of three or four colors. Also keep in mind that since the wall and cabinets will make up the largest area in a kitchen, their colors should be chosen first. Relatively quiet colors are usually preferable for large areas; unless a person really wants it, a bright red wall will normally be a little disquieting to live with. However, the secondary colors can be bright and exciting, since they will serve mostly as accents and dramatic highlights.

On the other hand, if a person really likes bright colors and daring patterns, do not be afraid to use them. Just because most people prefer softer colors does not mean that there is anything wrong with the bright ones. They can be extremely effective if used properly. For instance, unequal areas of color are most interesting. It is best to let the major color cover about two-thirds of the room. And to avoid a spotty look do not concentrate the strong colors or patterns in one area; balance both color and patterns throughout the whole kitchen.

Colors should be selected under the light which

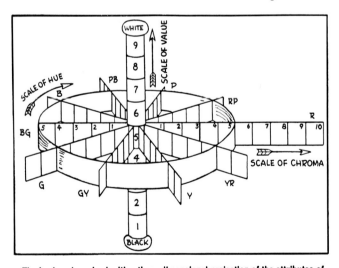

The basic color wheel with a three-dimensional projection of the attributes of color — hue, value and intensity as shown in their relation to one another. The circular band represents the hues: G-green, B-blue, P-purple, R-red and Y-yellow. The upright center axis is the scale of value. Paths leading from the center indicate color intensity.

will be predominant in the end usage of the room. Daylight, in most cases, can be controlled but should be given consideration as to cool or warm exposure. Artificial light can do strange things to some colors and the need to check the colors under the type of lighting that will prevail cannot be stressed too strongly. For instance, a kitchen with cool fluorescent lighting and a blue-green color scheme will be decidedly greener than if the illumination wire were changed to yellowish incandescent.

The psychological factors of color must be considered, too. The one who has to live with the colors is the person who will live with the kitchen. Blue might be the decorator's rage this year, but if the color blue happens to make the homemaker feel sad and lonely, then a brand new blue kitchen will be just a sad and lonely kitchen as far as he or she is concerned. And who needs it?

Color and Pattern

Color and pattern work hand in hand as kitchen decorating tools. It is very important to remember the value of patterns in selecting an overall color scheme. They can be a dramatic accent used with the color scheme and they can be handy inspirations in choosing a good color scheme. Many a striking kitchen began with a swatch of cloth that combined several beautiful colors in an attractive pattern. The same colors can be simply picked up and extended throughout the kitchen with very happy results. When remodeling, patterns can brighten, cover flaws, or unify a room chopped up with too many doors and windows.

Although today there is a trend of "freely" combining many patterns with great daring, some points which should be remembered when working with patterns in the kitchen are:

1. Be careful in using two strong patterns close together in large amounts. If the cabinets forms are already patterned visually, the addition of a patterned wall treatment could create visual confusion.

2. Be especially careful in using large-scale patterns. The size of the pattern should conform to the wall and other surface areas for which it will be used. On the other hand, the use of a supergraphic, which is a large pattern, can be very effective, if it is used carefully.

3. A window form or other opening which may interfere with the total harmony of the kitchen can be removed visually by using a pattern to tie it in with its nearby surroundings.

4. Large areas of strong pattern, such as the floor and countertops, can be very dominant, and are most effective when other patterns and textures remain supportive to it.

5. Repeat the dominant shapes that occur in the kitchen forms in the choice of fabric or wallcover patterns. If the dominant forms are geometric, a smaller-scaled geometric pattern with some subordinate curves would be a good choice. This procedure will aid in establishing harmony and unity.

The wallpaper used on cabinets.

The color scheme of the room is based on the wallpaper. Note that the window shade, lamp shade, window valance and shelf edging are the same design as the wallpaper.

Other Design Fundamentals

Applying some other fundamentals of art besides color to kitchen concepts means considering basic elements of structure — line, form, and texture.

Line. Line may move in any direction — up or down or in diagonals to form zigzags or curves. Line forms the boundaries which define the shape or silhouette. And within these silhouettes, line divides the whole into parts or spaces. Lines can also be used to decorate, form patterns, create illusions, or express emotions.

How does this apply to kitchen design? A kitchen which is too low can be given the feeling of height by using strong vertical lines such as contrasting strips between cabinets or striped wallpaper. It is the old idea of "verticals heighten and horizontals widen." Yet, a series of narrow vertical lines close together can create just the opposite effect — widen instead of heighten.

Vertical lines are also strong, like a person standing; horizontal ones suggest rest. Applying these values to the open-shelf concept, horizontal shelf lines convey a restful effect in kitchens — perhaps even suggesting the kitchen itself is relaxed and is a room in which to relax. Green plants of varying size and fullness always add softness to the many straight lines and hard surfaces of a kitchen, and when placed on open shelves, they are especially great in juxtaposition with glass walls of modern apartments.

Form. Form is the mass or the volume and the shape of the object. Each item displayed potentially adds pleasure according to its shape and size. Glass canning jars and well-designed ceramic bowls and coffee mugs on a shelf have a visual pleasure all their own. There is no visual treat in seeing stacks of plastic cereal bowls piled up.

Visual form is closely allied with the apparent weight of the object. While actual weight is important, frequently it is the apparent weight which is the deciding factor in a design's success. A shape strongly contrasting with its background will have

A real modern-designed kitchen. Note the storage closet behind the doors at the end of this corridor kitchen.

forms can be just as dominant visually as the mass form, and it is important to learn to use both of them in appropriate ways. A skeleton form can occupy as much space as a mass form, but it usually defines, yet does not enclose, space; consequently it may appear to be smaller than it actually is.

Texture. All forms and surfaces have texture, that is, they give a tactile sensation when touched. They feel smooth, rough, jagged, slick, soft, hard, warm, or cold. Some have a regularity of surface. Others are varied with no apparent order to the surface. But touch is not the only sense which is affected. Sight also plays an important part in the study of textures. What of the surface which has a pattern on it rather than in it? This frequently gives an equal sensation.

There are two kinds of texture. One, the actual texture, which is the tactile quality of a surface. The second is a simulated texture or applied pattern, which does not affect the tactile quality but does affect the visual quality. The eyes "feel" the surface rather than the fingers. Often both texture and pattern are combined, and further aesthetic tendencies are established.

All forms in the kitchen have texture and pattern — fabrics, stone, wood, glass, metal, plaster, brick, china, plants, and plastics. The surface of a form has a great deal to do with its inherent qualities of weight and density. A form will take on more importance when its surface contrasts greatly with the surface

more visual or apparent weight than one which is similar. Thus, if application to kitchen design is made, a large white refrigerator might be too dominant for a room having dark walls and cabinets, but with light walls the refrigerator might assume less importance. Conversely, the refrigerator could be dark and the same desired result would be achieved with dark walls.

Another aspect of form that is important is the difference between mass form and skeleton form. An appliance which has the visual appearance of a solid box, with the structure within, is an example of a mass form. A mass form frequently suggests weight, apparent if not actual, and may require compensatory treatment, such as color or surface decoration. The above reference to the refrigerator is such an example.

The second type of form is called the skeleton form. A group of open shelves, a wire hanging planter, or a room divider, all having their structure revealed, would be classified as skeleton. These forms will be linear in quality and will generally appear to have less apparent weight. However, these

A picture can take the place of a window.

144

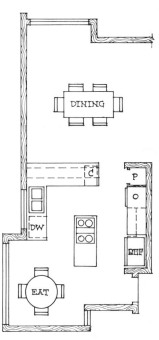

This kitchen offers such features as a spacious breakfast nook, a pantry, a center island cooktop with work space and a long counter/divider, which is also used as a snack bar or a service bar for the dining room.

This big, eat-in kitchen, with its sliding glass doors, offers not only a view but also easy access to a broad deck for open air dining.

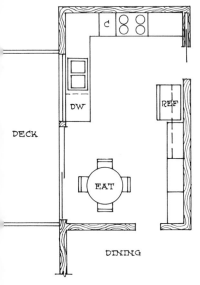

(Above—Top) A well laid out U-shaped kitchen that features a butcher-block countertop area.

(Above—Bottom) Another U-shaped kitchen that features an eating/planning area. Note the rocking chair for complete leisure.

(Left) This vacation kitchen in a one-bedroom/loft beach retreat is right in the center of things. A large serving bar, which is used for snacks or a buffet, divides it from the living/dining area.

(Top-Left) This open kitchen which is directly off the living room features both eating table and snack bar.
(Top-Right) No doubt about it, this kitchen makes a person feel that they are down in Mexico.
(Bottom) This two glass walled kitchen brings the outside in. The island provides a work center for the range as well as an eating area.

Several features that would fit nicely in most kitchens. The kitchen shown at top right features plastic molded countertops and built-in appliances. The molded plastic overhead cabinets contain built-in lighting units.

The kitchen shown above features a built-in barbecue next to the oven center. A separate table and chair arrangement provides eating space in the kitchen. The kitchen at the left features an eating counter. The remaining portion is a simple L-shaped arrangement.

Various cabinet finishes and drawer/door styles. The kitchen cabinet units shown (top center) are used as built-in units in the den. Kitchen cabinets are becoming increasingly popular as built-in units for other rooms.

151

(Right) With one end wide open to a large family room and the other closed off from the dining room, this kitchen lets a family entertain casually or formally without problems.

(Bottom) A well-designed kitchen with a breakfast nook. The countertop is ceramic tile.

A one-wall kitchen into a good-sized eating area. The same wallcovering is used to decorate both areas.

The cabinets in this kitchen have easy-grip doors and drawers which eliminates the need for pulls and knobs. The kitchen is well-lighted by the octagonal skylight.

Two open planned kitchens. The one above ties the living room, dining room and kitchen together. The U-shaped kitchen makes for an efficient layout. The arrangement at right has no wall between the kitchen and dining room. The kitchen and dining room both open upon an attractive patio/terrace arrangement.

154

(Top) Two kitchens featuring eat-in areas. One has a table while the other an eating island.
(Bottom) The kitchen overlooks the family room and — an unusual feature — the front entry as well. It is easily reached from the front path (through the double door is the family room) or from the garage (through the laundry, lower right on plan). And it is closed off from the formal part of the house but open to the informal family room, and accessible from the secondary bedrooms. This setup is ideal for families that entertain formally and who may have older children living at home.

This island kitchen is surrounded on three sides by windows or sliding glass doors; on the fourth, a table-height eating counter separates it from the family room, which also has a large glass sliding door. It was designed for a waterfront site, but a similar plan would make sense wherever there is a good view of a garden, a wooded area, or even of other houses on a hillside. All that openness, however, cuts down on places to hang cabinets. The problem is solved with a storage wall that includes a good-sized pantry.

156

(Above) There is a counter for snacking, a corner nook (foreground in photo) for informal dining and convenient access to a patio for outdoor meals. In addition, there is a large formal dining room, which can be served easily through the family room when the kitchen door is closed for privacy.

(Left) A well-planned sink/work center. The pull-out board is very handy.

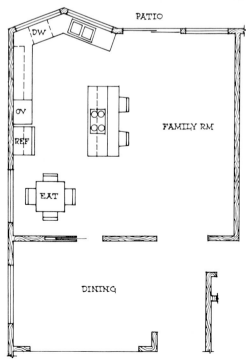

PATIO

DW

OV

REF

FAMILY RM

EAT

DINING

An L-shaped island with a second cooktop — this one with a grill — and a marble slab for pastry-making provides added luxury in this large kitchen. And note the warming drawer below the double ovens. The painted cabinets were built on the job.

When a couple loves to cook, here is what their kitchen should look like. The cabinets, walls and ceilings are all of redwood, and three 2-by-8-foot stained-glass panels brighten the ceiling. The countertop is laminated strips of rosewood, teak and walnut. The center island holds a vegetable sink, and half its base pulls out to become a serving cart. Other built-ins include two microwave/oven combinations, warming drawers and a blender.

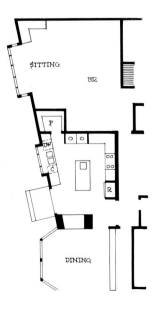

The tile eating counter in the above kitchen is at tabletop height and is an excellent selling point. From the kitchen at left, the occupants can look across the family room to the mini-greenhouse below.

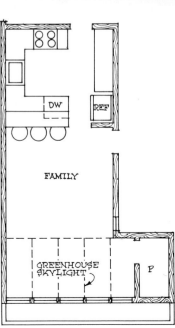

(Above) This kitchen is a very efficient corridor design. Various accessories give it a Colonial effect.
(Right) This kitchen is very modern. The molded plastic cabinets are most interesting.

160

texture and/or pattern of its background. In fact, frequently the size or form is changed visually by the use of texture and pattern. For example, a large, plain-surfaced form might almost disappear against a plain-textured background or a pattern against a pattern. Sometimes, however, a boldly patterned large form will be broken visually into smaller parts and can be camouflaged, almost appearing as a group of small forms.

In general it is always safe to combine similar textures, but a carefully considered contrast in textural quality can enhance both surfaces. Rough wood, fieldstone, and homespun fabrics are quite compatible, but often by adding plate glass, chromed steel, or other hard surfaces, all the surface qualities are immeasurably enhanced. Use contrasting textures for variety where contrasting colors or patterns might destroy unity. This is especially true when a very limited color scheme might tend to be dull and drab. Finally, remember that all surfaces have texture and must be considered in the total design, not just in the surface treatments of the major appliances.

Five Other Principles of Design. The proper use of line, form, texture, and color are considerations that can generally make a major improvement in the appearance of any kitchen. There are five other principles of design that can also improve appearance. A sense of order is needed for an aesthetically pleasing design. Order can easily be achieved by unity of all parts. But if all parts are exactly alike, monotony or boredom may be the result. Therefore variety must be introduced for interest. The first principle then, can be expressed as *unity with variety.*

An experienced kitchen designer is one who knows just how much variety is needed to produce a pleasing effect. Variations of colors, textures, or lines can be used. But if there are several variations of one of these components, then the others should remain more constant in order to retain the harmony of the whole. For example, if several colors or many intensities and values of one color are desired, then closely related textures and lines could hold these color variations together. So the second principle to be considered is *balance* in the use of colors, textures, and lines. To minimize the confusion that might occur when using a number of colors, textures, and types of lines in the kitchen, one dominant idea should be emphasized.

Briefly, the third principle to remember to employ is the need to maintain *one center of interest* instead of many strong features vying for attention.

But this point of emphasis might be too shocking if it actually is so different or unusual in color, line, or texture that it stands out by itself. Some means of leading the eye to this dominant spot should be used. This can be done in various ways such as grouping smaller or less important articles or accessories in an attractive arrangement near the main object. Or, the color of the main object can be repeated in other parts of the room to lead the eye to the dominant point. Another way might be a gradation of color from light to dark or dull to bright to carry the eye to the darkest or brightest point. Gradation of size is also pleasing.

Any method that will lead the eye to the center of interest will produce *rhythm*, the fourth principle that should be considered when creating good design. The scale of sizes and shapes within a kitchen should be in relation to the whole.

The fifth principle, the use of good *proportion*, or scale, should never be overlooked when choosing the sizes and shapes to be combined. But use of the knowledge of all these principles in handling the elements (line, texture, and color) will not necessarily produce beautiful results. Imagination, understanding, and personal taste must be developed to a point where the combining of these elements becomes a natural skill instead of a maneuvered or set pattern of arrangements.

STYLE

The only important rule about style or theme is, "have one." Any kitchen should have a common look that coordinates the different elements in it and makes it uniquely personal. The style or theme that is selected is strictly up to the homemaker.

The more one knows about the classic styles of the past and present, the easier it will be to find the style for the new. But if names like Duncan Phyfe, Regency, Bauhaus, and Shaker are strangers to you, do not despair. Because kitchens are basically utilitarian and need little real furniture, they do not have to be decorated in traditional style to tie in with the rest of the home — Spanish, Early American, Traditional, Oriental, or Scandinavian Modern, for example. The decorative scheme can just as successfully be picked from a less conventional theme like turn-of-the-century Americana, a spring garden, or an old-fashioned farm kitchen.

As previously mentioned, the kitchen's decorating theme or style is determined by the

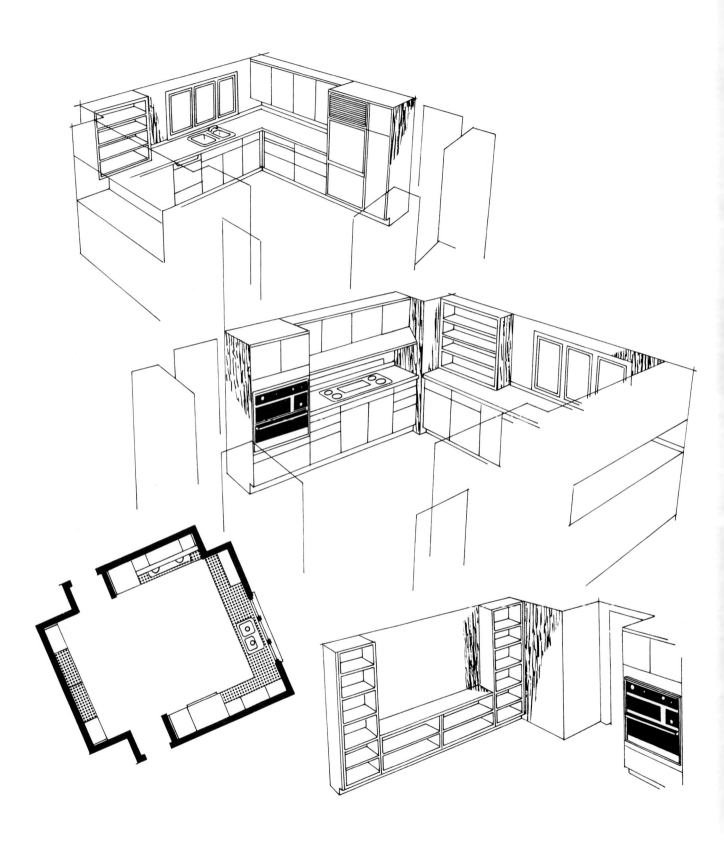

The basic layout of a many styled kitchen.

Country-style kitchen.

Contemporary-style kitchen.

Spanish-style kitchen.

Modern-style kitchen.

Early American-style kitchen.

Oriental-style kitchen.

choice of materials, colors, and accessories. To illustrate this point and demonstrate how easily a decorating theme or design motif can be established, we have selected six kitchens each in a different style — Contemporary, Early American, Oriental, Spanish, Modern, and Country Living. The same kitchen plan and arrangement of work centers are used in each kitchen, only the basic materials (cabinets, floor and ceiling coverings, light fixtures, and wallcoverings), colors, and accessories have been changed in each case.

So often kitchens are not of one particular style, but their theme reflects the personality and interests of those who use them. It is common to find quite functional cabinets, combined with late nineteenth-century accessories and a table or chairs suggesting eighteenth-century France or England. The rough brick of seventeenth-century American fireplaces might also be combined with the stainless steel and glass of twentieth-century architecture. And why not? Such combinations might express the family. The contemporary human being is not just a product of today, but is the sum of all that has come before. Perhaps such combinations or "mixes" are also more truthful to today's way of life than a strict period or even modern kitchen or interior. The personality of the householder must always be evident, and it is the responsibility of whomever is making the decorative plan to be cognizant of this and to make suggestions and selections accordingly.

When planning such an eclectic kitchen, it is necessary to employ the principles and elements of design. It is in this area of free selection that many people falter because, with little prescribed historic combinations upon which to base the design, the person must truly "create" the atmosphere and look which the resultant kitchen will have. The kitchen may be designed as formal in appearance as any kitchen could be, or it can be made as informal as the client wishes. The cabinets, appliances, accessories, seating, tables, storage pieces, floor and wall surfaces, and textiles must be gleaned from all that is available, and the form, color, balance, etc., of each individual component must be scrutinized and evaluated not only for its intrinsic self but for how it will fit into the conceived whole; it is certainly not just a conglomeration of individual items, but a carefully selected assemblage.

Although it cannot be emphasized too strongly that eclectic kitchens are the most difficult to achieve successfully, they often give the most pleasure to the homemaker. They are never quite "done," nor should they be. Personal and family items and treasures of large or small inherent value can be added to make the kitchen a most personal room, a truly living kitchen.

ACCESSORIES

After selecting the kitchen's main decorating elements, the only thing that remains is to add the accessories — the personal touches that give a

Furniture and decorative touches such as a striped canopy will add style to a kitchen.

Shelves are an excellent method of displaying one's accessory items such as canned food, plants and cooking items.

166

Window shelves are an excellent place for plants.

A cabinet display case is a point of interest.

kitchen charm and make it personal. Most interior designers would agree that accessories properly selected for style and design can make a kitchen, while poorly chosen accessories can defeat even the most imaginative decorating scheme. A few well selected and strategically displayed kitchen utensils and accessories help define the kitchen's style theme, and give it a professionally decorated look.

When accessorizing the kitchen, it is not necessary to cover the entire countertop, nor create a cluttered look throughout the room. A few attractive, tastefully selected accessories are much more effective. It is important, though, to choose accessories that are compatible with the kitchen's style. Do not place them in a spot where they might interfere with kitchen tasks.

Some accessories are always popular. Plants, if they are live herbs, will perk up a kitchen and

enhance cooking. Flowers in an outside window box, set on a shelf or hanging near a sunny south window, are always colorful and cheering.

Cooking utensils can be decorative as well as utilitarian. Copper pots and pans are excellent decorations. Hang them on a pegboard, over a cooking island, or on a wall. In addition, plates or mugs can be attractively displayed. A mug rack or stand puts mugs within easy reach for morning coffee or late-night cocoa; beautiful plates should be on display, not hidden in a cupboard for occasional use. Kitchen clocks, calendars, spice or wine racks, and other functional items are also popular accessories.

Works of art are now considered popular kitchen accessories. The reason is simple: today's kitchens are just as clean and beautiful as any room in the house. A decade or so ago, art would have been impractical to consider due to the moisture and

Thanks to the attached greenhouse, plants are the main decoration.

Pots and basket collections add interest to this kitchen.

The rocking chair sets a relaxed mood in this kitchen.

Wine racks are now part of many kitchens.

grease problem. But now, thanks to modern ventilating fans, these problem cooking by-products are quickly removed from the room. Any type of contemporary or traditional art form — acrylic or oil paintings, water colors, pastels, collages, bright graphics, photographs, ceramics, weaving — can be used successfully in the kitchen. Try an exciting graphic on the ceiling above an island, or suspend a mobile over the sink. Water colors, pastels, photographs, drawings, and graphics are best preserved under glass. Only in unusual circumstances is glass put over an oil painting. The backsplash over the sink is one place in the kitchen where oils should not be considered. It is a good location, however, for a line-up of prints protected by glass.

Another good accessory item, if space permits, is a comfortable chair or two. Remember the kitchen is also a place to relax. The Early American idea of the "keeping room" is sometimes desirable. An easy chair or two or even a couch where members of the family can relax while waiting for a meal is a welcome addition to the kitchen. It has been suggested that an easy chair, where family members can talk and share the day's events while the cook is finishing the preparation of the meal has helped many a family.

For additional accessory ideas, think about particular items that would enhance the kitchen decorating theme. If planning a country kitchen, how about hunting for a pot-bellied stove, antique iron pots, or other old cooking utensils? Or select a pastoral print to hang over the kitchen table. For a super-modern kitchen, put bold-patterned fabric on a canvas stretcher for instant modern art or find an unusual plexiglas wine rack or free-form plastic storage unit, a wire sculpture, or unusual spice rack.

With a little imagination and searching, it is possible to provide a kitchen with the added sparkle, that touch of uniqueness that sets *that* kitchen apart from any other.

CHAPTER 10

FROM PLANNING THROUGH COMPLETION

The final step in planning a kitchen is making the plan or blueprint. To accomplish this, the designer or remodeler will first make a rough sketch of the room, usually on a grid or graph paper. Of course, when a new room is being added onto the house, or a kitchen is being designed for a new home, work from the architect's or contractor's blueprints. They will help greatly in making the rough sketch.

MEASURING THE OLD KITCHEN

The first step in making the rough sketch is to measure the room. Start at any corner above the counters at a comfortable height, measure the room and mark all dimensions on a rough sketch. (Write all dimensions in inches.) Show the thickness of walls, door, and window widths, including trim and door "swings." Note all critical measurements and irregularities: chimneys, closets, pipe raceways, radiators, or any other similar structures. Also note items in the existing kitchen that are not going to be replaced in the new kitchen — the exhaust fan, for example. Indicate the location of light switches, electrical outlets, exhaust fans, heat registers, and plumbing, using the symbols shown in this chapter. Make note of window stool heights, window heights, and the height of the ceiling. Add all overall measurements for each wall and prove with the overall measurement check.

When taking the measure, try to determine what is inside the walls — gas, electric or water pipes, duct work, stacking and chimneys — by reference to blueprints if available, or by careful examination of the area all around the kitchen. That is, on remodeling jobs, it is necessary to check and take notes on the following:

1. Present drain location and distance from the plumbing stack or vent.

2. Air ducts concealed in walls, soil pipes, vent pipes, and water pipes.

3. Exterior walls for construction type.

4. Heating and locate on sketch the ducts, radiators, pipes, etc.

5. Electrical system and size and type of service, condition of wires, and general condition.

6. Any unusual situations.

7. Which walls are bearing or non-bearing.

8. If windows or doors are to be changed, determine what size and style are to be used.

On new construction, when finished dimensions are established, the kitchen planner is generally limited to the existing conditions, since any changes at this point would prove quite costly. In the case of a complete remodeling job, considerable latitude is usually allowed and consequently more specific, detailed information is required. But, as mentioned several times in this book, it is less expensive to plan around plumbing and heating systems, and other obstructions than to relocate them.

MAKING THE BASIC LAYOUT

Again using grid or graph paper, lay out the perimeter of the kitchen from the measurements made on the rough sketch. Be sure to transfer measurements accurately, and include all the details noted while measuring the room. Try several room arrangements by drawing on tracing paper or by making cut-outs from the templates on pages 170 to 171 and moving them around. The dimensions of these appliance and appliance templates — ⅜ inch to 1 foot scale — are typical. Be sure for the final drawing, however, to consult specifications in manufacturer's literature for cut-out dimensions, required clearances, and exact size of appliances and cabinets that are going to be used. Any appliances that are presently in the kitchen and are going to be used in the new one, should be measured accurately, with their indicated door swings.

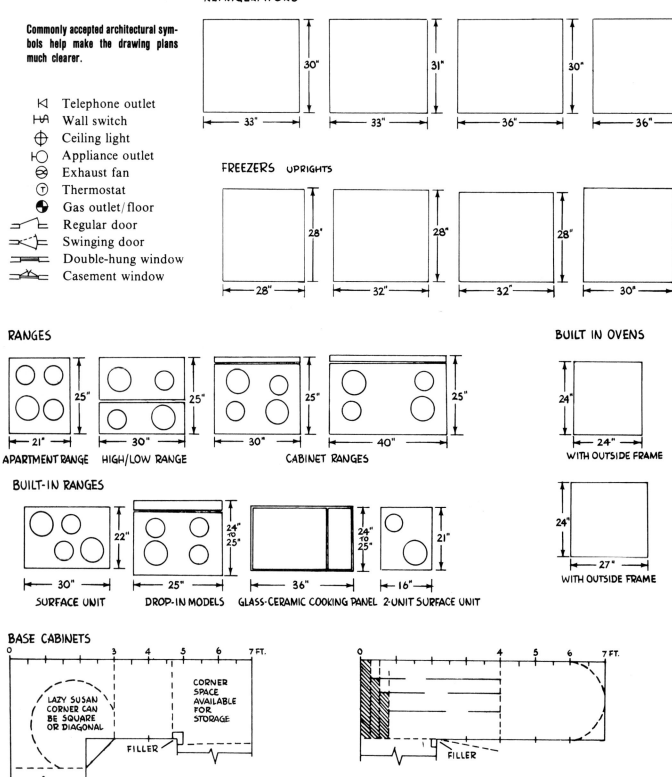

REFRIGERATORS

Commonly accepted architectural symbols help make the drawing plans much clearer.

⊲ Telephone outlet
⊢ᴀ Wall switch
⊕ Ceiling light
⊢◯ Appliance outlet
⊖ Exhaust fan
Ⓣ Thermostat
◓ Gas outlet/floor
⌐⊏ Regular door
⤝⊏ Swinging door
═══ Double-hung window
⌐△─ Casement window

30"   33"
31"   33"
30"   36"
36"

FREEZERS UPRIGHTS

28'   28"
28"   28"
28"   32"
30"   32"
30"

RANGES

25"   25"   25"   25"
21"   30"   30"   40"
APARTMENT RANGE   HIGH/LOW RANGE   CABINET RANGES

BUILT IN OVENS

24"
24"
WITH OUTSIDE FRAME

24"
27"
WITH OUTSIDE FRAME

BUILT-IN RANGES

22"   24" TO 25"   24" TO 25"   21"
30"   25"   36"   16"
SURFACE UNIT   DROP-IN MODELS   GLASS-CERAMIC COOKING PANEL   2-UNIT SURFACE UNIT

BASE CABINETS

0   3   4   5   6   7 FT.

LAZY SUSAN CORNER CAN BE SQUARE OR DIAGONAL

CORNER SPACE AVAILABLE FOR STORAGE

FILLER

0   4   5   6   7 FT.

FILLER

Typical templates for kitchen components. Check manufacturer's specifications for exact dimensions. Scale: ⅜" = 1 ft.

170

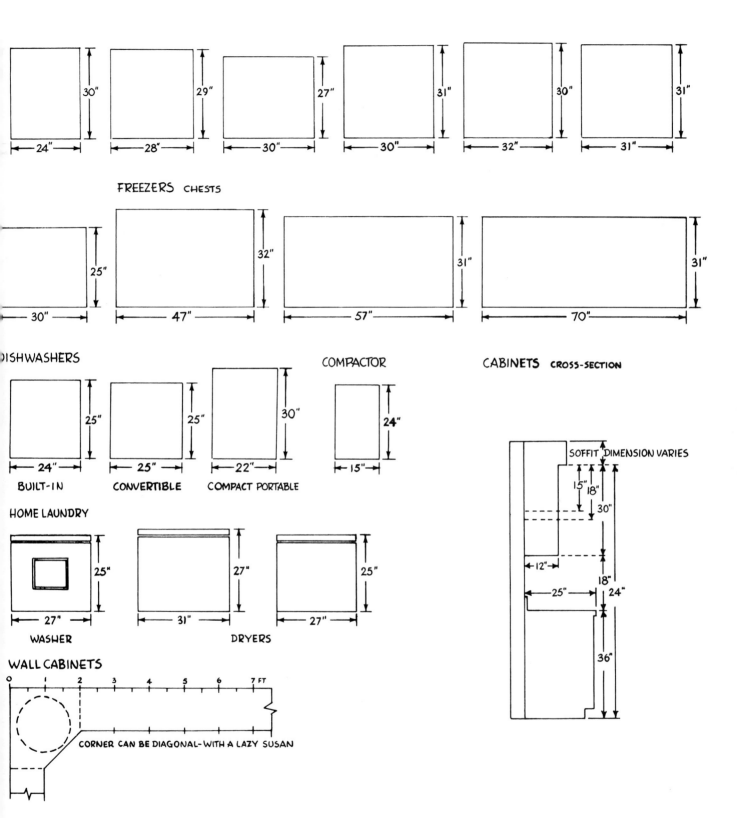

FREEZERS CHESTS

DISHWASHERS

BUILT-IN   CONVERTIBLE   COMPACT PORTABLE

COMPACTOR

CABINETS CROSS-SECTION

SOFFIT DIMENSION VARIES

HOME LAUNDRY

WASHER   DRYERS

WALL CABINETS

0 1 2 3 4 5 6 7 FT

CORNER CAN BE DIAGONAL-WITH A LAZY SUSAN

Using the material detailed in the previous chapters, proceed as follows:

1. Locate the three main activity centers with the appliances in place. Because the clean-up center is the most used, it is often easiest to start by drawing in the sink, then the dishwasher. Then place the other appliance on the grid in the position desired. In each layout, check the work triangle and traffic patterns.

2. Lay a faint line 24 inches out from the wall. This is the base cabinet line. Lay in another light line 12 inches from the wall for wall cabinets. Surround the main appliances with scaled representations of storage cabinets and work counters, using the templates on page 170.

3. Provide aisle and adequate clearance for cabinet doors and drawers and for appliances, windows, and doors.

4. Draw in the other activity areas that the householder desires — dining area, desk, laundry, pantry, pet area.

As was already discussed, more than one arrangement on the graph paper should be tried before deciding on the final one. Illustrated here are four plans that show the variety possible in a single large kitchen.

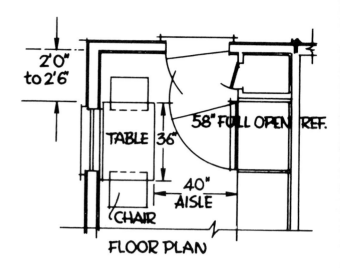

"Clearance" is of prime importance when making the floor plan. Space must be available for chairs to be pushed back, for the oven door to open and for the refrigerator door to open completely.

FINAL PLANS

Once the basic layout is made as desired, the final plans or blueprints can be made. Prepare the layout of the kitchen to scale — either ⅜ inch to the foot or ½ inch to the foot. Indicate all measurements, obstructions, and peculiarities. Review all original survey notes and the householder's desires. Lightly lay in the three work center areas as per the basic layout. Lay in a line along the walls of the kitchen, 24 inches from the wall. This line will indicate the base cabinet line. Lightly lay in a line 12 inches from the walls, and this will indicate the area for the wall cabinets.

When placing any cabinets or appliances in any given area, always use the subtraction line method for computing the remaining workable area. This is important in order to avoid errors and replanning. Everything must fit in its place, and its place must fit everything.

Basic floor plans of a large kitchen.

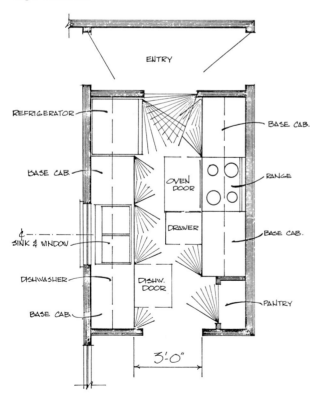

Narrow aisle considerations.

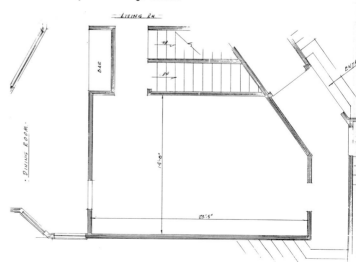

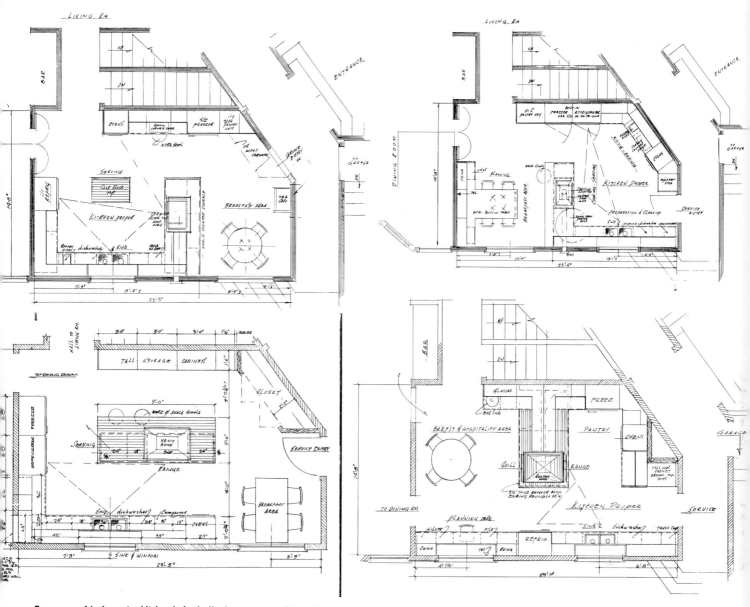

Four ways of laying out a kitchen in basically the same area. The design at the lower right was the one selected. Below is the perspective view of this kitchen taken at the range elevation (left) and sink-refrigerator-desk elevation (right).

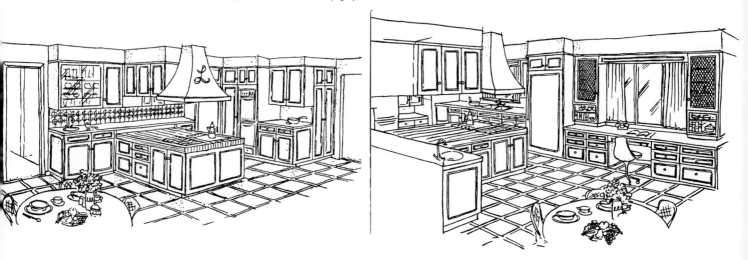

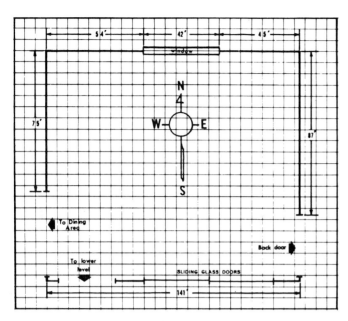

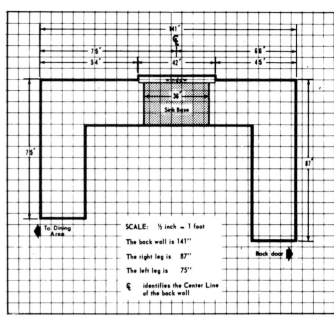

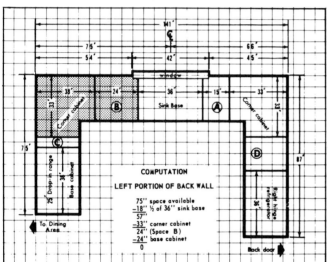

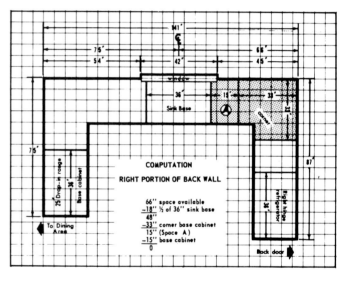

Laying out the base cabinets on the back wall.

Subtraction Method

The subtraction method is very simple. All room measurements should be converted to inches and the size (width) of each cabinet or appliance used is deducted (subtracted) from the space available (wall dimension in inches). After deducting the width of all items there should be zero inches of space remaining and you will have the exact number of inches of cabinets needed to fill the wall space — neither too many nor too few.

To understand the subtraction method concept, study the illustrations on this page and the next. For

our purpose, let us assume that the U-shaped kitchen includes the following items:

33-inch double-bowl sink (requires a 36-inch cabinet)

36-inch refrigerator

25-inch drop-in range (can use any size base cabinet above 30-inches in width). The back wall is 141 inches with a window in the center. The right leg of the "U" is 87 inches while the left leg is 75.

As shown, the total space from the sink center (or window center) to the right wall measures 66 inches. Deducting 18 inches (½ of the 36-inch sink cabinet) from this leaves 48 inches of space to be filled. The first cabinet to be selected, once the sink

174

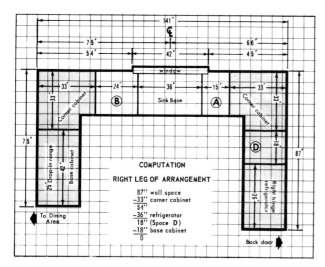

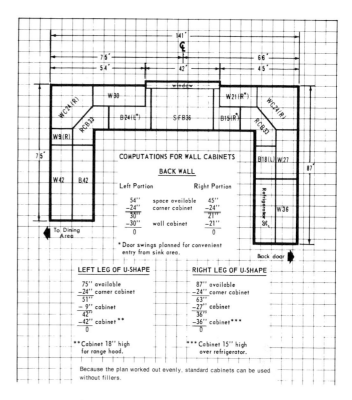

COMPUTATION

RIGHT LEG OF ARRANGEMENT

87" wall space
−33" corner cabinet
54"
−36" refrigerator
18" (Space D)
−18" base cabinet
0

COMPUTATIONS FOR WALL CABINETS

BACK WALL

	Left Portion		Right Portion
	54"	space available	45"
	−24"	corner cabinet	−24"
	30"		21"
	−30"	wall cabinet	−21"
	0		0

* Door swings planned for convenient entry from sink area.

LEFT LEG OF U-SHAPE	RIGHT LEG OF U-SHAPE
75" available	87" available
−24" corner cabinet	−24" corner cabinet
51"	63"
− 9" cabinet	−27" cabinet
42"	36"
−42" cabinet **	−36" cabinet***
0	0

** Cabinet 18" high for range hood.   *** Cabinet 15" high over refrigerator.

Because the plan worked out evenly, standard cabinets can be used without fillers.

Complete computations for wall cabinets. Because the plan worked out evenly, standard cabinets can be used without fillers. Key to the letters above: B = base cabinet; RCB = revolving corner base cabinet; SFB = sink front base; W = wall cabinet; WC = wall corner cabinet; (R) = right hinge: (L) = left hinge; and number = width of cabinet in inches.

cabinet has been determined, is the base corner cabinet. If a 33-inch rotary (lazy susan or revolving) base corner cabinet is selected, this leaves 15 inches (Space A) to fill.

An all drawer unit should be next to the sink, for convenient storage of the utensils used at this cleaning center: cutlery, dishtowels, etc. Since there is a 15-inch all-drawer cabinet available, the back wall of the U-shaped kitchen plan is neatly filled from the center of the window to one corner.

To complete the back wall, let us plan another convenient 33-inch rotary corner cabinet. Space B in the illustration can be neatly filled with a 24-inch cabinet or dishwasher.

Now that the entire back wall is filled we are ready to fill the 87-inch right leg of the U-shaped arrangement. The rotary corner cabinet previously selected occupies 33 of that 87 inches and the refrigerator occupies 36 inches so we have only 18 inches (Space D) to fill. There being an 18-inch base cabinet available, the right leg is complete.

The computation for the left leg is somewhat different. On the preceding page the illustration shows a 33-inch rotary corner cabinet plus a 36-inch base cabinet for the drop-in range, leaving Space C to be filled. Since there is no 6-inch base cabinet (it would be uneconomical) and since fillers should be limited to a maximum of 3 inches in order to minimize waste storage space, the easiest way to fill this 6 inch space would be to increase the size of the

range cabinet by these 6 inches substituting a 42-inch cabinet for the 36-inch cabinet previously selected. This completely eliminates Space C.

To complete the U-shaped kitchen layout, cabinets for the upper wall are needed. For maximum storage and beauty, the width of each wall cabinet should correspond to the width of the appliance or base cabinet beneath it, except at the end of the arrangement when open shelves are frequently more attractive and economical.

The subtraction method can be used in planning any shape kitchen: single wall, corridor, or "L" shaped.

Drawing Floor Plans and Details

To make the final plans and details proceed as follows:

1. Working from the clean-up center, place the sink cabinet, using the centerline of the window as a guide. The sink is generally placed beneath the window, however, this is not a firm and fast rule. If design, function, or aesthetics require it to be elsewhere, place it freely in that area and then concentrate on making that area the focal point of the kitchen. Design around it.

2. Place the dishwasher next, if one is to be incorporated into the plan. Remember that for better

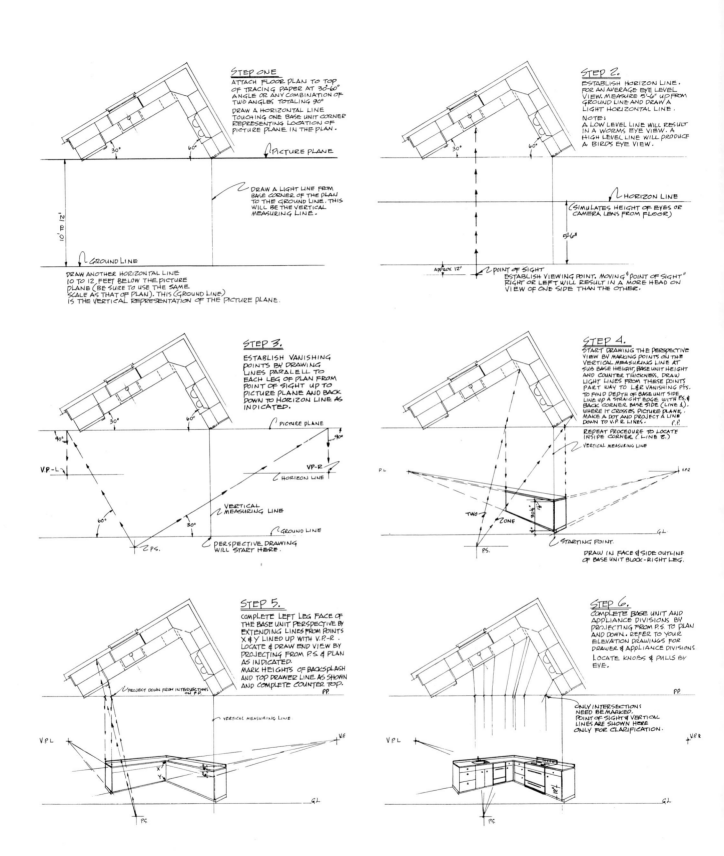

STEP ONE
ATTACH FLOOR PLAN TO TOP OF TRACING PAPER AT 30°-60° ANGLE OR ANY COMBINATION OF TWO ANGLES TOTALING 90°.
DRAW A HORIZONTAL LINE TOUCHING ONE BASE UNIT CORNER REPRESENTING LOCATION OF PICTURE PLANE IN THE PLAN.

↙ PICTURE PLANE

DRAW A LIGHT LINE FROM BASE CORNER OF THE PLAN TO THE GROUND LINE. THIS WILL BE THE VERTICAL MEASURING LINE.

10', 12'

↙ GROUND LINE

DRAW ANOTHER HORIZONTAL LINE 10 TO 12 FEET BELOW THE PICTURE PLANE (BE SURE TO USE THE SAME SCALE AS THAT OF PLAN). THIS (GROUND LINE) IS THE VERTICAL REPRESENTATION OF THE PICTURE PLANE.

STEP 2.
ESTABLISH HORIZON LINE. FOR AN AVERAGE EYE LEVEL VIEW, MEASURE 5'-6" UP FROM GROUND LINE AND DRAW A LIGHT HORIZONTAL LINE.
NOTE:
A LOW LEVEL LINE WILL RESULT IN A WORMS EYE VIEW. A HIGH LEVEL LINE WILL PRODUCE A BIRDS EYE VIEW.

↙ HORIZON LINE
(SIMULATES HEIGHT OF EYES OR CAMERA LENS FROM FLOOR)

5'-6"

APPROX 12"   ↙ POINT OF SIGHT
ESTABLISH VIEWING POINT. MOVING "POINT OF SIGHT" RIGHT OR LEFT WILL RESULT IN A MORE HEAD ON VIEW OF ONE SIDE THAN THE OTHER.

STEP 3.
ESTABLISH VANISHING POINTS BY DRAWING LINES PARALELL TO EACH LEG OF PLAN FROM POINT OF SIGHT UP TO PICTURE PLANE AND BACK DOWN TO HORIZON LINE AS INDICATED.

↙ PICTURE PLANE
90°   90°
V.P-L   VP-R
↙ HORIZON LINE
VERTICAL MEASURING LINE
60°   30°
↙ GROUND LINE
P.S.   PERSPECTIVE DRAWING WILL START HERE.

STEP 4.
START DRAWING THE PERSPECTIVE VIEW BY MARKING POINTS ON THE VERTICAL MEASURING LINE AT SUB BASE HEIGHT, BASE UNIT HEIGHT AND COUNTER THICKNESS. DRAW LIGHT LINES FROM THESE POINTS PART WAY TO L & R VANISHING P'S. TO FIND DEPTH OF BASE UNIT SIDE LINE UP A STRAIGHT EDGE WITH P.S. & BACK CORNER BASE SIDE (LINE 1). WHERE IT CROSSES PICTURE PLANE, MAKE A DOT AND PROJECT A LINE DOWN TO V.P.R LINES.   P.P.
REPEAT PROCEDURE TO LOCATE INSIDE CORNER (LINE 2.)
↙ VERTICAL MEASURING LINE
P.L   V.P.R
TWO ZONE   36¾"
P.S.   GL
STARTING POINT.
DRAW IN FACE & SIDE OUTLINE OF BASE UNIT BLOCK-RIGHT LEG.

STEP 5.
COMPLETE LEFT LEG FACE OF THE BASE UNIT PERSPECTIVE BY EXTENDING LINES FROM POINTS X & Y LINED UP WITH V.P-R. LOCATE & DRAW END VIEW BY PROJECTING FROM P.S & PLAN AS INDICATED.
MARK HEIGHTS OF BACKSPLASH AND TOP DRAWER LINE AS SHOWN AND COMPLETE COUNTER TOP.   P.P.

PROJECT DOWN FROM INTERSECTIONS ON P.P.
↙ VERTICAL MEASURING LINE
V.P.L   V.P.R
X Y
GL
P.S.

STEP 6.
COMPLETE BASE UNIT AND APPLIANCE DIVISIONS BY PROJECTING FROM P.S. TO PLAN AND DOWN. REFER TO YOUR ELEVATION DRAWINGS FOR DRAWER & APPLIANCE DIVISIONS.
LOCATE KNOBS & PULLS BY EYE.

P.P.

ONLY INTERSECTIONS NEED BE MARKED. POINT OF SIGHT & VERTICAL LINES ARE SHOWN HERE ONLY FOR CLARIFICATION.

V.P.L   V.P.R
GL
P.S.

Steps in making a two point perspective kitchen plan by using the projection method.

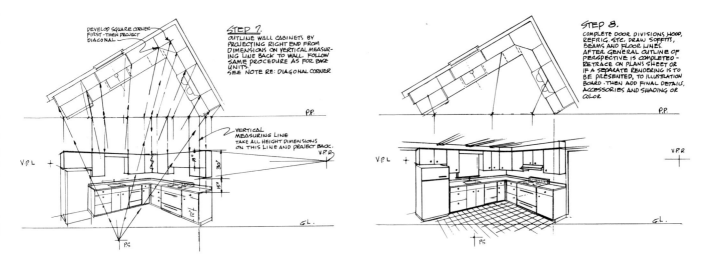

STEP 7.
OUTLINE WALL CABINETS BY
PROJECTING RIGHT END FROM
DIMENSIONS ON VERTICAL MEASUR-
ING LINE BACK TO WALL. FOLLOW
SAME PROCEDURE AS FOR BASE
UNITS.
SEE NOTE RE: DIAGONAL CORNER

DEVELOP SQUARE CORNER
FIRST—THEN PROJECT
DIAGONAL

VERTICAL
MEASURING LINE
TAKE ALL HEIGHT DIMENSIONS
ON THIS LINE AND PROJECT BACK.

STEP 8.
COMPLETE DOOR DIVISIONS, HOOD,
REFRIG. ETC. DRAW SOFFITS,
BEAMS AND FLOOR LINES.
AFTER GENERAL OUTLINE OF
PERSPECTIVE IS COMPLETED-
RETRACE ON PLANS SHEET OR
IF A SEPARATE RENDERING IS TO
BE PRESENTED, TO ILLUSTRATION
BOARD. THEN ADD FINAL DETAILS,
ACCESSORIES AND SHADING OR
COLOR

The final steps in making a two point perspective drawing.

The completed two point perspective drawing.

function, if the homemaker is right-handed, it should be placed on the left of the sink; if he or she is left-handed, it should be placed on the right side. This should be the order of first preference; however, if a compromise is necessary due to space limitations, place it as near to the sink as possible.

3. Next, work toward the nearest corner. Subtracting the size of the dishwasher and half of the sink cabinet size from the measurement of the wall to the centerline of the window.

4. Decide what method and the size of the cabinet that is going to be used in turning the corner. Place this cabinet in the appropriate area, noting visually the appearance.

5. Work back toward the sink and dishwasher area and adjust the location of the sink and dishwasher, if necessary and within acceptable limitations. Place base cabinets, if space permits, between the dishwasher and sink cabinet and the corner cabinet, noting every cabinet that is placed,

according to function and type of storage required.

6. Place the range in the area originally designated and adjust to accommodate necessary cabinetry on both sides of the range. The normal flow for right-handed people is from left to right, and the opposite for left-handed people. When laying out a kitchen plan, work toward this end with this rule in mind.

7. Check wall cabinet function and operation in this area and develop swing of the single-door cabinets to guarantee full-door opening and accessibility. Place the balance of cabinetry on this leg, again reviewing function and type of storage required. When working between two walls incorporate a filler somewhere in the layout of this leg in order to compensate for walls that are out of plumb.

8. After the left leg is completed, return again to the base leg (the leg with sink and dishwasher) and work from the right side of the sink and dishwasher toward the right-hand corner or right leg, whichever the case may be. (We are assuming that the corner nearest the window was the left corner, or left leg.) If another corner cabinet is required, determine the type of cabinet according to intended use, and the size of the cabinet according to the space availability. Place it in the appropriate space required.

9. Place all other necessary cabinetry in line, using the subtraction method, and ending the run or right leg with the refrigerator and possibly the utility or broom cabinet.

10. After all of the base cabinets have been placed and the measurements checked, proceed to place the wall cabinets in their proper sequence. Use the subtraction line method again to prove out wall measurements. Contrary to popular belief, it is not necessary for the stiles of the wall cabinets to align themselves with the stiles of the base cabinets; however, where possible to do this, it will tend to balance the design of the kitchen and layout.

To give a better idea of what the kitchen will look like, you may wish to add a two point perspective drawing to blueprints. The steps in making such a drawing are given on pages 176 and 177.

Once the final blueprint drawings are made, the kitchen is no longer in the planning stage, but the room is now ready for the construction phase.

THROUGH COMPLETION

Once the rough plan for the new kitchen is complete, the next task is to determine how the plan is going to carry on through completion. There are several ways this can be done:

1. Turn the job over to an architect or kitchen modernization specialist. They will handle the entire project: translating the plan into a workable blueprint; writing specifications for materials; contracting with suppliers and tradesmen; and obtaining necessary permits. For these services, a professional will usually charge you a specific price.

A Certified Kitchen Designer (CKD) is a trained professional and a member of the American Institute of Kitchen Dealers (AIKD). You can buy materials and services through the designer. The kitchen design comes as part of the total package. To find a reputable kitchen designer, ask friends or look in the Yellow Pages for a Certified Kitchen Designer, under "Kitchen Cabinets and Equipment."

An architect will supervise the project in addition to designing the kitchen, if you wish, hiring and directing the subcontractors. The local chapter of the American Institute of Architects should be able to give you the names of several residential architects who specialize in remodeling. An architect will know several good contractors and can act as your agent in any dealings with them.

2. Draw your own blueprints, or have them drawn, and turn the job over to a contractor. You may obtain blueprints from a kitchen designer (for a flat fee), from a blueprint-drawing service, from cabinet dealers when you buy their cabinets, or from an architect. Or, draw up your own plans from the directions given earlier in this chapter.

A good contractor will carry out your plans according to the blueprints and specifications. To find a reputable contractor, ask friends who have had work done. Find out how long the contractor took, how much he or she charges, whether he or she was easy to work with, and whether the work was of high quality. Other sources for contractors' names are your local bank, Chamber of Commerce, or Home Builders Association.

To choose an architect, contractor, or kitchen designer, visit several firms, then narrow your choices down to two or three reputable companies. Check to make sure the company has an established place of business. Make appointments to have someone from each firm come to your home to discuss your needs. Ask each for a written bid, and let each firm know you are asking for other bids. You should ask for the company's bank references and for the names of several clients for whom the company has completed remodeling jobs. Ask to see one or two of the jobs they have done. Check the references.

To ensure that the bids are based on the same work, each company should bid on the same specifications. Write up identical specifications, outlining what materials and equipment will be used in the project. The kitchen designer will usually submit a floor plan and sketches with the bid. If you are dealing with a contractor, give him or her a copy of the blueprint. If possible, provide brand names of products to give a more exact idea of price.

Once you have decided on an architect, designer or contractor, you will sign a contract. This will state the specifications and plan for the kitchen, as well as such details as approximate completion date, procedures for breaking the contract or making changes and corrections, terms of payment, and length of guarantee on the work. Before you make any substantial commitment, have your lawyer look over the contract.

3. You can save money by acting as your contractor, performing some labor yourself and subcontracting the more difficult jobs, or subcontracting all the work. This means more work on your part, and the job will probably take more time. This method is well suited, however, to less extensive remodeling projects or to a project done in phases over several years.

To handle the job yourself, you will need to draw your plan and write up the exact specifications for the work you want the tradespeople to complete.

You may be working with many experts: carpenters, cabinet installers, painters, electricians, plumbers, plaster or drywall experts, appliance installers, and flooring specialists. Send a set of blueprints with the written specifications to each prospective subcontractor. The bidder should visit your home to see the job before he or she bids. You may also need to obtain local permits and schedule inspections as work is completed.

You will need to make up a schedule for completing each stage of the work, and see that the workers and the materials arrive at the right time. The remodeling usually proceeds in this order: removing old cabinets, installing appliances, installing countertops, decorating the walls, and installing flooring.

Budgeting

Even with unlimited funds to spend on a new kitchen, you will want to know ahead of time how much the total kitchen will cost. And, if you are the average person, you will have to stick to a carefully controlled budget. Few families can afford everything new, all at once.

How much your kitchen will cost depends on many factors: how much work needs to be done, and what kind; whether you choose economy, medium, or luxury components and decorating accessories; and how much of the work you do yourself. If the budget for everything you would like is out of reach

The U-shaped kitchen (left) opens to a small family room. If the breakfast area is relocated (right), the plan provides a much better family room.

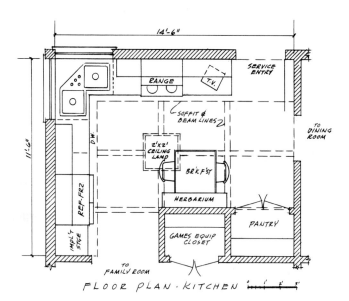

A kitchen from plan (left) to completion (right).

of your pocketbook, you have several choices.

1. Do most of the work yourself. If you can lay the floor tile, do your own painting, or install cabinets, you can save a significant amount of money.

2. You can make a list of priorities. Your kitchen flooring may be a wreck, but you can get many more years out of your existing kitchen cabinets, if they were given a new paint job. You may insist on a dishwasher, but decide to refinish your old kitchen table and chairs rather than buy a new set.

3. You can do the remodeling or decorating in stages over a period of months or years. Separate your list of priorities into phases; for example:

First Stage: Buy a new cooktop and built-in oven. Install new kitchen cabinets. Modernize wiring.

Second Stage: Buy a new kitchen dining table and chairs. Install dishwasher and disposer.

Third Stage: Install kitchen carpeting. Install a new luminous or "light" ceiling. Decorate with a new coat of paint.

Financing. If you do not have the money, financing is the answer. The options are many:

1. *Life Insurance Loan*. This may be the lowest-cost method. If you have a life insurance policy that has built up cash value, you may borrow against it, at relatively low interest rates.

2. *Passbook Loan*. You may pledge your savings account as security for a low-interest bank loan.

3. *Collateral Loan*. You may put up securities as collateral, to secure a lower interest rate.

4. *Remodeling Loan*. This loan is similar to a personal loan, but allows you several years to pay it back. You may usually borrow several thousand dollars, perhaps more if you are a good customer of the lender.

5. *Credit Union*. If you belong to a credit union, you probably can borrow money there more cheaply than from another lender.

6. *FHA Title I*. These government insured remodeling loans are getting difficult to obtain, but offer lower-than-market rates and several years to repay.

7. *Bank Note*. If you are a commercial customer of a bank, you may be able to obtain a note at the going commercial rate, which is usually lower than for personal loans.

8. *Refinancing Your Mortgage*. For an extensive remodeling job, you may want to refinance your old mortgage. You will probably have to pay new closing costs, but you can stretch payments out over many years. If your mortgage is fairly old, however, you may not want to trade its lower interest rate for today's higher ones.

9. *Appliance Loan*. This may include not only the appliances, but also the cost of the entire remodeling project, and can usually be obtained through your major appliance dealer.

Now that we have the full course of planning through completion, it is time to use this knowledge to create the most beautiful room that anyone has ever dreamed of — the truly personalized kitchen.

Appendix A
Glossary of Kitchen Planning and Building Terms

The following terms are used in the planning and remodeling procedures necessary for obtaining a good kitchen.

AIKD. American Institute of Kitchen Dealers — an association of kitchen retailers.

ANSI. American National Standards Institute — an association that sets construction and performance standards.

Apron. The trim board placed immediately below the window stool.

Appliance. The range, refrigerator, diswasher, garbage disposer, trash compactor, and kitchen sink are considered *major* or *large appliances. Small* or *portable appliances* include toaster, blender, mixer, coffee maker, can opener, etc.

Back Panel. The piece of material making up the back of a cabinet.

Back Rail. The top and bottom horizontal members on the back of a cabinet. They are used for mounting the cabinet to the wall with screws.

Back Splash. The portion of a countertop which extends up the wall at the rear of a base cabinet.

Baseboard. The finishing board covering a finished wall where it meets the floor.

Base Bread Board. A base cabinet which includes a bread board.

Base Cabinet. Those cabinets which rest on the floor and support the countertop to provide a working surface.

Base Corner Filler. A special accessory item which is used to "turn a corner" in the most economical way.

Base Drawer Unit. A base cabinet composed entirely of drawers.

Base Drawers and Bread Board. A base cabinet composed of several drawers and a bread board.

Base End Panel. An accessory item which is used to provide a finished end next to items such as dishwashers and lazy susans.

Base Filler. An accessory which is used to fill spaces resulting from "odd" wall dimensions which cannot be filled using standard base cabinets.

Base Pantry. A deluxe base cabinet which includes a bread board, bread box, and cutlery divider.

Base Slide-Out Shelves. A base cabinet with shelves that can be pulled out of the inside of the cabinet.

Base Tray Unit. A base cabinet designed to accommodate large items, such as cookie sheets, trays, etc. This cabinet contains no shelves or dividers.

Bearing Wall. A wall carrying more than its own weight, usually supporting floor or ceiling joists.

Blind Corner Base. A base cabinet used to "turn a corner" and utilize all available storage space.

Blind Corner Wall. A wall cabinet used to "turn a corner" and utilize all available storage space.

Bottom Panel. The material used in the bottom of a base or wall cabinet.

Bread Board. A solid maple board included in certain base cabinets and used as a cutting surface.

Btuh. British thermal units per hour; a measure of heating or cooling.

Butt Joint. A joint framed by butting the ends of two pieces together without overlapping.

Canned Goods Storage Cabinet. A tall cabinet featuring a "swing-out" storage unit.

Center Stile. The vertical member which separates doors on two-door base and wall cabinets. Also used on blind corner wall and base cabinets.

Certified Cabinet. A cabinet which through testing has been verified as meeting the quality and performance requirements of the standards program of the NKCA.

CKD. Certified Kitchen Designer. To qualify to use the initials CKD after his or her name, a designer must pass a rigid examination and submit affidavits of competence and integrity to an accrediting body known as the Council of Certified Kitchen Designers of the AIKD.

Clearance Space. A term used to describe the space necessary for the safe and convenient use of appliances, working surfaces, and storage, and for passage in the kitchen.

Close Grain. Small closely spaced pores or fine texture.

Corner Block. The piece of wood which is used to square and strengthen the corners of base cabinets.

Corridor. The surface on which mixing, cutting, cleaning, and other kitchen food preparation and cleanup activities take place.

Counter Frontage. The measurement of the counter along its front edge.

Countertop. The item that rests on the top of the base cabinets to provide a work surface.

Countertop Fasteners. The mechanical items used to secure the countertop pieces together.

Cutlery Divider. An accessory item used in certain cabinet drawers to provide separate storage areas for silver and cutlery items.

Diagonal Sink Front. A cabinet front designed to enclose a sink in a corner area.

Diagonal Wall Cabinet. A wall cabinet designed to "turn a corner" on an angle.

Dimensional Stock. Solid lumber pieces of specified length, width, and thickness.

Dishwasher Front. An accessory item which is used to cover a dishwasher door. It is often finished to match the cabinets.

Door. A cabinet component used to cover an opening in the cabinet base frame. Also an entryway to the kitchen.

Door Frame. The outside portion of a "frame and panel" door.

Door Panel. The inside portion of a "frame and panel" door.

Door Samples. A sales and display aid constructed of a face frame door and a drawer front.

Dovetail. A projecting part that fits into a corresponding indentation to form a joint.

Drain Stack. The portion of the plumbing in the kitchen or bath which is used to remove waste waters.

Drawer. A part of a base cabinet, shaped like a topless box, which can be pulled in and out of the base cabinet.

Drawer Back. The rear portion of the drawer box.

Drawer Front. The exposed front portion of the drawer box. Same as **drawer face.**

Drawer Bottom. The lower portion of the drawer box.

Drawer Pull. The hardware which is held onto when opening and closing a drawer.

Drawer Side. The side portion of the drawer box.

Drawer Suspension. The mechanism used to guide the drawer box when it is being opened and closed.

Elevations. Drawings of the walls of a kitchen, made as though the observer were looking straight at the wall.

End Panel. The material which makes up the sides of a cabinet.

End Splash. The portion of the countertop which is used to protect walls and tall cabinet sides where the countertop joins them.

Equipment. The appliances, plumbing fixtures, storage units, and counters used in a kitchen.

Face Frame. The exposed front portion of the cabinet which provides shape and strength to the cabinet.

Fascia. The front of a soffit area.

Fiber-Core. Sheet core material made from compressed wood fibers which have been impregnated with a waterproof phenolic resin. Density of material develops great dimensional stability and resistance to warping and twisting. Core is veneered on both sides for use as doors, drawer panels, and overlays.

Filler. An accessory which is used to fill spaces resulting from "odd" wall dimensions that cannot be filled by using standard cabinets.

Finish Coat. The final covering applied to cabinets to provide a tough durable surface.

Finished Paneling. Prefinished sheets which can be used to provide a matching surface for walls, cabinet ends, and peninsula backs.

Floor Plan. The horizontal section of a kitchen showing the size, doors, windows, etc., in the walls.

Frame and Panel Door. A type of door constructed of several separate pieces which are fastened together to form a door.

Frontage. A measure equalling the horizontal dimension across the face of an appliance, base cabinet, counter, or wall cabinet. To be credited as having "accessible frontage," a component must be directly accessible from the area located in front of the component. In accordance with this definition, cabinet space (base or wall) and counter surface located in corners are not credited in counting accessible frontage.

Full-Shelf Option. Base cabinets are manufactured with half-shelves standard. A full shelf can be added at an additional cost.

Furring. The building out of a wall or ceiling with wood strips.

Grain. Pattern arrangement of wood fibers.

Gusset. Brace installed in corners of base cabinets to provide strength and a means of attaching the countertop. Also used in peninsula wall cabinets to insure positive installation.

Hanging Strip. A portion of the cabinet back through which screws are attached to the wall.

Hinges (self-closing). A type of hardware which is used to attach doors to the face frame. They are spring-loaded and as a result will close automatically if the door is partially closed.

Hinging. A term applied to single-door cabinets to identify whether the hinges attaching the door to the face frame are on the right or left side.

Hollow Core. A panel construction with plywood, hardboard, etc., bonded to both sides of a frame assembly.

Island. A cabinet or group of cabinets which are free-standing (not attached to a wall).

Island Corner Base Cabinet. A base cabinet used to form an **Island.**

Jamb. The inside vertical finished face of a door or window frame.

Joists. The framing members that are the direct support of a floor.

Kiln-Dry. To remove excessive moisture from green lumber by means of a kiln or chamber, usually to a moisture content of 6 to 12 percent.

Kitchen. The area containing the equipment and floor area necessary to prepare and serve meals and to clean up after meals. The kitchen may be a room in itself, or it may be a part of a larger room and open into space for other activities, such as dining or family relaxation.

"L" Shape. One of the basic kitchen shapes where two sides join to form an "L" shape.

Laminate. Layers of wood, plastic, or other material bonded together, usually by having heat and pressure simultaneously applied.

Lap Joint. Two pieces of dimensional stock overlapping each other and bonded together.

Layout. A drawing showing how cabinets and appliances will be arranged within a kitchen.

Lazy Susan Corner Base Cabinet. A base cabinet which contains revolving shelves and is installed in a corner.

Level. Flat when measured horizontally.

Liberal Kitchen. A kitchen that meets liberal-ample cabinet space requirements.

Liberal-Minimum Kitchen. A kitchen that meets limited-ample or liberal-minimum cabinet space requirements.

Lintel. The horizontal structural member supporting the wall over an opening.

Magic Triangle. A technique used in a kitchen design to insure efficiency.

Metal Bread Box. An accessory item inserted in certain base cabinet drawers. It is used to maintain the freshness of breads and similar foods.

Millwork. Finished woodwork, machined, and partly assembled at the mill.

Minimum Kitchen. A kitchen that meets the limited-minimum requirement of cabinet space.

Modular. Pertaining to a module or a standard or unit of measurement. Kitchen cabinets are generally manufactured in 3-inch modulars.

Molding. Prefinished pieces of various shapes which are used to improve visual appearance of areas where cabinets meet walls, ceilings, etc.

Monorail. Metal center guide or rail for supporting and guiding a drawer roller.

Mortise. A notch or hole, cut into a piece of wood to receive a projecting part (tenon) shaped to fit.

Mounting Rail. Top and bottom horizontal members on back of cabinet, used for mounting cabinet to the wall with screws.

Mullion. The large vertical division of a double-width window.

Muntins. The small members that divide the glass in a window.

NKCA. National Kitchen Cabinet Association — an association of cabinet manufacturers.

Obstructions. A term applying to exposed obstacles, such as pipes, in a kitchen area.

One-Wall. One of the basic kitchen shapes. It is composed of a single row of cabinets.

Open-End Shelves. An accessory item which is attached to the end of base and wall cabinets to provide exposed shelf space. Primarily used for decorative purposes.

Open Grain. Large pores or coarse texture.

Oven Cabinet. A tall cabinet designed and engineered to house a built-in oven.

Overlay. Decorative panel fixed to a door or drawer panel surface rather than inlaid.

Peninsula. A group of cabinets which extend at right angles to a wall to create a divider. A peninsula is usually used to separate the food preparation from the dining area.

Peninsula Base Cabinet. A base cabinet used to create the base extension of a peninsula.

Peninsula Blind Corner Wall Cabinet. A base cabinet used to "turn a corner" and begin the extension of a peninsula.

Peninsula Diagonal Wall Cabinet. A wall cabinet used to "turn a corner" on an angle and begin the extension of a peninsula. This cabinet usually has access from two sides.

Peninsula Wall Cabinet. A wall cabinet used to create the upper portion of a peninsula extension.

Plumb. A term applying to a perfectly vertical measurement — straight up and down.

Plywood. A panel made of layers (plies) of veneer bonded by an adhesive. The grain of adjoining plies is usually laid at right angles, and an odd number of plies are bonded in order to obtain balance.

Preliminary Preparation. Steps to be taken in advance of cabinet installation.

Pull. Knob or handle on doors and drawers.

Racking. Twisting or warping out of square, due to uneven floors, walls, or pressure being applied as a result of forcing into position.

Rail. The horizontal members of a cabinet face frame.

Range. A cooking appliance. It can be free-standing, drop-in, or built-in.

Range Cut-out. The opening cut into the countertop so

that the cooktop unit will fit below and rest on the countertop.

Range Panel. A base cabinet front engineered to accept "drop-in" ranges.

Reveal. The offset or exposure of the jamb edge that is not covered by the trim.

Rough Opening. The rough-framed opening into which window and door frames are installed.

Sash. The framework which holds glass in the window.

Scribe Allowance. Small extension of sides beyond back, and frame stiles beyond sides for trimming to insure proper fit.

Scribing. A technique used to adjust for wall irregularities. Scribing is used in fitting countertops, molding, and fillers.

Sealer. A protective coating applied to the cabinet during the finishing process.

Self-Closing. A term applied to hinges which assist in closing a door.

Separate Oven. An oven unit which is not part of a range.

Shallow Drawer. A drawer less than regular depth.

Shelf. An interior storage surface.

Shelf Clip. An item used to support the adjustable shelves in wall cabinets.

Shim. A small angular piece of wood used in shimming is defined below.

Shimming. A technique using small wood pieces to compensate for unevenness in wall and floor surfaces.

Sink Cut-out. The opening cut into the countertop so that a sink unit will fit below and rest on the countertop.

Sink Front. A cabinet front, with no sides, back, or bottom, which is used as a low-cost substitute for a sink base cabinet.

Sink-Front Bottom. A piece of material used to cover the floor area behind a sink front.

Sink/Range Base Cabinet. A base cabinet designed to house and support either a sink or cooktop unit.

Slide-Out Shelf. A base cabinet option where shelves which can be pulled out are substituted for the standard fixed half-shelf.

Soffits. The area between the cabinet top and ceiling. When this area is closed off it appears to be part of the ceiling.

Stain. The material which is used to color cabinets.

Stile. The vertical members of a cabinet face frame.

Storage. A general term used to denote any space that is used for storing food, utensils, small appliances, etc., in the kitchen. Generally the refrigerator space is excluded from this term, although in reality it provides *cold storage*. Most storage space is provided in cabinets, but other special storage devices such as closets, pantries, etc., may be employed.

Studs. Two-by-four wall framing members to which cabinets are to be attached.

Style. A term referring to the design and decorator effect

of the cabinet door.

Sub-Rail. Horizontal interior framing member, not a part of the front frame assembly.

Subtraction Method. A technique used to check and insure layout accuracy.

Surface Cooking Unit. Cooking units which are not part of a range, but are usually installed in a counter work surface. Same as a *cooktop*.

Tall Cabinets. Large cabinets which are 84 inches high. These cabinets are designed to supply a large quantity of storage space or house built-in oven units.

Tenon. A projecting part cut on the end of a piece of wood for insertion into a mortise to make a joint.

Toe Space. The open area at the lower portion of the base cabinet. This space allows a person to stand close to the cabinet without kicking it with their feet. Same as *kick space*.

Top Panel. A piece of material making up the top of a wall cabinet.

Twin-Track Hardware. The item which guides and directs the drawer when it is being opened and closed.

Trim. The finishing frame around an opening such as doors and windows.

'U' Shape. One of the basic kitchen shapes where three rows of cabinets are joined together to form a "U".

Utility Cabinet. A tall cabinet providing large amounts of storage space.

Utility Filler. An accessory which is to be used next to tall cabinets to fill spaces resulting from "odd" wall dimensions that cannot be filled by using standard cabinets.

Valance. An accessory which is usually used to fill the area between wall cabinets next to a sink.

Veneer. A thinly cut slice of decoratively marked wood. Produced by sawing, slicing, or rotary process.

Wall Cabinets. Those cabinets which attach to the walls and provide storage space above the countertop work area.

Wall Filler. An accessory which is used to fill the space resulting from "odd" wall dimensions which cannot be filled with standard wall cabinets.

Wide Bottom Rails. A wide bottom rail is used to replace the toe space on base cabinets.

Window Sill. The exterior slanting ledge of a window frame.

Window Stool. The interior horizontal ledge that seals a window at the bottom.

Working Surface. This term refers to the surfaces which are used for the preparation of food and for other work done in the kitchen. Same as *counter* or *counter surface*.

Appendix B
HUD's Minimum Property Standards for Kitchens

In some instances a kitchen design must comply with the Minimum Property Standards Issued by the Department of Housing and Urban Development of the federal government. Compliance is required whenever the loan on the property is to be insured through one of the mortgage insurance programs sponsored by HUD (formerly referred to as an "FHA-insured loan") or when the property owner or renter is to benefit from one of the HUD subsidy programs.

In 1973 the Department of Housing and Urban Development issued for the first time a "single unified set of technical and environmental standards" for housing. These standards are intended to define the minimum level of acceptability of design and construction standards for housing approved for mortgage insurance purposes as well as for low-rent public housing. Two of the publications, the *Minimum Property Standards for One- and Two-Family Dwellings*, and the *Minimum Property Standards for Multi-Family Dwellings* contain minimum standards for kitchens.

The following excerpts relating to kitchens have been taken from *Minimum Property Standards for One- and Two-Family Dwellings*. Standards for seasonal dwellings have been omitted. The paragraph and table numbers are those of the original document.

401-4. 1 *Kitchen*

    a. Each dwelling shall have a kitchen area which provides for efficient food preparation, serving and storage, as well as utensil storage and cleaning up after meals.

    b. Kitchen fixtures and countertops shall be provided in accordance with Table 4-1.2. Required countertops shall be approximately 24 inches deep and 36 inches high. Clearance between base cabinet fronts in food preparation area shall be 40 inches minimum.

    c. Required countertops may be combined when they are located between two fixtures — stove, refrigerator, sink. Such a countertop shall have a minimum frontage equal to that of the larger of the countertops being combined. This combined counter may also be the mixing counter when its minimum length is equal to that required for the mixing counter.

    d. In housing for the elderly, a refrigerator below the countertop may not be used.

TABLE 4-1.2
COUNTERTOPS AND FIXTURES

Work Center	Number of Bedrooms				
	0	1	2	3	4
	Minimum Frontages in Lineal Inches				
Sink (1)	18	24	24	32	32
Countertop, each side	15	18	21	24	30
Range or Cooktop Space (2, 3, 6)	21	21	24	30	30
Countertop, one side (4)	15	18	21	24	30
Refrigerator Space (5)	30	30	36	36	36
Countertop, one side (4)	15	15	15	15	18
Mixing Countertop	21	30	36	36	42

Notes

    (1) When a dishwasher is provided, a 24-inch sink is acceptable.

    (2) Where a built-in wall oven is installed, provide an 18-inch-wide counter adjacent to it.

    (3) A range shall not be located under a window nor within 12 inches of a window. Where a cabinet is provided above a range, 30-inch clearance shall be provided to the bottom of an unprotected cabinet, or 24 inches to the bottom of a protected cabinet.

    (4) Provide at least 9 inches from the edge of a range to an adjacent corner cabinet and 15 inches from the side of a refrigerator to an adjacent corner cabinet.

    (5) Refrigerator space may be 33 inches,

when a refrigerator is provided and the door opens within its own width.

(6) When a range is not provided, a 30-inch-wide space shall be provided.

e. Kitchen storage shelf area shall be provided in accordance with Table 4-1.3. At least one-third of the required area shall be located in base or wall cabinets. At least 60 percent of the required area shall be enclosed by cabinet doors.

TABLE 4-1.3
STORAGE AREA

SQ. FT.	Number of Bedrooms				
	0	1	2	3	4
Minimum Shelf Area (1, 2, 3, 4)	24	30	38	44	50
Minimum Drawer Area (5)	4	6	8	10	12

Notes

(1) A dishwasher may be counted as 4 square feet of base cabinet storage.

(2) Wall cabinets over refrigerators shall not be counted as required shelf area.

(3) Shelf area above 74 inches shall not be counted as required area.

(4) Inside corner cabinets shall be counted as 50 percent of shelf area, except where revolving shelves are used, the actual shelf area may be counted.

(5) Drawer area in excess of the required area may be counted as shelf area if drawers are at least 6 inches in depth.

General MPS requirements

For more general requirements of the MPS, see the section GENERAL REQUIREMENTS - MPS.

Index

ILLUSTRATION ACKNOWLEDGMENTS

We wish to thank the following manufacturers and photographers for use of the illustration material seen in this book:

ARMSTRONG CORK COMPANY: Pages 16 (left); 64 (center-left); 98 (top-left); 104 (top-left); 113 (top and bottom-left); 125 (top); and 139 (right).

AZROCK FLOOR PRODUCTS, INC.: Pages 104 (top-center); 104 (bottom-left); and 115 (center).

DEL MAR, INC.: Page 89 (top).

EXCEL WOOD PRODUCTS COMPANY, INC.: Pages 51 (left); 64 (top-left); 65 (top-left); 112 (bottom); 136; and 140 (right).

FASCO INDUSTRIES, INC.: Page 133 (left).

FRIGIDAIRE, INC.: Pages 26 (right) and 40.

GAF, INC.: Pages 15 (top); 65 (bottom-right); 104 (bottom-right); and 111.

GENERAL ELECTRIC COMPANY: Pages 8; 22; 23 (left); 30 (right); 31; 45 (right); 47; 54 (left); 56; 57; 84; 95 (top); 96 (top); 97 (right); 98 (bottom); 101, 106 (top); 114 (bottom-left); 123; 124; 129 (left); 140 (left); 166 (left); 170; 171; and 179.

IXL FURNITURE COMPANY: Pages 32 (right); 65 (bottom-left); 93 (left); and 139 (left).

JENN-AIR CORPORATION: Pages 55 and 59 (bottom).

KOHLER COMPANY: Page 42 (bottom).

MAJESTIC COMPANY, INC.: Page 26 (left).

MANNINGTON MILLS, INC.: Pages 104 (top-right and bottom-center); and 168.

MONTGOMERY-WARD COMPANY: Pages 174 and 175.

MUTSCHLER, INC.: Pages 58; 85 (top-right); 92 (top-center); 112 (center); 116 (bottom); 125 (bottom-left); 138; and 168.

NEWELL COMPANIES, INC.: Page 143 (right).

QUAKER MAID COMPANY: Pages 25 (right); 26 (top); 85 (top-left); and 93 (right).

RIVIERA PRODUCTS, INC.: Pages 32 (left); 65 (top-center and top-left); 70 (left); 74 (bottom); 89 (bottom-left); 92 (top-left); 114 (top); and 126 (bottom-right).

RONSON, INC.: Page 62 (right).

ST. CHARLES KITCHENS, INC.: Pages 17, 24 (right); 28; 51 (left); 59 (top); 64 (bottom-left and right); 66; 70 (right); 71; 72; 75; 78; 89 (bottom-right); 92 (top-left and bottom-right); 94; 95 (bottom); 96 (bottom); 98 (top-right); 102; 106 (bottom); 114 (right); 115 (center); 117 (top); 125 (bottom-right); 126 (top-left); 128; 162; 163; 164; 165; 166 (right); 172 (bottom-right); 173; 176; 177; and 180.

SCOVILL, INC.: Page 62 (left).

SMALL HOMES COUNCIL/BUILDING RESEARCH COUNCIL: Pages 129 (right), 133 (right); and 135.

TILE COUNCIL OF AMERICA: Pages 49; 82 (right); 108 (right); 110 (top); 115 (left); and 117 (bottom-left).

UNITED CABINET CORPORATION: Pages 25 (left); 67 (left); 82 (left); and 97 (left).

U.S. INDUSTRIES COMPANY: Pages 87 and 116 (top).

U.S. PLYWOOD COMPANY: Pages 51 (center) and 117 (bottom-right).

WALLCOVERING INSTITUTE: Pages 109 and 139 (left).

WHITE-WESTINGHOUSE APPLIANCE COMPANY: Page 16 (right).

WHIRLPOOL CORPORATION: Pages 20; 21; 41 (left); and 54 (right).

WOOD-MODE CABINETRY, INC.: Pages 15 (bottom); 23 (right); 30 (left); 32 (center); 37; 41 (right); 42 (top); 59 (center); 65 (bottom-center); 72 (left); 74 (top); 82 (center); 85 (bottom); 91, 98 (top-center); 106 (center); 108 (left); 112 (top); 113 (right); 115 (right); and 132.

PHOTOGRAPHERS:

Del Carlo - Page 153 (top).

Joshua Freiwald - Page 159 (bottom).

Pat Harper - Page 149 (bottom).

Leland Lee - Page 148 (top).

Gordon Menzie - Page 145 (bottom).

Kent Oppenheimer - Page 156.

Dave Ross - Page 154 (bottom). Page 155 (bottom).

Julius Shulman - Page 147 (left).

Greg Wenger - Page 145 (top).